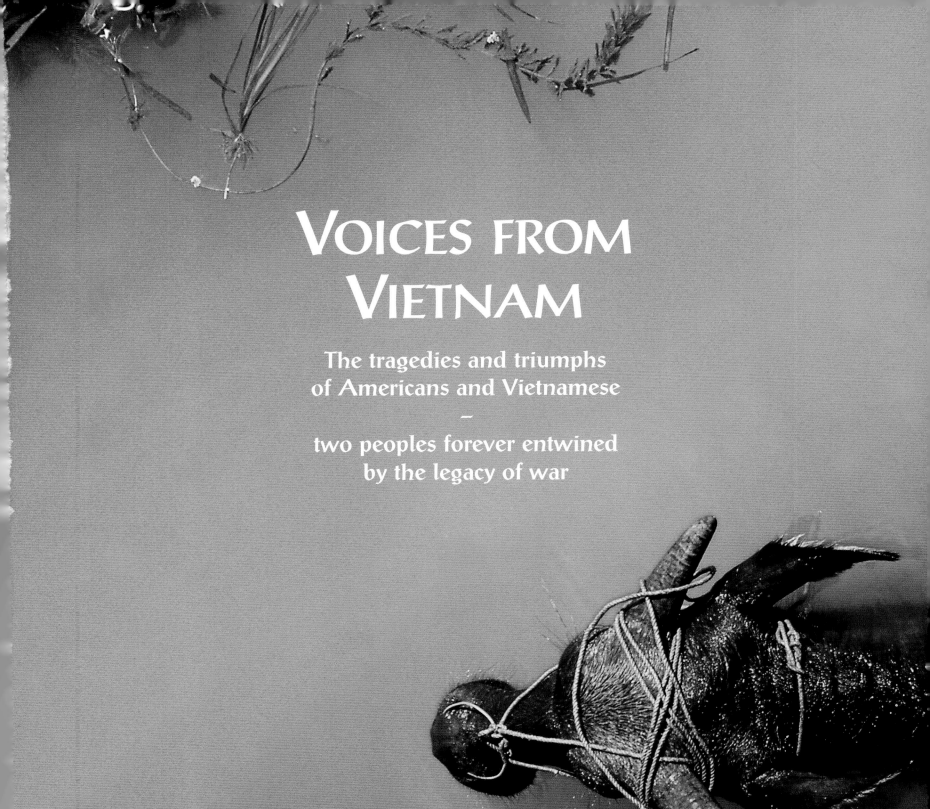

VOICES FROM VIETNAM

The tragedies and triumphs
of Americans and Vietnamese

–

two peoples forever entwined
by the legacy of war

VOICES FROM VIETNAM

The tragedies and triumphs
of Americans and Vietnamese

two peoples forever entwined
by the legacy of war

written and photographed by
Charlene Edwards

with a foreword by
Robin Moore

JOURNEYS

Library of Congress Control Number: 2002091761

Publisher's Cataloging-in-Publication Data
Edwards, Charlene.
Voices from Vietnam: the tragedies and triumphs of Americans and Vietnamese:
two peoples forever entwined by the legacy of war / written and photographed by
Charlene Edwards; with a foreword by Robin Moore.—1st ed.
p. cm.
ISBN 0-9714020-5-1 (hardcover)
ISBN 0-9714020-3-5 (softcover)
1. Vietnamese Conflict, 1961-1975—Personal narratives. 2. Vietnamese
Conflict, 1961-1975—Sources. 3. Culture conflict. I. Title.

DS557.7.E39 2002   959.704'3
QBI02-701343

Designed by Joe Gannon of Mulberry Tree Press, Inc. (www.mulberrytreepress.com)
Printed in Hong Kong by Overseas Printing Corporation

Foreword © 2002 Robin Moore.
Poem: *Bury Me With Soldiers* © 1980 Charles R. Fink.
Song: *Twenty Bucks For Billy* © 1997 John Taylor.
Song: *Children of the Dust* © 1986 Patricia Shih.
Map of Vietnam provided by the Vietnamese Embassy, Washington, D.C.

AUTHOR'S NOTE: After the war, the city of Saigon was renamed Ho Chi Minh City. For the sake of simplicity and familiarity, I have used the name Saigon throughout the book regardless of the time frame.

PROCEEDS: A portion of the profits from the sale of this book will be donated to help support those Vietnam veterans, Vietnamese and Amerasians still in need.

INTERNATIONAL EXHIBIT: A traveling exhibit of the images and stories in this book is available through JOURNEYS. Inquiries should be directed to the address below.

ACQUISITION OF PRINTS: High-quality prints of the photographs in this book and in the project archives are available for purchase through JOURNEYS. Further information about pricing and availability can be obtained by contacting:

JOURNEYS • PO Box 610260 • Bayside, New York 11361
email: vnvoices@aol.com • www.voicesfromvietnam.com

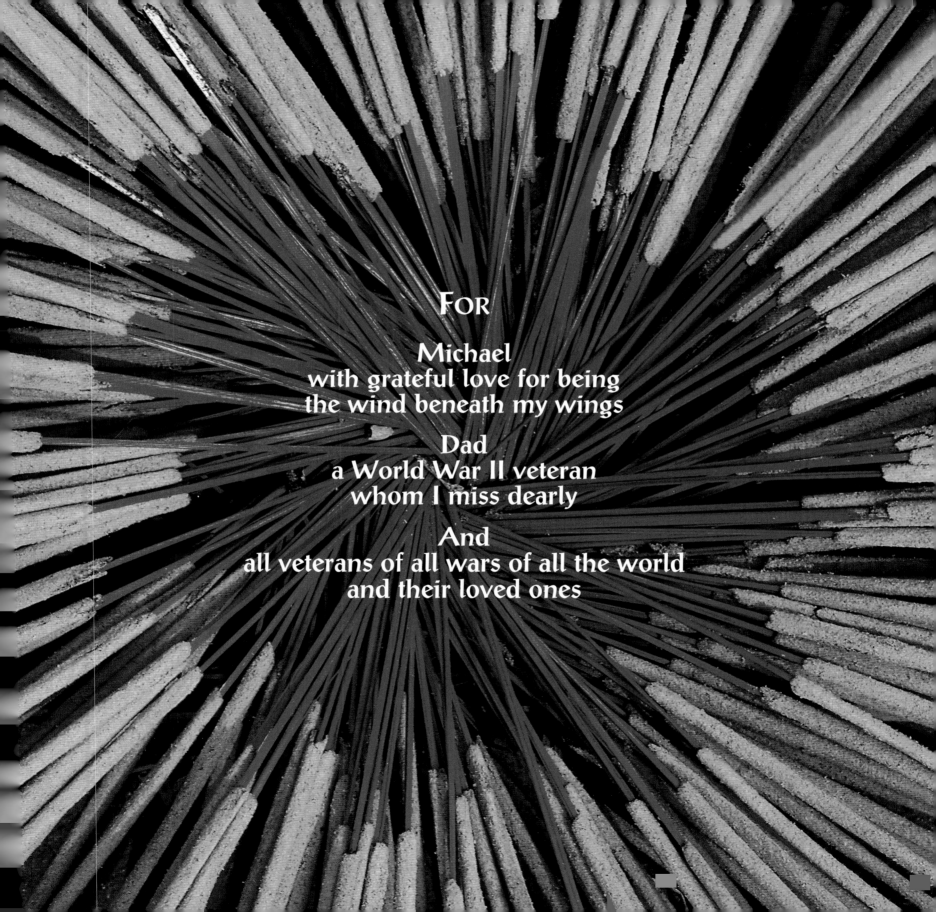

FOR

Michael
with grateful love for being
the wind beneath my wings

Dad
a World War II veteran
whom I miss dearly

And
all veterans of all wars of all the world
and their loved ones

CONTENTS

FOREWORD

by Robin Moore
author of *The Green Berets* and *The French Connection*

*A*nyone who was in any way touched by the Vietnam War will find this book deeply moving and hauntingly evocative. Whether you were a warrior, a correspondent, a draft evader, a picket line protester, a family member of a KIA or MIA, or just someone interested in the scene, there is a picture or a story that will reach into your soul.

Charlene Edwards has brought a photographer's eye, a journalist's ear and a crusader's heart to the story of the Vietnam War and its aftermath. She spent more than a decade absorbing the emotions of those affected by the Vietnam War and with passion and insight she transports you on a visual and emotional journey through the horrors of war and the resilience of the human spirit.

Her travels through Vietnam and America and the hundreds of hours she spent meeting people shaped by its legacies, enable her to acquaint you with the individuals behind the sterile and grim statistics: Three million Americans served in some capacity in Vietnam, and 58,000 did not return alive. Roughly ten percent of the entire Vietnamese population, accounting for more than four million soldiers and civilians, were killed or wounded.

Charlene introduces us to those who survived and relays their stories in their own words. There are the deeply moving stories of the veterans such as Gary, a Marine who wears a fatigue hat decorated with the Purple Heart, Bronze Star and Silver Star medals, and who still retains in his eyes "the look" of those who fought in Vietnam. He travels around the country with the Moving Wall, a replica of the Vietnam Memorial located in Washington. He now talks openly about his Vietnam experiences but deeply regrets that he was never able to tell his own wife that he was a Vietnam combat veteran before she died in 1980. Then there is the story and soulful picture of Quang, a Vietnamese Navy frogman, who saved thousands of American lives when he discovered and removed three mines from the hull of the U.S. Navy troop carrier *Upshur* in April 1972.

In her attempt to present a broad perspective, Charlene did not exclude the Viet Cong. She brings us the story of Toai, once a top commander of the Viet Cong and one of the planners of the Tet Offensive in 1968. Now, more than 30 years later, he is pictured still serving his famous noodle soup, as he did to the Americans who once ate downstairs while upstairs his people planned a victory over America.

The religious flavor of Vietnam is colorfully presented as well. A spectacular photograph of the Cao Dai temple in Tay Ninh Province brings me back to the time I spent in Parrot's Beak, that notorious section along the Cambodian border named for the shape of the deep incursion on the Vietnamese border line.

Charlene reminds us that those who fought in combat are not the only ones deeply touched by the war. More than one million Vietnamese fled Vietnam after the Communists seized control, and almost 400,000 of them, a somber number died in the attempt. Many, however, successfully escaped and emigrated to America, where they started new lives. Charlene introduces us to some of them and their children. For instance, we learn the story of Lana and her husband Byron who adopted a Vietnamese baby from Operation Babylift in April 1975. The child lived only for a month due to illness and malnutrition in Vietnam. Despite their heartbreak, they went on to adopt another baby from Vietnam and then another from Korea.

One of the most unforgettable and sadly lovely stories is the one of Bich, a beautiful Amerasian girl whose father Johnny never came back for her. Bich, however, triumphed over heart wrenching adversity. She was first placed into a relocation camp in Saigon, then sent to the Philippines and ultimately traveled to the United States, where she now lives with her young sons Trinh and Johnny.

Voices From Vietnam has something for everyone who had any connection to the war or Vietnam. I am an author who would like someday to return and recapture the emotional equity that went into researching *The Green Berets* and the three other books I wrote about Southeast Asia. In *Voices From Vietnam*, Charlene's photos and descriptions of the Vietnamese countryside I once knew, seem to indicate that it has changed little today, despite the war that raged through that small nation. This book makes me all the more interested in going back to see firsthand what she has portrayed so vividly in these pages. *Voices From Vietnam* reverberates with Charlene's passion for healing and her compassion for all of us—Americans and Vietnamese alike—who were at war in some way or another. Her work clings to your soul.

—Robin Moore

INTRODUCTION

A DENT ON MY HEART

*V*ietnam. The first time I heard the word Vietnam I was eleven. It was 1963, and I was studying the countries of Asia in my junior high social studies class. Vietnam. The second time I heard the word, I was thirteen. The Beatles invaded America in 1964 and the United States invaded Vietnam in 1965. Every day after school, my family compulsively watched as the Vietnam War invaded our homes via

mass media. Scenes of the mesmerizing violence played out in our living rooms with the sounds of bullets cracking and bombs exploding, and reports of body bag counts drifting through the air. Our lives were consumed with uncertainty in the constant shadow of this war half a world away. A world where tomorrow was not guaranteed. From that time forward, my adolescence was put on hold as I waited to see if my brother, cousins or dear friends would be the next to receive a draft notice from

Uncle Sam. A draft notice that would send them to this place where, in the great greenness of its countryside, thousands were to die—to this place of war that irrevocably changed my life, and the lives of a generation of Americans.

For the next few years, our countries remained embroiled in conflict. In 1968, the Communists attacked South Vietnamese cities, towns and military bases during the Tet holiday celebration, and in America, Martin Luther King Jr. and Senator Robert Kennedy were assassinated. In 1969, the year I graduated from high school, America's hippies descended upon a small farm in Woodstock; massive antiwar demonstrations were held in Washington; newspapers were filled with photos of North Vietnam's leader Ho Chi Minh, who died on September 3; and Americans landed on the moon.

I remember clearly where I was when it was announced that representatives of North and South Vietnam, the United States and the National Liberation Front had signed the Paris Peace Accords, ending direct U.S. military involvement in Vietnam. It was a snowy night, in January of 1973. I was in the restaurant of a ski lodge in southern Vermont. I never heard the entire announcement, because everyone in the restaurant was immediately on their feet screaming and cheering. Tears streamed down our faces as we hugged both our loved ones and strangers alike. Shortly afterward, in early 1973, American ground troops left the fighting behind and our POWs came home. Just two years later, on April 30, 1975, images from this place called Vietnam deluged our television screens again with Marine CH-46 helicopters as they evacuated the last Americans in Saigon from the roof of the embassy just hours before South Vietnam surrendered to the North. The images of panicked American and South Vietnamese military and support personnel scurrying beneath

whirling chopper blades and being hurriedly lifted off to safety burned into our nation's collective psyche, symbolizing for us the end of America's longest war.

The Americans called it the Vietnam War; the Vietnamese refer to it as the American War. By whatever name, it was a great tragedy. Three million Americans served in Vietnam; over fifty-eight thousand of these men and women did not return alive from its jungles, rice fields and cities. Nearly four million Vietnamese soldiers and civilians on both sides were killed or wounded. By war's end, more than 2,200 U.S. soldiers were missing in action, as were 300,000 of Vietnam's own sons and daughters. The Communists interned a few hundred thousand vanquished soldiers and South Vietnamese officials to reportedly brutal "re-education" camps. More than a million "boat people" fled their ancestral homes in leaky vessels to escape the continuing nightmare and nearly 400,000 died in the attempt. There was virtually no one in Vietnam whose life went untouched.

The war cost the American people billions of dollars. It left the Vietnamese country in shambles and its infrastructure in ruins. Six million tons of ordnance were dropped on Vietnam (the equivalent of a 500-pound bomb for every human being in that small country)—more than three times the amount dropped during World War II. Left behind were huge depressions in the rice paddies where the bombs fell. Many have filled with stagnant water and now harbor malarial mosquitoes. It is estimated that twenty million such craters litter the landscape.

And in the Vietnamese countryside, especially the area near Khe Sanh, tragedy still strikes as the remains of the war continue to kill and maim. Various kinds of wartime refuse, ranging from nearly 27,000 tons of munitions to unexploded bombs to hand grenades are scattered about. They can be found in a farmer's field or a child's playground; on, or just beneath the soil's surface. There they lie in wait, just as deadly as the day they were dropped some thirty years earlier. Even with this imminent danger, Vietnamese continue to comb the former battlegrounds searching for unexploded artillery, mortar shells, grenades, or any war material to sell for scrap metal. One day a scavenger might earn a couple of dollars, and, on another, he might lose his life. In this country where war supposedly ended long ago, the wailing of widows and the sobbing of parentless children continues.

Eleven million gallons of the defoliant Agent Orange were also left behind. Designed to kill trees by stripping the foliage—thus exposing the enemy—it was sprayed repeatedly over central and southern Vietnam during the war. This silent killer poisoned everything its vapors touched before seeping into the soil and water table. Today, Vietnam has an unusually high amount of children born with defects—everything from cleft palates and crossed eyes to spina bifida—believed to be a long-term result of this chemical pollutant.

Although Washington lifted the trade embargo against Vietnam in 1994, allowing American companies to get a foothold in their emerging market, Vietnam remains an impoverished nation with a per capita annual income of about $350. While billboards decorate the cities with ad-

vertisements for Coca-Cola, IBM and Seiko, electricity and fresh running water remain only a dream in many rural areas. While shops are making money from the remnants of the war by selling vintage American wristwatches, an array of bullet casings, metal helmets and Zippo lighters embossed with war rhymes, the people of the land eke out a living toiling in the once bloody rice paddies.

A new generation has been born in Vietnam since the war's end. Nearly two-thirds of the country's 77 million inhabitants are under 35 years of age and seem firmly focused on the present and the future, not the past. To them, the American War was three wars ago, merely a part of their country's history. Someday soon the elderly of yesterday's war will die, allowing the young to carry on without that war's memories.

After its soldiers came home, America wanted to forget about the war it lost. There was almost a conspiracy of silence surrounding the war. Even the veterans and their families rarely talked about it. But, whether it was talked about or not, combat changes a person, sometimes beyond all consideration. For most veterans, spending time in a war zone created a bitter battlefield inside and emotional wounds that won't heal.

The average age of the men who served in World War II was 26. Most already had life experience, while the young men who fought in Vietnam were 19 on average, and just out of high school. For most, the plane ride to Vietnam was their first trip away from the safety of their parents' home. The WW II soldiers went to war as part of a trained troop of men who had spent time together and who cared about one another. The soldiers heading off to Vietnam went as individuals, usually knowing no one else in their platoon. The World War II soldiers returned at war's end to be greeted by accolades and welcome-home parades, but the Vietnam soldiers returned home one by one throughout the many years of the war, often to jeers and questions like "How many babies did you kill?" One day a soldier was in a bloody battlefield using his wits to stay alive, and a few days later he was in his parents' living room watching the war on TV while listening to the latest family gossip. These soldiers had no one to talk to, no time to cry and no way to decompress their feelings.

The returning veterans did attempt to repair the broken threads of their lives, and despite the handicap of their war memories and a mostly ungrateful nation, the majority have gone on to lead productive, successful lives. Some others returned emotionally shattered and turned to drugs and alcohol to drown out memories of the horrors they experienced. Thousands of others have died since the war's end by their own hands, perhaps brought on by an unwelcome homecoming, by survivor guilt, or by post-traumatic stress disorder.

Slowly, long-overdue recognition was given to American soldiers and nurses for their efforts and sacrifices during our nation's longest and most divisive war. In the late 1970s and 1980s, movies like *The Deer Hunter, Apocalypse Now* and *Platoon* again brought the battlefields of Vietnam close to home. In 1982, the Vietnam Veterans Memorial was dedicated in Washington and created a place for vets and family members to bring their memories and to weep for the loss of more than 58,000 abbreviated lives. The Wall, which attracts 3.7 million visitors each year, helped to bring together this generation of silent sufferers. It has allowed this group of men and women to share their buried pain. It has allowed them to understand that, although they went to Vietnam as individuals and strangers, they did come home as brothers and sisters. And what they experienced in those 365 days of their innocent youth only they can understand. When they meet, hug, and whisper "Welcome home brother," into each other's ears, it allows a floodgate of tears to flow and cleanse, further helping to heal their wounds.

Do we know the exact moment day fades into night or when the direction of a person's life is altered forever? I believe all those involved in the Vietnam War know when that exact moment happened to them.

For me, a world traveler, landing in Vietnam on my first journey there in 1992 was that exact moment. No other country affected me the way Vietnam did, maybe because this country was a part of my history, part of my own memories and part of my adolescence. I was drawn like a magnet to this stirringly beautiful place that had haunted my soul for years. The patchwork of lush, brilliant emerald green rice paddies enriched with the varied scenes of everyday life; a coastline with stretching, pristine beaches; the exotic limestone outcrops of Halong Bay dotted with the silhouettes of junks and sampans; the remarkable minority tribes who still hunt with bows and arrows; the atmospheric old French villas; the rickety bridges of logs and bamboo spanning muddy watercourses; the offshore coral reefs and mysterious primal forests; all contrasting dramatically with the modern-day sights, sounds and pace of the cities whose busy streets overflow with humanity traveling along on the rising tide of cyclos, bicycles, motor scooters, cars, buses and trucks.

I spent my days photographing small explosions of rich color and faces that had a story to tell, and I spent my nights listening to those stories—stories of the old blending with the new from those Vietnamese whose eyes had lost all their innocence so many years ago. It was impossible for me to come away from Vietnam untouched. Upon returning home, I started compiling the stories of the amazing people I had met. Stories they shared with me as moments of their own past rushed back through their memories. Moments of history, of hope and despair that defined their lives. Moments that bring tears to the eyes, touch the heart and offer inspiration from those who have healed to those who still suffer.

My experiences in Vietnam made me curious to know more about the American soldiers and nurses and the Vietnamese in America. Not just the stories of the South Vietnamese, but also those of the North Vietnamese. I had so many questions. What happened to the Amerasian children created from this war; or those who chose to go to Canada to evade military service; and how had life changed for the family members of all those involved? As I did my research, I found that each story was unique, yet each was so similar. What began as a four-week journey during a six-month backpacking trip throughout Asia soon became a roller coaster out of control. One story led to just one more story and to two more journeys back to Vietnam, one in April and May of 1997 and again in April 2000. It was important for me to bring together all the threads of the war from which I eventually chose 70 of the most compelling stories I heard—the ones that have left the deepest tracks across my heart.

Creating this book has taught me so much about how dysfunctional war really is. And how, although the shooting stopped in Vietnam in April 1975, the war rages on in a different way in the consciousness of Americans and Vietnamese alike. It continues to shape and color the lives of everyone involved. Several generations of both American and Vietnamese carry with them visible—and more often invisible—scars of war.

As with all wars, the memories are a tapestry woven of fact and myth, of romance and savagery. Now, over a quarter-century since the Vietnam War ended, the passage of time has only slightly begun to erode its harsh legacy. It has taken ten years to create this book, and in that time I have spoken to many people, learned many facts,

and seen much pain. Through it all, the only things I know for sure—and that are historically consistent—are the grave sites left behind. There are no real winners in the cemeteries of war.

The irrationality and horrors of war, or for that matter, any of life's great traumas, are extraordinary events that transform everyday life in unimaginable ways. By reading the stories, meditating on the photographs and referring to the resource guide, I hope that those of you who are still troubled begin to find solace and that any unhealed emotional wounds may begin to melt away when you discover that you are not alone in your pain. It is also my hope that out of the depths of mankind's darkness will come a light, if only a flicker at first, that allows you to begin to reclaim your life from the constant shadow of Vietnam. By getting in touch with the feelings of today brought on by the actions of yesterday, my wish is that your broken spirit will embrace the paths of empowerment and healing and that peace will begin to echo inside the troubled corners of your heart.

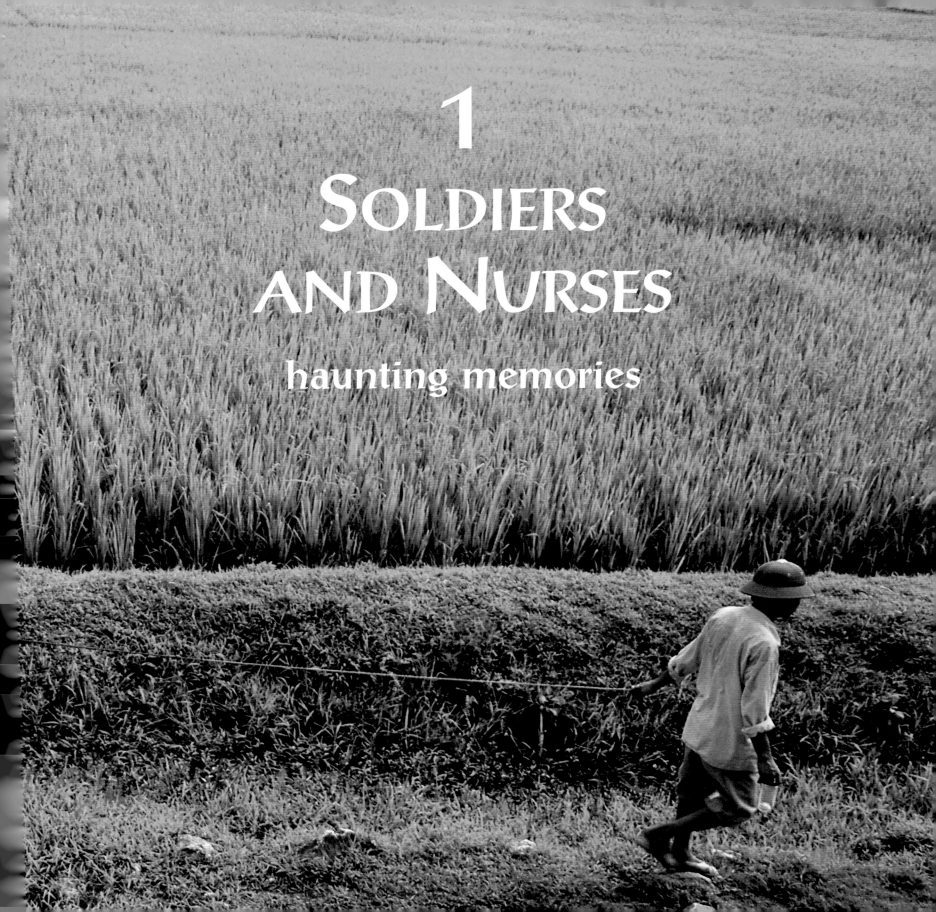

1
SOLDIERS
AND NURSES

haunting memories

As an 18-year-old soldier in 1966, Michael spent his tour of duty as a door gunner in a medevac helicopter, retrieving the wounded and dead. *(photo courtesy of Michael)*

I Can't Carry It Anymore

"*I* landed in Saigon on Thursday, April 21, 1966. Although I was with a hundred other soldiers, I was feeling very much alone and scared." Assigned to one of the war's most dangerous jobs, Michael would perch precariously in the open doorway of a medevac helicopter waiting to leap into the rice paddies, jungles, or ocean below to pick up wounded and dead soldiers—at times being shot at by the enemy as he attempted these rescue missions. "My best friend Mark's body was one of these soldiers." Staring intently, he continues, "My job felt like suicide in a war that I knew was crazy."

"My only real objective became to simply stay alive." The enemy was everywhere: It was a farmer, a woman in a rice paddy, a small child wired with explosives, unseen snipers, hidden booby traps, home-made spike balls, Agent Orange, poisonous snakes, "friendly" fire, and disease-ridden mosquitoes. Worst of all, themselves. "We were inexperienced, hardly more than boys, in the adult world of war, and we were terrified. I spent the entire year I was in 'Nam experiencing life in the extreme. Death was all around me." Michael stands up as he talks and crosses the room. "To relieve the terror, I began using alcohol and drugs."

Three hundred and sixty-five days after landing in Saigon, Michael's tour of duty ended and he was sent home. "Home? Nowhere felt like home anymore, especially not inside my own skin! It was awful. I couldn't handle the daily barrage of questions— 'Gee, how was it over there? Did you see any action? Did you kill anyone?' Over and over again, always the same questions. I just wanted to be left alone!" He constantly felt nervous and disconnected. "My parents and closest friends didn't know who I was anymore. There was only one buddy who could help me cope with what was happening. Only one that could help drown out the voices of Vietnam that were living in my head. Only one—my dear old buddy, Jack. Jack Daniels."

Michael's drinking escalated as the years passed. "In January 1989, I finally bottomed

> "**We were inexperienced, hardly more than boys, in the adult world of war, and we were terrified . . .**"

out. At that same time, I almost lost my oldest daughter—she was 19 then—to drugs. The day I brought her to long-term drug rehab was the day I stopped drinking."

Slowly, the memories of the war that he had managed to bury with alcohol began to take over his life. "My every day no longer took place in New York, but instead, it felt like the battlefields of Vietnam. I became a living time bomb." Michael's eyes close as his face falls forward into his cupped hands. "By 1990, my most private moments were consumed with thoughts of suicide. Thankfully, at this same time, someone new came into my life—someone who I trusted with my story. With her guidance, I took my pain to a Vietnam veterans counseling service and began my long journey home."

Michael attended group therapy with other vets, received private therapy, and went to daily AA meetings. After many long years of courage and a lot of hard work, he slowly learned to let go of his guilt and come to a place of healing. Time passed and, "The more I let go of my suffering and let peace and balance into my life, the more I wanted to share what was happening to me. As I did, strange things started to happen. People began to come to me and warmly, openly hug me. Through their tears, they would whisper 'thank you' for changing their lives and sometimes for saving them. It was amazing."

"On my birthday in 1994 I gave myself a special gift," he says, almost shyly. "I went to Washington to visit the Wall." The Vietnam Veterans Memorial Wall had been open for twelve years and this was his first visit. Michael's body shook as he slowly approached the Wall. He stood quietly for a long time looking at the seemingly endless columns of names carved into the black granite that reflected his own tearful image. "I searched the Wall and finally found Mark's name." His fingers trembled as he traced the letters. "And I said to him—'You bastard, it's been 28 years, and I still miss you every day.' I took a deep breath and said, 'Mark, we need to talk. That's why I'm here. Remember the day I carried you from the helicopter to the jeep for transport to the States? Well, I took on some very heavy baggage that day. I felt responsible for what happened to you. And guilty because you were dead and I was alive.' I fell to my knees, 'Mark, please help me. I can't carry it anymore.'" The tears came in choking sobs as he felt the weight of many years of suffering disappear.

"In the months and years that have passed since I visited the Wall, my life has changed forever." Michael's eyes are now clear and free of pain. "The demons that once lived inside me have finally moved out."

After many years of therapy and healing, Michael has finally banished the burden of anger, fear, and guilt that he carried since the war, and he has reached a place of peace. Michael continues to share his story with veterans in America and in Vietnam.

A Different Drummer

"Ask not what your country can do for you, ask what you can do for your country." John Kennedy's famous words were the driving force behind Pat's decision to join the Army Nurse Corps and volunteer to go to Vietnam. "After listening to President Kennedy back in the early sixties, I truly believed it was my obligation to somehow help out with the war effort. And, after watching the haunted looks on the faces of the young soldiers I saw on television every night, I knew I had to go to Vietnam. It was that simple."

Pat landed in Vietnam six weeks after being sworn into the Army Nurse Corps. She went almost instantly from studying diagrams in books to assisting real-life triage and tracheotomies. "Most of our casualties came right out of the field. We pasted them together and shipped them out. They were babies, 18 or 19 years old." Pat was only 22 at the time. She not only mended American soldiers, but also tribal people and locals from the surrounding villages. She mended not only adults, but also children and infants.

"Everything over there moved at such a rapid pace. A chopper lands, doors bang open, you're in the middle of hell. The boy is smoking from phosphorus wounds. His cries can be heard above the noise of the rotor blades. I run over to him. He grabs me and screams, *'Don't let me die. Help me!'* I didn't help him—I froze. At that very instant, I knew I couldn't let

my feelings get in the way ever again." Pat stares blankly as she remembers every detail. "I had to learn all too quickly to detach and numb all my feelings so I would survive. So I would survive and be able to help."

"The boys would have horrific nightmares and cry out at night. I remember this one young boy from the Midwest was wailing in his sleep. He was in terrible pain and very scared. Personal boundaries no longer existed—I climbed into bed with him and cradled him, protecting him from the enemy. After a while you have no idea of where you began or ended, or if you ended. Never for one minute did I recognize the emotional jeopardy that I was in."

Then in December 1967, the jeep Pat was traveling in flipped over and her right leg was nearly severed. She was now one of the wounded. "I was a nurse, not a soldier, and it never occurred to me that anything horrifying would ever happen to me. They rushed me to my evac hospital and the commanding officer temporarily glued me back together. 'Paste them together—ship them out.' When they told me they were sending me back home to the States to recuperate, I didn't want to go! Vietnam was now my home."

Pat was sent against her wishes to Walter Reed Hospital in Maryland, where they put her leg in a cast up to her thigh. The hospital staff seemed uncaring and unsupportive, and this added to Pat's already poor emotional state. She became deeply depressed and struggled with anorexia, a problem she had since childhood. "It's as if everything I thought was, well, it just wasn't anymore."

During her stay in the hospital, Pat met John, a veteran who was recovering from a sniper wound. They were married six months later. After almost a year in a field hospital, three-and-a-half years at Walter Reed going from cast to cast and surgery to surgery, Pat was finally released from the hospital. She went home with John, but the transition to housewife and mother in suburbia and the stresses of two veterans raising adopted children were taking a serious toll. "Both John and I were anxious and depressed all the time, but failed to recognize the connection between these feelings and our personal troubles to Vietnam."

Pat sought solace with various therapists and veteran groups. "I was in so much pain that my hair hurt." Pat finally found a therapist who understood about the aftermath of war and post-traumatic stress. "It has taken me years to untangle the haunting memories of Vietnam." Pat's voice breaks with emotion. "A lot of my work with the therapist revolved around the nightmares I was having about the war, especially the one which plagues me regularly. I'm in a VA [Veterans Administration] hospital and walk through two doors. On the other side of the door I step into Vietnam today, as a middle-aged woman. A boy walks out of the jungle with a bandage wrapped around a wound that wasn't treated for days. He appears a bit disoriented. I walk over to him and tell him

> *"I was a nurse, not a soldier, and it never occurred to me that anything horrifying would ever happen to me . . ."*

31

An emotionally strong woman, Pat survived the trauma of being a nurse in an Army field hospital and a long hospitalization for her own war injuries. She works today to survive her haunting memories.

that everything is going to be okay. I start to unravel his bandage. From behind the layers of blood-soaked gauze, maggots begin to fall onto the floor. He's talking to me and I have to keep his eyes trained on mine so he won't notice the maggots infesting his wounded arm. His eyes—his hollow, pale, green eyes—haunt me to this day."

"I have come to understand that I will never look at the world the same way everyone else does. I now realize I have a profound inner strength that I wouldn't have had if I didn't volunteer to go to Vietnam and follow a different drummer."

Torn By Two Nations

"The noise of the war was always in the background when I grew up in Saigon in the 1960s. I didn't pay much attention to it, though, until 1968 when the fighting came to my city's streets." Hoi Quang was in the eleventh grade when his city came under attack. "I remember houses in flames, people screaming and dead bodies lying in the streets." After hesitating for a long moment, Hoi Quang goes on to say, "I was really scared." Because he was born into a wealthy family, he could have avoided military service. But, despite his family's status and his own fears, Hoi Quang felt compelled to do what was right. At the age of 17, he enlisted in the South Vietnamese Navy.

Shortly after joining the Navy, he had the opportunity to become a Navy frogman. He trained for a year, learning to become a skilled scuba diver and studying explosives disposal. He graduated in 1970 and joined the EOD (Explosive Ordnance Disposal) Team Five. He married the same year.

"I was sent all over the south of Vietnam to check for enemy booby traps planted on American and South Vietnamese ships." During silent nights and quiet early mornings, Hoi Quang would dive into the calm sea just after low or high tide. He discovered and defused many bombs on both American and Vietnamese boats. The most terrifying situation he encountered was on April 22, 1972. During a routine check, he spotted three mines attached to the Upshur, an American Navy troop carrier that held thousands of sailors. "After evacuating everyone from the ship, I removed the bombs and towed them 500 yards out to sea, where I set up explosives and blew them up." The pumping adrenaline of that dark, intense night is felt as Hoi Quang retells the story. Six months after this successful mission, the United States

Hoi Quang joined the South Vietnamese Navy at the age of 17. He was awarded the Bronze Star medal for discovering and then removing three mines attached to a U.S. Navy ship, saving the lives of thousands of men. *(photo courtesy of Hoi Quang)*

government awarded him the Bronze Star medal for heroic achievement in connection with combat operations against the enemy.

Hoi Quang remained in the Navy until the war ended in 1975, at which time he went home to his wife and children. His service records indicated only that he was a low-ranking regular Navy man; therefore, he was interned in a re-education camp for only three days. After being released from the camp, one of his neighbors betrayed his friendship and informed the Communists what Hoi Quang's job had really been during the war. He was immediately arrested and hauled off to another camp, where he was sentenced to one year of hard labor.

After being released from the camp, Hoi Quang worked as a diver for a private company that lifted sunken boats out of the sea for salvage. But within two years, the new government of the North took over the company. "When that happened, I quit! I would not work for a company run by the Communists." From that day on, Hoi Quang expended all his energies pursuing a better life for his family. "It took me two years, but one of my sons and I finally escaped on a small boat that left from the southernmost part of Vietnam." Hoi Quang captained the boat, which took 32 others to safety.

"We were stopped three times by pirates. The first time was the worst. It was our second day at sea. They held us captive from eight in the morning until two in the afternoon." Hoi Quang remembers as if it were yesterday. "They stole all of our valuables and without any care or concern, they used a hammer and screwdriver to extract the gold teeth from the mouths of the old people." After taking a deep breath, he continues, "They raped one of the women. At first, she tried to escape by jumping into the ocean and killing herself, but they pulled her out of the water, and then fifteen of the pirates gang-raped her."

"One hour later, another boat came. This time they took the only thing remaining—our tool box. After they left, our engine stopped working. We were drifting in the middle of the ocean, and I was sure we were all going to die." With that thought in his mind, Hoi Quang turned to his six-year-old son to talk to him. "My son knew me so well. I will never forget his words and the look of hope on his young face. He looked up at me and said, 'No, Father—we aren't going to die. You can fix the engine.'" Somehow, Hoi Quang did fix the engine, and on the third day another boat came. "Surprisingly, this last boat gave us food and water, and showed me the way to Thailand. We were lucky, very lucky."

After spending some time in a refugee camp, Hoi Quang and his son came to America, and settled in California. They immediately sent for the rest of their family in Vietnam. "My wife's reply shocked me. She and my two other children were staying in Vietnam." Hoi Quang plummeted into despair. He did not know what to do. He felt torn by two nations and by two families. "I decided to stay in the States, go to school for automobile mechanics, and raise my son—alone."

In 1987, Hoi Quang's childhood girl-friend phoned him. They reunited and married in 1988. "I'm really lucky to have come to the United States. We have so much freedom here. I won't go back to Vietnam as long as the Communists are there, not even to visit." Hoi Quang turns and reaches for a picture of his children who are still in Vietnam. "I miss my kids so much." Even though they are now grown and married, Hoi Quang dreams about them as they were the last time he saw them, as little children. Today, Hoi Quang spends his days working as an automobile mechanic, but some of his nights are still consumed with fear. As the past lurks in the dark, quiet shadows, he waits for the Viet Cong to break down the door and take him away.

Today in America, there are still some dark nights when the former frogman waits for the VC (Viet Cong) to come and take him away.

And He Taps...

*U*nlike most of the American soldiers in Vietnam who had grown up in places with concrete sidewalks or wide-open spaces, John had grown up in a place with lush, tangled jungles. Unlike most of them, gunfire and fear were as familiar to him as weekend walks in the park were to most Americans. Born in Guatemala and raised there and in Belize, John grew up during a time of intense guerrilla warfare in his homeland. He came to the United States to attend college and then entered the United States military.

As a child in Central America, John walked to and from school on a trip fraught with terror. "The worst part of my walk to school was when I had to cross the railroad tracks early in the morning." John starts tapping lightly on the arms of his chair as he describes the vivid memories of his youth. "We lived in a small community where everyone knew each other. The rebels came and killed my neighbors during the night, then took their bodies to the tracks. In the morning, the coal trains that chugged along the tracks would run right over the bodies and the fire produced beneath the train created from the burning coal would burn them."

John's tapping increases its pace—louder and faster. "When I was in Vietnam and a Skyraider dropped its deadly cargo, the napalm would eat right through the flesh of anyone who got in its way." As the memory of the smell of burning flesh fills his nostrils, John's tapping fills the room with noise. "You know, your senses are a powerful thing. A smell, a taste or a sound can bring you back to a time and place stored somewhere deep in your memory. In the Vietnamese jungle when the smell of stagnant pools, rotting vegetation and our own filthy bodies were mixed with the smell of burning flesh, that was the worst imaginable." Suddenly, the tapping stops. The total silence is a shock.

John begins to speak again, tears filling his eyes, "When I was growing up in Guatemala, the old folks taught us how to beat the Carib drums to create music for dancing and celebration. Today, whenever I get upset or nervous, I tap or drum on anything that's nearby. It feels comforting, like the drums of my youth."

No one at the draft board told John, a Belizian who was attending college in America, that he was eligible for a deferment, so he was sent to Vietnam where the terrain and warfare were a brutal reminder of his war-torn homeland.

When John first came from Central America to the United States, he attended Fordham University for three semesters, from February 1965 to May 1966. Before the next semester began, "Uncle Sam" called. "I was told that as a resident of the United States I had to register for the armed forces. What they neglected to tell me was that I could have applied for a college deferment." When John left for the service, his wife was three months pregnant with their first child.

John trained in the States as a paratrooper and later as an air traffic controller. By December, he was stationed in Bien Hoa, where he worked as an air traffic controller. After Tet, he was reassigned to Phu Bai to work LRRP (long-range reconnaissance patrol). He and his troop would go on dangerous, endless jaunts, slogging through the forest to gather information on the enemy. "The forest canopy felt very familiar to me—it was my home as a child."

They spent weeks at a time in the thick jungle confronting not only the Viet Cong, mines and punji stakes, but the hostile jungle itself. John tightens up as he reflects on his days in Vietnam. "We would walk on the soggy ground for miles on end—our hands sweaty against the plastic stock of our M-16 rifles. Our blood pumped loudly through our temples. We ate C-rations, didn't bathe and had a good chance of getting ringworm, dysentery, hookworm, malaria or all of these." The tropical jungle can be a mean place with stinging ants, blood-sucking leeches and over 100 species of poisonous snakes lying in wait. A bite from a five-foot-long cobra, a black and yellow colored krait or a bright-green bamboo viper could kill a soldier in a matter of hours.

"By July, I was vomiting all the time and my eyes had turned yellow. They tried telling me I had hepatitis from the water or the food, but I believe I was sick from Agent Orange." This was not the only symptom that John endured that might have been caused by the toxic defoliants that were sprayed on the jungles when he was in Vietnam. "It started the summer I returned home. Whenever I got hot and sweaty, I developed lesions on my hands and white blotches on my forehead. I went to a dermatologist who took scrapings that showed the problems stemmed from a chemical compound. I believe they were caused by Agent Orange. The scars and blotches have never gone away."

The hepatitis was John's ticket out of Vietnam. After months of hospitalizations, he was discharged on October 31, 1968. "I was in Staten Island, walking toward the ferry and home to my wife and new baby girl and still wearing my Army uniform. Then from out of nowhere, a woman came up to me and asked, 'Were you in Vietnam?' I innocently answered, 'Yes, but I've been back since July.'" What happened next was a bitter surprise. "She screamed at me—'You are a baby-killer!'—and then she spat on me." John's fingers are again tapping on his chair. "It was unbelievable. It took a long time for those words to register. I just stared at her for what seemed like forever, trying to decide what to do next. My gut reaction was to grab her by the neck and choke the life out of her. Lucky for this lady, my mother had lectured me to never lay a hand on a woman. If that was a man who had just spit on me, I would still be doing jail time, 'cause I would have killed him in a minute."

John went home to his family, hung up his uniform and never talked about Vietnam to anyone. Life went on. He had a son, went back to school and earned a bachelor's in computer science. He now works as a programmer.

"The one thing I learned when I got home from Vietnam was to never talk about my experiences there. I promised myself I would never talk about it and tried not to even think about it." Today, as he breaks that promise to himself, the memory of his uniform comes back and his eyes flood with tears. "I used to feel proud to wear my uniform. When I put it away all those years ago, I never even had it cleaned." His fingers tap the chair arm. "That horrid woman's spit is still on my jacket." And he taps his drums.

"Westy"

General William C. Westmoreland, or "Westy," as he was commonly known, commanded all United States military operations in Vietnam from 1964 until 1968. At 84, he is still a handsome West Pointer with a strong chiseled chin. He stands straight and tall with his hands clasped in front of him, altar-boy style, as he shares stories of his childhood. "I was born in 1914, the son of a cotton mill manager and a housewife from rural South Carolina." Westmoreland grew up a country boy who played the flute and trained in boxing in his spare time. At the age of fifteen, he had the good fortune to attend a World Boy Scout Jamboree in England. "I got to mingle with boys from all over the world, and this gave me an international perspective. It was a great experience and instilled in me a love of travel, greatly influencing the rest of my life."

> **"My father wanted me to become an attorney and my mother wanted me to be a doctor."**

Shown in the Oval Office in November 1967, General Westmoreland and President Johnson discuss war tactics. *(photo courtesy of Rip Westmoreland)*

"My father wanted me to become an attorney and my mother wanted me to be a doctor." He shrugs, "Instead, I went to West Point Military Academy." Westmoreland graduated in 1936 as the Cadet Corps' first captain and won the coveted John J. Pershing sword, an award for leadership and military proficiency. Following this honor, he was commissioned as a second lieutenant and served in the 18th Field Artillery at Fort Sill, Oklahoma. With humor in his voice he explains, "It was the 1930s, and horses and mules were still an artillery officer's means of mobility."

During World War II, Westmoreland commanded artillery battalions in Sicily and North Africa. While there, he suffered two bouts of malaria and a brush with a land mine that blew a truck out from under him, but left him mostly unharmed. By 1946, he was promoted to captain; in that same year he received airborne training at the Infantry School and commanded the 504th Parachute Infantry, 82d Airborne Division. One year later he married Kitsy. Westy stands up from his comfortable-looking armchair, crosses the room and looks lovingly at the painted portrait of his life's companion.

In 1952, Westmoreland volunteered for duty in Korea and went overseas as the commander of the 187th Airborne Regimental Combat Team. After Korea, following a round of Pentagon assignments, Westmoreland became the Army's youngest major general at the age of 42. In 1964, he was sent to Vietnam, where he assumed command of all United States military operations and 190,000 men.

"When I was in Vietnam, I woke up every morning at 6:30, did 25 push-ups and a few isometric exercises, then ate breakfast. I was at my desk by 7:30 and stayed till nightfall, usually bringing work home each night." As the war ground on, he tried to spend at least two days a week in the field, meeting as many of his men as he possibly could. Westmoreland knew how hard it was for his men to fight in the Vietnamese jungles day after day. Still his philosophy was, "If the other guy can live and fight under these conditions, so can we." Sadly, he watched as his young soldiers turned too quickly into aged men.

General Westmoreland was replaced by General Creighton Abrams in late 1968. After his assignment in Vietnam, Westy served as the Chief of Staff of the Army, a post he held until his retirement in the summer of 1972. Westmoreland chuckles with restraint as he reflects on his 36-year military career, "My first mount in the Army was a horse and my last was a helicopter . . . I feel privileged to have commanded American soldiers in three wars." He proudly adds, "The American soldier is the best in the world."

Following retirement, he traveled, lectured extensively, and wrote his autobiography, *A Soldier Reports: A Memoir of 40 Years in Uniform*. Westmoreland earned five honorary degrees, 17 battle campaign stars from three wars, and four distinguished service medals. He was decorated by 16 foreign countries and, in 1965, his photo appeared on the cover of *Time* magazine as their "Man of the Year." Today, Westmoreland plays golf and receives visits from his three children, six grandchildren, and people around the world.

William C. Westmoreland, always a straightforward, determined man, talks about his life, "I feel very fortunate with the opportunities I've had. Some were tough assignments, but the tougher the assignment, the greater the chance to fill it in an honorable way." With a hint of sorrow in his weary eyes and voice he continues, "I never look backward. I deal with that which was, not that which could have been." He stares in the distance before lowering his eyes. When he looks up again he says in an even tone, "People always ask me how I want to be remembered. I'd like to let history take its course. I don't know what it will say about me, but I hope that history will take note of the last sentence I wrote in my book, 'As a soldier prays for peace, he must be prepared to cope with the hardships of war and bear its scar.' I bear its scars."

Westy, although retired, remains a soldier—scars and all.

General William Westmoreland commanded soldiers in three wars, and says he bears the scars of war.

"Uncle Ho"

Ho Chi Minh was affectionately nicknamed "Uncle Ho" by his admirers. Known by some as a man who loved children, here he sits surrounded by delighted students. *(photo courtesy of the Embassy of Vietnam)*

He might have been small in stature, but he was large in reputation. He is remembered by some as a great leader, a patriot, and a humanitarian, and by others as a schemer, manipulator and tyrant. Who was Ho Chi Minh or "Uncle Ho," as he is more affectionately remembered by his admirers?

His birth name is disputed, probably lost to history, but many say he was born Nguyen Sinh Cung on May 19, 1890, in a small village southwest of Hanoi. In accordance with Vietnamese custom, at the age of ten he received a new name, Nguyen Tat Thanh. During his lifetime, he assumed over 50 aliases, each marking a new phase of his life, mastered many languages, including English, German, Russian, Mandarin, Cantonese, Thai, and French, and was employed as a teacher, waiter, photo retoucher, gardener, snow sweeper, cook's apprentice, writer, and ultimately revolutionary.

Ho left Vietnamese soil for the first time at 21, and began an apprenticeship to a cook on a French ship. This was the beginning of a three-year journey that took him to France, England, America and North Africa. While living abroad, he began reading revolutionary literature and became acquainted with the ideas of the political theorist Karl Marx. This helped shape his

ideas about communism and gave direction to the rest of his life. After his three-year voyage, he lived briefly in London, then moved on to France. He stayed there for years, engaging in radical activities and eventually becoming a founding member of the French Communist Party in 1920. In 1923, he left for Moscow, where he was trained to work as a spy and to promote revolution throughout the world by the Communist International, an organization created by then Soviet leader Vladimir Lenin. From there, Ho Chi Minh traveled to Canton in southern China where he helped to found the Vietnamese communist movement, which evolved into the Indochina Communist Party in 1930. During these years, he was arrested many times for participating in subversive activities, and spent time in, and escaping from, a number of prisons.

Disguised as a Chinese journalist, Ho slipped back into Vietnam after a 30-year absence. By then a highly influential man, he helped to establish the Viet Minh Front, also called the League for the Independence of Vietnam. Their objective was to gain independence for Vietnam from French colonial rule and Japanese occupation. A few years later, in 1945, Ho Chi Minh led the August Revolution, which succeeded finally in taking control of the country and proclaiming the formation of an independent Democratic Republic of Vietnam. Ho was made president, and wrote Vietnam's Declaration of Independence. Around this time, he changed his name to the name that he always would be remembered by: Ho Chi Minh, which roughly means "Bringer of Light" or "Enlightener."

The Viet Minh rule was short-lived, because the French returned and forced him and his men to flee into the mountains. There, they took up arms and fought the French in the rice paddies and mountains for the next eight years. Ho's Viet Minh, who started as an unknown, poorly armed force, soon became a strong military threat. Their fervor to win was indomitable. Ho Chi Minh's own words to a French official said it best, "You can kill ten of my men for every one I kill of yours, but even at those odds, I will win and you will lose." They did suffer heavy losses, but their desire to win back their country from foreign dominance prevailed. The final showdown came in 1954, when the Viet Minh succeeded victoriously against the French at the Battle of Dien Bien Phu. The Geneva Accords provided for a temporary partition of the country at the 17th parallel, with elections scheduled to occur throughout Vietnam in 1956 to vote on the eventual fate of the two halves. But the American-backed government of Ngo Dinh Diem, who controlled the southern part of the country, refused to hold them, knowing that Ho Chi Minh would win. Ho Chi Minh led the North until his death in September 1969, six years before Vietnam was reunited.

Ho never married and, to anyone's knowledge, never fathered any children. He was known by some to be a charming man, with a great wit, humility, simplicity and sincerity that impressed people, from fishermen to priests, wherever he went.

"You can kill ten of my men for every one I kill of yours, but even at those odds, I will win and you will lose."

Like Lenin and Mao Zedong, Ho Chi Minh requested to be cremated upon his death. He did not want to be put on public display and laid out for the world to see. In his will, he specified that his ashes were to be placed in three urns to be positioned on three unmarked hilltops, one in the North, another in the South and the third in the center of the country. Despite his wishes, in September of 1975, his body was laid to rest in Hanoi in a glass sarcophagus set inside a huge, imposing, gray stone mausoleum. Guided tours are conducted daily throughout the year to view his remains. An armed guard wearing a starched military uniform escorts visitors as they stand in two-by-two columns on a bright red carpet. The rules are recited: No hats, no shorts, no tank tops, no cameras, no gum chewing, no smiling, no hands in pockets.

Frigid air shocks the body when entering the overpowering gray mausoleum. Narrow hallways connect to a large room, creating the appearance of a castle surrounded by a moat of ominous guards. In this castle is an elevated platform where Ho Chi Minh's embalmed corpse lies in repose under a glass casket. A pink light shines on the platform, giving his face a peaceful glow. This slight-looking man wielded an enormous power over countless people's lives, and his power can still be felt through all the protective layers of his tomb.

Ho Chi Minh, the founder of the Vietnamese Communist Party and President of the Democratic Republic of Vietnam, is laid to rest in this stone mausoleum, although he requested to be cremated and have his ashes left in the mountains.

Michael's Welcome Home

They spit on me.
I came home after 365 days of uncertainty and fear.
And they spit on me.
I am angry and confused.
But I fought the war for you, for your children,
and your children's children.
For freedom.
Freedom for all of us.
My anger builds.
I killed the Viet Cong. Our enemy.
I gave up my youth in the jungle, to hidden booby traps,
claymore mines, and mists of Agent Orange.
I used my body as a shield to protect you from communism.
My anger becomes rage.
I jumped out of helicopters into enemy territory to pick up the bodies of my
wounded buddies. Soldiers who were your sons and your brothers.
I glued and bandaged them back together. I saved their lives.
Then they were sent back into the battlefield to be killed.
It's not my fault. I'm not the one who sent them back.
Sadness overwhelms my rage.
Please understand.
I did my best. The best I knew how.
For God's sake, you should be thanking me.
Not spitting on me.
My rage lies buried, ready to erupt.

Coming home after 365 days in the battlefields of Vietnam, veterans were sometimes cursed instead of thanked. This only served to intensify their confusion and rage.

We're Sure to Go to Heaven

"*I*t's a terrible thing to live your life in constant fear." Gene clears his throat nervously, and presses the palms of his hands tightly together. "When I go to sleep at night, the helicopters still loom overhead and the Viet Cong still hide in the shadows." More than 30 years have elapsed since Gene last set foot on Vietnamese soil, yet memories from his past continue to visit him daily with extreme clarity.

His mother was an Abenaki Indian, his father, an Ojibway. Born in Hartford, Connecticut, when his mother was only fifteen, Gene was sent to Canada when he was six weeks old to be raised by his great aunt and uncle on an Abenaki reservation. "Although we were real poor when I was growing up, we still had a wonderful connection to our heritage and a love of our family. We never lacked for food because we lived off the land and even chopped wood to heat the stove. My family earned about eight dollars a week from making baskets. On the downside, a new pair of pants would have to last us at least two years." Gene attended school on the reservation until the sixth grade, when he was main-streamed into the public school system; at fourteen, he left school all together. "It was an Indian tradition to work as a guide and take tourists into the woods to hunt moose and fish for trout. I only did this for a year because when I was fifteen I took off for New York to live with my mother. We spent the next couple of years getting to know each other." Gene sits

Gene is shown here in August 1966 at Hill 55 holding a sniper rifle.
(*photo courtesy of Gene*)

46

on his couch, a beer in hand as he continues, "During my days I worked as a roofer, but the nights were consumed with a lot of drinking."

His stepfather was concerned that Gene was headed down the wrong track so one day he made him a dare, a dare that altered the course of Gene's life. "He bet me 100 dollars that I couldn't make it through boot camp in the Marine Corps. I was determined to show him!" Gene accepted the challenge and eagerly went to the induction center with his mother, who had to sign his enlistment papers because he was too young to enlist. "On May 6, 1965, I left for boot camp training and in less than a year I was headed to Vietnam." Gene sits back comfortably, as an ironic grin takes form on his face. "The Marines took an arrogant young Indian construction worker and made him into a 'warrior.'"

"Vietnam seemed real familiar to me. The primitive wooden houses, the dusty dirt roads and the absence of cars made me feel right at home, like on the Indian reservation." Gene also felt more familiar with the long hours of isolation and quiet the jungles brought. His fellow soldiers were used to constant distractions and entertainment like television and radios; they had a hard time dealing with the silence and their own thoughts. Gene, on the other hand, felt comfortable and at peace. Reservation life tended to foster an environment of self-reliance, a meditative way of thinking and introspection—all great skills for a lonely jungle life.

Gene served two tours in Vietnam with the 1st Battalion, 9th Marine Division. He worked as a scout sniper and participated in numerous patrols, reconnaissance, and operations, eventually advancing to the rank of sergeant. "I tried to use my time in Vietnam to better myself. I was in a bunker at Hill 55 when I took and passed my high school equivalency test." But Vietnam was no vacation for Gene. One day during an ambush by a division of NVA (North Vietnamese Army) regulars, Gene was wounded. Mortar rounds blew up next to him and when he got up to run for cover, his leg failed. Shrapnel had destroyed his knee and damaged the nerves on the right side of his face. "I was medevaced to a hospital where they threw on a cast, and as soon as that healed, they sent me back out to the war." Gene left Vietnam on October 20, 1967, and the service two years after that.

Once out of the military and back in the States, he spent eight years working construction and tending bar. But he spent all of his down time isolated. Afraid of his own thoughts, he tried to drown his emotions in alcohol. "Things had gotten really bad with everything in my life. I remember when I was near the bottom. It was 5:30 one morning and I had a .357 Magnum in my hand. I was ready to pull the trigger when 'the guy upstairs' said to me—'I didn't pull you through Vietnam for you to do this!'" Gene got it together long enough to make a different choice than suicide. He decided to return to his roots as a Native American in hopes of finding peace.

> *"I remember when I was near the bottom. It was 5:30 one morning and I had a .357 Magnum in my hand."*

Back on the familiar reservation, Gene faced the deep guilt he felt about having killed other human beings. "I couldn't understand why I was alive, especially when I wasn't a good enough person." For the next three years, Gene worked as a school bus driver on the reservation, but would not accept a salary for the job. It was a kind of payback for all the children who had been killed in Vietnam. He married a few times and had three children, but his relationships always ended in failure.

Ultimately, Gene realized that he needed professional help for his emotional problems. "I did go to three different therapists and none of them worked out. My family problems were so awful and getting worse every day. I was impossible to live with—who should have to live with my mood swings, my flashbacks, and my alcohol abuse? A lot of times I would cry for what seemed like no reason at all." Gene suffered from chronic depression and suicidal thoughts. "Finally, in 1985, I did find a wonderful psychiatrist. He was a Vietnam veteran himself, so he understood my pain—he truly saved my life! We worked together for thirteen years until he retired. I really miss him."

"Of all the problems I worked on with my therapist, probably the hardest one concerned the government. I felt like what the American government had done to the American Indian in the last few hundred years, the VA was now doing to the American veteran. Not even an enemy would do to another enemy what our own government did to us. What were we? Guinea pigs for the economy? Do they think we don't know that they made an economic decision to start that war?" Gene's eyes are filled with rage, his voice escalating in fury as he goes on. "But why don't they do what they said they were going to do? 'We take care of our vets.' Ha! What a lie!"

Gene's anger at the government did not change once he crossed the Canadian border. As a nation, Canada was not involved in the war, but Canadian men did cross into the States to enlist. (It is estimated that more Canadian men came to the States to join the American war effort than Americans went to Canada to avoid military service.) Upon returning from Vietnam, Canadian veterans, like many of their American counterparts, were ignored or treated with open hostility by the Canadian government and people.

Even now, Gene sleeps only when he is totally exhausted or self-medicated with alcohol. "I sleep only an hour or so, then I get up in a cold sweat, walk around, have a smoke and a soda, then sleep another hour, get up and do the same, all night long. At night I still live on the battlefields of Vietnam, even after 30 years. Funny thing though, I couldn't imagine life today without my experiences from Vietnam in it. And as crazy as this sounds, I would do it all over again. Since then, I have never found—and am sure I'll never find again—the kind of friends I had then. It was the kind of friendship, brotherhood, and people I would put my life on the line for anytime, anywhere, all over again." Sobbing like a little boy, Gene finishes by saying, "We all went to hell in Vietnam, so we're sure to go to heaven when we die."

Approximately 42,000 Native Americans, more than 90% of them volunteers, fought in Vietnam. Gene, a Native American, continues to fight the VC every night in his nightmares.

49

I Didn't Cry
in Vietnam

> *"Even today, I cry. I cry in my room where no one can see. I cry over the pain and needless suffering I've seen. Over all the lost lives. Over my life."*

Today, Erin looks like a kindly grandmother. Upon first meeting her, no one would suspect that she is, in fact, a courageous warrior who dedicated her life to mending and healing soldiers. "My career as a nurse spanned three wars. It began in February 1945, when I was commissioned as a second lieutenant in the United States Army and assigned to the 319th Station Hospital in Bremerhaven, Germany. During the Korean War, I was attached to a MASH unit that relocated every two or three days." Erin had the distinction of being the youngest nurse to participate in the Korean War.

After earning a master's of science degree in nursing service administration and attaining the rank of lieutenant colonel, she was sent to Cantho, Vietnam in 1968. "Each war was different from the last, but the first two were nothing like Vietnam," Erin says as she reflects on her days there. "I worked as the chief nurse at the 29th Evacuation Hospital and took care of wounded and sick soldiers and local tribal people. I remember the sheer terror I felt when the enemy fired mortar rounds into the camp at night. My nurses and I would run to take cover in sandbag bunkers, where we sometimes stayed for hours. I still keep in contact with many of those nurses today." Erin continues with sadness in her voice, "The bonds that Vietnam created are hard for outsiders to understand."

Erin was a colonel when she retired from the Army in 1974 with many honors and medals, including the Bronze Star for bravery during her tour in Vietnam. "When I retired, I set out to enjoy my life. I bought a mobile home and started to travel all over the United States." But her journey was cut short when, in 1981, she suffered a severe aneurysm. "The doctors found an unusual amount of swelling in my brain and suspected that chemicals, perhaps Agent Orange, had caused my problem." This did not stop Erin; once out of the hospital, she drove her mobile home from Washington, D.C. to Alaska by herself.

Erin's career as an Army nurse spanned three wars. She still cries privately over the lost lives she witnessed.

Today, Erin cries as she speaks of the past. Tears that were never allowed to fall in Vietnam are finally escaping from their hiding places. "I didn't cry, drink or do drugs in Vietnam. I kept the pain inside because I had to be strong for my nurses." Erin then admits, "But I cried when I got home to America. Even today, I cry. I cry in my room where no one can see. I cry over the pain and needless suffering I've seen. Over all the lost lives. Over my life."

The Silent Vet

"Yeah, I was in Vietnam. No big deal. I never think about being there. It's not a part of my life and who I am today, and I really don't want to talk about the past. Please stop asking me questions about the war. Dammit! Can't you hear me? I don't want to talk about it. Get out of my face before I get into yours!!!"

Joe, like many Vietnam veterans, tuned out a piece of his life—the piece he spent in Vietnam. He believed that if he did not talk about it, then it did not happen. And if it did not happen, it cannot hurt. Unfortunately, this enforced silence did not make Joe's pain go away.

Joe positions his M-60 machine gun in his bunker near the airport in Chu Lai, where his unit guards radar and communication controls for aircraft in 1965. (*photo courtesy of Joe*)

Many veterans like Joe have repressed and denied the tremendous grief and shame that engulfs them. Approximately 30% of the Americans who are Vietnam veterans do not admit to being involved in the war. Many have told their families not to ask them about the war or to even mention the war in general. Some of these veterans have hidden their feelings about the war so well that their own spouses do not even know that they were in Vietnam. Others, while admitting their participation in the war to their wives, have never told friends or co-workers that they served in Vietnam. Sometimes that silence takes a deadly toll on a veteran's life.

Joe says that people who fail to understand why he and other Vietnam veterans would choose to be silent about the war did not experience the fear of living day after day, for 365 days or more on the brink of death. They did not watch their dearest friends lose their lives prematurely, violently, and pointlessly. They did not walk down the tarmac next to these young men when they returned to American soil to be greeted by ridicule, horrific accusations, and spit. And they have never been looked down upon and harassed by total strangers asking them, "How many babies did you kill?"

These silent veterans often live in emotional isolation and with buried sadness. Their only crime was answering their country's call in an age of flawed authority. They are heroes of quiet courage.

Joe has been living in emotional isolation since the war. He rarely admits to anyone that he served in Vietnam.

Toai's Noodle Soup Shop

*T*oai stands motionless at the window of his noodle soup shop on Ly Chinh Thang Street. As he gazes out at the Saigon of today and its chaotic pace of change, he reminisces about the 86 years of his long and astonishing life.

"I was born in Thai Binh, in the North. Life was hard back then. By the time I was twelve, I was working full-time as a silk weaver in my home village. I joined the anti-colonial underground when I was in my teens." Toai's decision to fight against France's domination of Vietnam changed the course of his life. It was not long before the French jailed him as an insurgent for taking part in the Xo Viet Nghe Tinh (Nghe Tinh Soviet uprising). While in prison, he was taught by experts—prison became his school of revolutionary education. Upon his release, he resumed his political activities as the commander of a Viet Minh guerrilla fighting squad in the North.

Years later, after escaping another French prison, he obtained a false identification card and moved to Saigon in 1951. "I needed an occupation so I could live unnoticed in the South. I decided to open a noodle soup shop. It would be a great place to shelter revolutionaries on the run." Toai married, and after eight years he and his wife discovered a great secret they had hidden from each other—they were both spies working for the North.

Ironically, Toai, who knew nothing about making noodles, soon became the owner of a very popular noodle soup shop. The shop also became an increasingly important place for senior Viet Cong operatives to meet, and eventually became the secret headquarters of the Viet Cong in Saigon. With a sly grin, he adds, "Most of my customers were U.S. diplomats, military brass and soldiers." Sipping their soup in the friendly *pho* shop, American soldiers and high-ranking Saigon regime officials had no idea that the owner and his wife, and even the waiters, waitresses, and cooks, were infiltrators. "I'd be smiling and serving soup to the Americans downstairs while the high command upstairs was planning their victory over the United States."

It was from Toai's shop that the VC planned the attack on the United States Embassy and other targets in Saigon during the bloody Tet Offensive of 1968, perhaps the single most important coordinated series of battles during the American War in Vietnam. Eighty-four thousand Communist troops simultaneously attacked targets in 105 urban centers. One month before the Tet Offensive, the building connected to the noodle soup shop housed more than 100 cadres, commandants and messengers.

On the third day of Tet, South Vietnamese, American, and Korean troops surrounded Toai's business, burst inside and hauled Toai and his comrades before a firing squad. "That day, two of my closest aides were shot dead right in front of me. My captors tried to get me to tell secrets of our high command by setting my hair on fire." For a brief moment, Toai stares blankly. He touches the top of his head where his hair would have been, "But I would never tell." He was then brought to the Saigon police headquarters, where he was stripped and put into a metal box too small to stand in. "I thought I was going to die in that box. My belief in communism is what kept me alive."

After two months of torture at the police headquarters, Toai was in such bad shape that he had to be carried by two other prisoners to his next place of imprisonment—Con Son Island. There, he barely survived for the next five years in a "tiger cage" cell. The cage contained about 700 men. They slept sandwiched together. "It was like a bunch of fish in a can that was so tightly packed." Their food consisted of poor quality rice, salt, a small amount of vegetables and about a half cup of water a day. At first, they were imprisoned with no clothes. Then they were issued jail clothing, but the guards stopped giving them clothing because too many men used it to kill themselves. Whenever a protest erupted among the prisoners, the South Vietnamese guards doused them with powder made of ground oyster shells, causing some to go blind.

Toai would smile as he served soup to American diplomats, military brass and soldiers downstairs in his noodle soup shop in Saigon, all the while hiding Viet Cong infiltrators upstairs.

Many died in prison; many of those who did not die were permanently crippled by the time their confinement ended. Toai's brother lived to tell of his 19 years in such a cage.

Toai was set free after five years. He was only skin and bones by then and at first, he was unable to walk. But he got back in shape enough to run his noodle soup shop again and even cautiously resumed illegal political activities. Finally, in April 1975, when the Communists declared victory, he was able to celebrate his past openly.

Voices of the past still echo in the thick humidity that hangs in the air of this room where Toai orchestrated the Tet Offensive. Although a little more tattered, the room remains unchanged over 30 years later.

Today, even at his advanced age, Toai stands straight and offers a firm handshake. He awakens at five each morning and goes to the local park to perform his *tai chi* exercises. He also plays tennis daily. Gazing out the window of his noodle soup shop he resembles a sweet grandfather—he has five children and, to date, four grandchildren—rather than a man who topped the South Vietnamese government's list of public enemies. He insists that he is still a Communist and shrugs as he says, "I was born to do this. I had a mission." He adds, "Today I meet so many people from around the world. There are no more enemies, we are all friends now. The important thing is that we are at peace today." When asked if the long struggle was worthwhile, he smiles broadly and says, "Oh yes, yes! We are a proud, independent people now."

Assassinate by Christmas

As John leans against the worn, black, iron fence outside one of his favorite pubs, he jokes and clowns with friends and strangers alike, but the smile that fills his face never quite reaches his hollow eyes. John has been married three times and has four children with whom he does not keep in touch.

"My life didn't start out like this. My childhood wasn't the best, but it wasn't the worst either," John says as a look of sadness takes over his face. "In my youth, I was a world-class athlete. I held the all-American record in swimming. After I finished prep school, I went to Cornell University and graduated with a business degree in 1965." John, who always had a premonition he would go to war, enlisted in the Marines nine months out of college—on his 23rd birthday. From that day on, his life would never be the same again.

John's first assignment in the Marine Corps was in California, where surfing filled his free time. Over two years later, in 1968, he was sent to Vietnam as a first lieutenant at the tail end of Tet. By June, at the age of 25, John advanced to the rank of captain. "I was a pretty bad soldier, but somehow, I always got my men home safe. For me, there was nothing like the thrill of combat, except maybe the thrill of the black market." John's face beams with boyish pleasure. "I thought my life was worth more than the $12,000 a year I received for combat pay, so I added another $30,000 or so by way of the black market."

In December 1968, two weeks before Christmas, he was sent to the Dai Loc District, a very hot area 18 miles south of Danang. This particular area was involved in a project that the Marines called CAP, or Combined Action Program. CAP was a specially-trained Marine squad that worked and lived with the South Vietnamese in their villages. "We would spend our days in the villages eating, sleeping, and hanging out, and our nights

> "My heart was beating a mile a minute. I approached silently from behind and put my .45 to his temple."

on patrol protecting the area. Our platoons were a mixture of U.S. Marines and local South Vietnamese who were paid to carry a gun."

In the center of the area was a main command post surrounded by barbed wire. From there, John commanded the entire operation. "When I first arrived, I was greeted by notes the Viet Cong had planted in the barbed wire fencing. They read, 'The new company commander will be assassinated by Christmas.' Rewards had been offered to the South Vietnamese to help kill me." After reading the notes, John dumped the contents of his duffel bag onto the bamboo floor and began opening the Christmas presents he had been carrying around with him. "Just in case the VC succeeded in their mission, I didn't want to miss out on opening my gifts. Needless to say, I got very little sleep. I spent my days trying to whip my unit into shape, and as night fell, I tried my best to protect my own back. The feeling of imminent death was always with me."

About three in the morning, a few days after John arrived, while doing a random check of the perimeter, he spotted a dark figure through the inky night. Someone was standing at the special section in the barbed-wire fence that was rigged by the Marines for emergency use only. It provided a quick escape route if needed. "My heart was beating a mile a minute. I approached silently from behind and put my .45 to his temple." John looked the perpetrator straight in the face with disbelief. Then rage set in. "I couldn't believe my eyes. The dark figure was our camp interpreter. He was supposed to be on watch protecting us, and instead, he was in the process of undoing the quick-release system in the fence so the Viet Cong could get in. I completely lost it. I jumped on him and beat him to a pulp. When I finally took him back to headquarters, a very strange thing happened. The interpreter was let go and reassigned to another unit, and I was reprimanded for hours and threatened with a court-martial!"

Christmas came and went and John was still alive. Through John's leadership skills, the team was shaped into a tight fighting machine. "By May, I was supposed to be headed home, but my replacement was late. I didn't want to leave my men in the field alone, so I stayed." Little did John know how that one decision would greatly impact the rest of his life.

On the evening of May 28, 1969, as John and his men watched the tiny lights of the fireflies dart among the trees, their conversation centered around childhood days and heading home from Vietnam. Five different times, mortar fire interrupted their nostalgic reminiscing. "I was in my rugby shorts and combat boots, and holding a .45 in my hand as one went off right behind me. I didn't know what hit me. That sucker hurled me right through the air. I felt okay and thought I was just scratched up a little, but boy, was I ever wrong."

John left Vietnam for the States a few days later, on June 1. When the plane landed in America and he stood up to get off, he staggered and fell down. "It felt like I had broken my leg. What I later found out was that the trauma of the mortar hit had set off arthritis throughout all my major lower joints." For the next seven years, John was in and out of hospitals. Twice, he had to learn to walk all over again. "They prescribed mega amounts of anti-inflammatory drugs, which had the added danger of eating away at my stomach. It took me ten years to wean off those terrible drugs to just 30 aspirins a day." The pain had gotten so bad that John became suicidal, and the VA psychiatrist had to intervene.

Sometimes, serving in a war creates an even bigger war inside. John suffers from flashbacks and fits of rage. "I lost my best friend to the war." Blankly, John proceeds, "He was captured by the Viet Cong, tortured, beheaded, and hung upside down on a cross. I would have given up my life for him. I wish I had been killed in Vietnam, because surviving has been too difficult." His eyes turn away and, in a flat voice, he continues, "Going through three marriages, putting up with the VA's nonsense, and trying to make a living in this country have all been too much to handle. Sometimes I feel like I'm living in the constant shadow of fear and death. When things get real bad, I turn on the Stones' *Sympathy for the Devil,* drink a bunch of beer, and write things about the war."

John has found one relief to help him through all the pain—marathon running. "Believe it or not, running has saved my life. The movement helps with the arthritis, and I take out my aggression on the highway, instead of on the people in my life. That's been the best therapy for me." Maybe someday John will no longer hurt when he remembers the past. Maybe someday he will not need to run to heal the wounds of war.

John was a captain in the Marines. When he arrived at his new command post, he found notes from the Viet Cong to the villagers pinned to the fence. They read, "The new company commander will be assassinated by Christmas."

"The Look"

My dearest Cindy,
Well, another day in Vietnam is drawing to a close
and I am 24 hours closer to home—and you.

> *"As soon as I saw him stepping off the plane, I knew my husband had come home with the look — the eyes of the dead."*

Gasper wrote to Cindy every day while he was in Vietnam. "We were newly married and we shared all our feelings—feelings of longing, isolation, hope, and fear—in those letters." A devilish smile crosses Cindy's face. "We even fought through the mail, and we made up through the mail." Then her smile turns to one of deep sadness. "I remember reading Gasper's letters and sensing the riveting terror hiding just beneath the ink and paper."

"But I'm getting ahead of myself. I was only 18 when I joined the Army, but I grew up fast. I had no choice." Most of the women with her in Fort Gordon, Georgia, where Cindy worked as an Army medic, were demeaned and sexually harassed by the men, and their disillusionment with their government was almost overwhelming. Cindy soon felt like a very old, young woman. "War is ugly. A little bullet can destroy not only one person's life, but that bullet has a rippling effect on the family and friends left behind. That bullet is forever devastating. There is no glamour in the tortured faces and bodies of the boys who came home. Many of them had 'the look.'" The look, as Cindy and so many others called it, is the expression she saw regularly on the faces of the guys traumatized by the war.

Cindy had been assigned to the administration of a hospital specializing in amputees and psychiatric cases. "We worked twelve-hour shifts, six days a week. The admissions room was always full, and we saw a little bit of everything imaginable." They not only dealt with the soldiers wounded from Vietnam, but also those recently given orders from Uncle Sam who had never left stateside. Some of these came in with self-inflicted wounds, others with psychiatric problems, but all were trying to get released from their assignment to Vietnam. "I remember once this guy comes in screaming at the top of his lungs, doubled over in pain. After examining him, the doctor comes out chuckling. The soldier had self-diagnosed the problem—he was pregnant and in labor. Their imagination for excuses never ceased to amaze me."

Then Cindy talks about Gasper. "One day, this cute guy, a social worker, came into my office to copy some reports. We chatted a little and he left. Later, back in my barracks, I told my closest friend about this guy. I didn't know his name, but I did know I was going to marry him." Days after first meeting Gasper, Cindy was injured in a flash fire in her barracks. Her sergeant was killed, four others were injured, and Cindy was overcome by toxic smoke and fumes. The remaining months of her service time were spent in and out of the hospital because of severe respiratory problems. This misfortune brought Cindy and Gasper closer together very quickly. They met in October, and Gasper proposed in January.

Generally, no one was sent to Vietnam unless he or she had at least a year of service left. "When Gasper had only ten months remaining, we thought he was in the clear, but in May 1969, he received orders." Three weeks after the orders arrived, Gasper and Cindy married; eighteen days after the ceremony, he left for Vietnam. Before he left for war, Gasper asked Cindy if she would still want him if he returned without an arm or a leg. An affirmative answer slipped out readily. "A part of me really was afraid of his coming home physically wounded, but a bigger part of me was terrified of his coming home with the look."

Cindy was honorably discharged from the Army early because of her respiratory illness. She tried to make a life for herself in New York while Gasper did the same as a social worker in Vietnam. She worked in an office pushing paper while he treated soldiers suffering from post-traumatic stress disorder or drug abuse. Their daily letters kept their relationship alive and flourishing.

When Gasper returned after ten months in Vietnam, Cindy was there at the base in California waiting for his plane to land. "As soon as I saw him stepping off the plane, I knew my husband had come home with the look—the eyes of the dead. It was almost like aliens had taken hold of him in Vietnam. Like they had plucked out his soul and inserted distance, anger, and rage instead. Our lives were shattered. He was no longer the loving man who left me ten months earlier. He wouldn't talk or share, he just stared off into space for hours at a time. I wanted to shout—*'I don't know who the hell you are, but whoever you are, you go back to Vietnam and send my husband home to me!'*"

The couple relocated to California and carried on as best they could. Gasper began work as a social worker at UCLA while studying for his master's degree. Cindy soon became pregnant and gave birth to Gabrielle and a few years later to Matthew. They eventually returned to New York to be closer to family and friends. Gasper worked in a state psychiatric center, started a therapy group for Vietnam veterans on Long Island, and helped to found the Vietnam Veterans of America Chapter 11. Eventually, he was offered

Cindy, an Army medic, worked stateside with men returning from the war. Later, she waited for her own husband to come back from a tour in Vietnam, terrified he would have "the look." He did. Here she is today with the letters Gasper sent to her when he was in Vietnam.

the job of treatment team leader for a vet center on Long Island. Cindy went back to school, and since 1984 has dedicated her life as an advocate for veterans and their spouses. The words "Sgt. Donald Grella, missing 12/28/65" are engraved into the POW bracelet Cindy still wears every day. A stranger to Cindy, Donald Grella never came home.

Through the years, Cindy and Gasper have reached a greater understanding of their relationship. "Once I stopped taking Gasper's silence personally and realized the depth of the trauma he and so many others who served in Vietnam were living with, I was able to come to a place of peace. We will be married 30 years this June. The older we are, the more mellow and forgiving we become. I reread Gasper's letters today and realized how young we were all those years ago. I also know how much passion we had and how much was taken from us because of this war on the other side of the world."

Well love, that's it for tonight. I miss you more than words can ever say.
I love you so very, very much. Good-nite and God bless.

Your husband,
Gasper

62

"Our Gang"

*T*he 1950s and early sixties were a time of streetcorner quartets, poodle skirts, pompadours, Elvis, and Camelot—a time of innocence. "Our gang was formed by the time we were in junior high," Barry giggles as he reminisces. "Our gang. It sounds so rough and tough when I say it today in the 1990s. Growing up in Bayside, New York—a sleepy neighborhood of tree-lined streets—was anything but rough and tough in the fifties and sixties."

"There were ten of us in our gang. We would meet at Pete's Candy Store in the morning before school and at the end of the day. Pete's was like a second home for us. A sort of safe haven where the guys met, talked, and ate Pete's two-cent pretzels." Barry recalls with nostalgia the sting of salt on his lips from those pretzels of yesteryear.

"After junior high, we all went to Bayside High School. Then we all enlisted in the armed forces. In the early '60s, protecting your country from the threat of communism was your sacred duty." Barry enlisted in the United States Air Force and, because he showed mechanical aptitude, was sent to Asia to repair B-52 airplanes. "Those babies were each capable of delivering over a hundred 750-pound bombs within 30 seconds and up to 54,000 pounds of bombs in a single mission! The North Vietnamese hated them. They nicknamed the planes 'Whispering Death' because the whistling of the approaching bombs was the first warning they had of an attack. And by then, it was too late!"

During the course of the war, two members of Barry's gang, John and Walter, were killed. Their deaths consumed him with uncontrollable rage. "How could they kill two of my friends? This was not supposed to happen to us!" Barry's face reddens with anger and pain as he remembers the loss of his two childhood buddies. "All I could think about was the John Wayne movies we used

Barry, on the right, was one of ten childhood friends who enlisted in the armed forces. Only eight returned. (*photo courtesy of Barry*)

to watch. The Americans never got killed. Never! So why did John and Walter? Fixing airplanes wasn't good enough any more. I wanted to get into the action. I wanted revenge!" Barry put in over fifteen requests to go into battle. Finally, he was allowed to join four bombing missions. Barry looks down at the floor, shifting in his chair. "As a kid, I saw everything in black and white. You kill my loved one, I'll kill you. It was that simple."

"I remember those bombing missions as if they were yesterday. I cheered, as the belly of my B-52 opened up, and I prayed that the bombs falling below me would land on the Viet Cong who killed my friends." Barry's face is consumed with remorse as he now realizes how many innocent men, women and children were also killed during those missions.

"My tour of duty came to an end in September 1967. One by one, the rest of the gang came home. Our lives were altered forever. Today, we're scattered across America, each living very different lives. I own a 100-acre chicken farm in Georgia—a far cry from the lazy street corners of Bayside and the blazing battlefields of Vietnam."

"The gang is still close and we get together often for reunions. When we do, we play as we did when we were young, tossing a football or sharing a few beers." Barry's voice drops, "But we are changed—changed forever by this war. It's a funny thing. No matter how much we share, no matter how intimate we are, the subject of Vietnam never comes up. Some things just need to remain stored away—under lock and key."

Today Barry owns a 100-acre chicken farm in Georgia and still keeps in touch with his childhood friends. "It's a funny thing...the subject of Vietnam never comes up."

Casualty of the War

"**M**y world changed forever the day the war hit our small village." Hai fumbles with his glasses as he begins to tell his story, "I was in my twenties at the time, a father of four and married to the love of my life. Our everyday life was simple. We worked the fields following the rhythm of nature. We sowed the seeds in spring, transplanted after the first rains and harvested in the fall. We grew enough food to feed our family. We were happy."

"When the North Vietnamese began to infiltrate our rural area, I joined the Navy and served as a lieutenant on a ship for the next ten years. When the war ended, I was captured and spent the next five years in a prison in the Highlands near Lao Cai. Images and thoughts of my beautiful wife and four wonderful children kept me alive through all that I was made to endure." Today, even in more peaceful times, Hai still harbors the memories of those torturous days in the darkest recesses of his mind.

"I was finally allowed to walk free in 1980. Weeks later, I arrived at my village. I ran to my home as fast as I could. It was gone. Only burned embers remained. I searched our village frantically for familiar faces. I looked everywhere for my wife, my children."

After piecing together bits of information, Hai came to learn what had happened during his fifteen-year absence. "One day, as my wife was working in the fields, a helicopter flying overhead started to receive ground fire from the forest below. A fight ensued and a stray bullet struck my wife. She spent the next six months in the hospital. My children were too young to care for themselves, so our relatives took them in. When she was released from the hospital, my wife began a slow decline as the years, the war and my absence took its toll." Hai still feels tremendous guilt for not being at his wife's side when she died and a terrible sense of loss because his children grew up without him.

Today, Hai—a five-foot-tall, 110-pound, 54-year-old man, who received an excellent education while in the Navy and who was honored for his leadership skills—works the streets of Saigon as a cyclo driver. A cyclo is a human-powered pedi-cab. This type of work is extremely demanding, but Hai perseveres as he maneuvers his cyclo around

> *"I ran to my home as fast as I could. It was gone. Only burned embers remained.*
> *. . .*
> *I looked everywhere for my wife, my children."*

the never-ending turns and hidden by-ways of Saigon's streets with the speed and agility of an athlete half his age. He, like tens of thousands of others detained after the war in re-education prisons, some for a decade or more, is today treated poorly by the government. According to the law, he is not allowed to obtain a residence permit. This permit is needed to attend school, seek employment or own a home or a business. Many, with no other recourse, must try to make a living begging on the streets, peddling cigarettes and lottery tickets, or, like Hai, driving a cyclo and working for very little money.

The government has recently announced that they will eventually ban the use of all cyclos in Vietnam. What will the future hold for men like Hai?

Hai served as a lieutenant in the South Vietnamese Navy and was later imprisoned. When he was finally able to return home to his family, they were gone.

My Old
War Locker

On January 31, 1968, North Vietnamese infantry battalions and Viet Cong units attacked the city of Hue, the gentle, old imperial capital of Vietnam. With only a small ARVN (Army of the Republic of Vietnam) force stationed there, they met with little resistance and soon the North Vietnamese flag was flying victoriously over Hue's ancient citadel. Ron, at the time a 28-year-old captain in the Marine Corps, was already married and the father of two children. Today, a retired three-star general, he looks back on the dark days of the Tet Offensive and describes what it was like for him. "The character of the war changed the night the Communists attempted to take over. South Vietnam exploded into violence and nowhere was the violence worse than in Hue."

Ron received the nation's second-highest medal given for extreme heroism: the prestigious Navy Cross. *(photo courtesy of Ron)*

"By the time we arrived on February 3, the enemy had strong points everywhere." Two days later, bogged down under thunderous fire from the enemy, Ron disregarded his own safety and darted across a large open area to assess the situation; he then crossed the area again to rejoin his platoon. Next, while hand grenades, satchel charges and small arms fire were striking around him, he sprinted across more open terrain to reach a tank. After issuing an attack order to his men, he climbed on top of the tank and directed fire against the enemy as rounds and two B-40 rockets assaulted the tank. Once the battle's intensity diminished, he jumped from the tank and personally led his troop in brutal combat until the enemy was defeated. For his selfless devo-

tion and dynamic leadership, Ron was awarded the second-highest medal given for extreme heroism, the prestigious Navy Cross.

"Urban fighting is the dirtiest fighting you can be involved in. It is no longer distant snipers—it is now face-to-face combat. Looking into someone's eyes before pulling the trigger and knowing you are killing someone's husband, brother or son made this a whole different kind of war. The adrenaline of the moment is the only thing that kept us going." After clearing their portion of the city, which was blanketed with an eerie fog, Ron's troop started heading west to a suburban area. Surprising both themselves and the enemy, they accidentally walked into a North Vietnamese command post. "Looking over my shoulder, I couldn't believe what I saw—an antitank weapon was aimed right at us."

Shrapnel flew all over. "One piece hit the back of my left leg and I fell over and rolled down into a hole." Ron hesitates and his face turns white as he finishes his thought. "I rolled on top of dead soldiers." In moments, mortar rounds started falling all around him. "Two of my men jumped on top of me and used their bodies to shield me from any more harm." Ron hesitates again as emotion overtakes him. "Marines take care of each other. It's a brotherhood." After quelling the fight, his men created a make-shift ambulance and evacuated Ron from the area. He was subsequently sent to a hospital in Danang and then to the Philadelphia Naval Hospital.

Once out of the hospital and back on his feet, Ron began to climb the military ladder and eventually advanced to lieutenant general. During this time, he and his wife Sherry had two more children. Two of their four followed in their father's footsteps, and are a captain and a major in the Marine Corps. After 34 years of service, Ron looks back on his days in the Marines with no regret. "I loved being a Marine."

When he was younger, Ron had no expectations of the magnitude his career would take. "The Marine Corps allowed me to grow up a great deal and helped me to appreciate what this country means to me. If asked what I felt was the greatest accomplishment of my career, I would have to say, next to my tour in Vietnam, it would be forming the Joint Task Force–Full Accounting in 1992." The task force works to pool information with the Vietnamese to find those still unaccounted-for Americans who did not return from the war in Southeast Asia.

Since the end of the war, Ron has traveled to Vietnam on four separate occasions; three were connected with the Joint Task Force. "When I went into the jungles with the men and women involved in this operation—young sailors, soldiers, airmen and Marines—and watched their dedication to this project, it brought joy to my heart." The task force workers use all available files and records to identify and excavate crash sites and to interview witnesses. When remains are discovered, they are sent to a lab in Hawaii, tested by forensic specialists, and processed through anthropological and pathological analysis for positive identification. "When all the pieces of this complicated puzzle are finally put together and the identity of the remains are certain, we notify the family, thus allowing for closure."

The other time Ron returned to Vietnam was to deal with his own closure. "I went to the places where I had lost men during the war." The experiences are still vivid and alive for Ron. "What we did in Vietnam was right. We were fighting for our nation. When we were at war, I had to stay above the emotion of the battle. If I allowed myself to become emotionally dragged in, I would lose my outfit. I've seen that happen often. Since 1775, we've been doing what our nation has asked us to do. Do I at times get a tear in my eye? Do I at times remember and think? Sure. What helps me to cope with the losses is intellectualizing them away. I store the memories on the top shelf of my old war locker, both the good and the bad."

Today, a retired Three-star General, Ron looks back on his life and sometimes gets a tear in his eye, yet he believes he has always done what is right.

A Shadow on Me

$\mathcal{A}$ndrew was born in Atlanta, Georgia in 1947, and grew up during the turbulent times of the American civil rights movement, yet fortunately, he escaped much of the bigotry and racism that many experienced in the South during the height of the movement. "It wasn't that I didn't know what was going on. I was actually baptized by my mother's childhood friend, the minister Dr. Martin Luther King Jr." Andrew beams with pride as he continues, "The thing was, I never ventured out of my own neighborhood. The closest I got to seeing the sit-ins and marches was in the news broadcasts on television." While civil rights workers protested by sitting-in at the lunch counters where blacks were refused service, held kneel-ins on the church steps where they were denied entrance, marched on Washington in 1963 and marched from Selma to Montgomery on March 25, 1965, Andrew quietly observed the movement from the safety of his childhood home.

Andrew dropped out of college in the fall of 1967, and that decision changed the entire course of his adult life because he was no longer exempt from the draft. With the Vietnam War in full swing, he received a letter from Uncle Sam just three months later. The next day, he enlisted in the Marine Corps. "On April 4, 1968, only four months before I had to leave for Vietnam, an assassin's bullet took the life of my family's dear friend, Dr. King, a pacifist who spoke out against the war."

"The prejudice against blacks that I watched on TV, pretty unaffectedly as a kid, became a reality in the Marines." For Andrew (and for many blacks in the 1960s), the military service was the first time they were closely enmeshed in day-to-day experiences with white people. "And boy, the discrimination and bigotry in basic training, on the plane ride to Vietnam and away from the battlefields, was so thick that you could cut it with a knife." There, the blacks and whites generally tended

Although blacks have served in both combat and support capacities in every war the United States has participated in, the military was not desegregated until after WW II. This occurred in 1948 on the orders of President Truman.
(photo courtesy of Andrew)

Andrew caresses his short-timer's stick in his hands. It is a memento from his days as a Marine. "It's as holy to me as anything I ever felt."

to be self-segregating. "But it sure was a different story once we were on the front-line. In the battle zone, the blacks and rednecks worked side by side as one unit and became one against our new enemy." As the sound of bullets faded, so too did the soldiers' skin colors. "In the line of fire, there was no prejudice, we all needed each other."

Andrew spent most of his tour of duty in the bush. "I spent one year and 24 days stationed as a radio operator on the DMZ [Demilitarized Zone]." He holds his short-timer's stick, a memento from his days as a Marine, caressing it with his hands as he talks. On this piece of wood, acquired near the end of his tour, he inscribed names like Dong Ha and Rockpile. Meaningless words to most people, each of these words tells a story Andrew will carry to his grave. "My short-timer's stick represented the magic day, the day I would leave my living nightmare. The day I would leave Vietnam." Andrew looks down at the stick with despondency. "Those days were really tough. There was no real food. We ate everything out of cans. There weren't even showers. We had to wait for the rains to come in order to bathe." When he was not in the heat of battle fearing his own annihilation, Andrew was bored to tears. "Marijuana was plentiful and helped the long, frightening hours to pass."

Andrew left Vietnam in September 1969 and returned to a new reality in America. "There were flags and welcome-home signs greeting me on my block, but everywhere else I went I was called a fool for even going to 'Nam. It was so hard for me to adjust to a 'normal' life when I felt so emotionally disjointed." He began drifting from job to job, and from relationship to relationship. "Rage, depression and isolation ruled my life." While marijuana tempered Andrew's fears in Vietnam, it took heroin to do the trick back in America—heroin, cocaine and liquid lunches of vodka and gin. "After a while, even that didn't work. Nothing could drown out the flashbacks."

By the 1990s, his estranged wife and five children could not compete with the alcohol, Andrew's real "significant other." "On the morning of May 3, 1994, almost 25 years after returning from 'Nam, I guzzled down a bottle of vodka and drove to the VA Hospital in Northport, Long Island. I spent three days in detox and 28 days in a drug and alcohol rehab. Then there was post-traumatic stress disorder counseling and Alcoholics Anonymous. Both individual and group counseling," says Andrew, sounding exhausted, yet proud.

"To this day, I am clean of all drugs and alcohol." Andrew is now a middle-aged man attending college and majoring in bio-medical engineering. "Everything has changed drastically since I chose the path of recovery. I now look forward to the rest of my life by taking it 'one day at a time.'"

While turning his short-timer's stick over and over in his hands, Andrew reflects on his life, "Vietnam is a permanent part of my life. It's a shadow on me. This short-timer's stick brings those memories close. It is my own personal piece of the Wall. The words on it represent powerful fragments of my life. It's as holy to me as anything I ever felt."

"Motorcycle Mike"

"**I**'d be sitting in a foxhole looking over the barrel of my M-60, daydreaming of climbing the mountains or exploring the forests around me, when gunfire would suddenly interrupt my thoughts and bring me back to my horrid reality." Fear of violence was not new to Mike. He grew up trying to avoid day-to-day battles with his abusive, alcoholic father, only to be beaten by nuns in his Catholic school. Mike chuckles about this today, but did not laugh about it much when he was a child. "I had learned the skill of anticipating the trouble that would follow my father's violent rages before the trouble happened, and that skill probably helped me to stay alive in Vietnam." Staying alive is what Mike, who was almost killed three times, did well.

In Vietnam's battle zones, the chance of an ambush or attack was greatest at night. And when the nights were moonless and coal black, the risk of peril was imminent. "One really dark night, near morning, all was quiet—too quiet. Suddenly, the sky lit up from a rocket attack. We charged out of the treeline and scattered. The adrenaline pumping through me disguised the fact that I was hit. My Achilles tendon had been severed, and I was running away from the gunfire with my foot flopping aimlessly in the air." Evacuated by chopper, glued and bandaged together, Mike was sent back to his base camp in a knee-high cast. He wore the cast for the next seven weeks.

A few months later, while patrolling a village street on a quiet Sunday, gunfire erupted from every direction. "I was lucky and went backwards over a fence. I sort of fell in what seemed like slow motion onto the ground. Rounds followed my fall." Most of the shrapnel from that incident embedded itself into his shinbone, thigh, back and elbow, and is still in him today.

"The third time I was wounded, it happened right in my base camp. We were overrun by the enemy and shrapnel penetrated my thigh—

Mike was almost killed on three separate occasions while in Vietnam. Each time he was patched together and sent back to the battle zone. *(photo courtesy of Mike)*

right down to the bone. I was again medevaced out, and again, sent right back to battle." Mike's voice goes flat. "Hadn't my body taken on enough metal from this war? Not according to the Navy doctor. The policy was, 'If you're able to walk and talk, you're going back out to do battle.' I was living proof of that—three times wounded—three times sent back."

At the end of his tour of duty, Mike was finally allowed to go home. "My head was swimming with a mixture of magnified joy, quiet sadness and a lot of confusion. When I stepped off the plane in California, I was immediately thrown into the twilight zone." Mike was greeted by a barrage of jeering and cursing protesters who spit on him, threw bags of feces at him and called him a "baby killer." "I couldn't understand why they were doing this to me. I felt so hurt and ashamed." Mike took his feelings and hid them deep inside, stuffing them away for many years. The only feelings he allowed to surface were those of fury. "I was always in a defensive mode, filled with anger and rage." Mike was in everyone's face. Total strangers walked away from him in fear.

"For many years I was torn because a part of me wanted to leave Vietnam behind and get on with life, and another part of me wanted to die." Unlike many other vets, Mike did not use drugs or alcohol to deaden his pain; instead, he immersed himself in his work with the phone company. He worked day and night trying to disconnect from the rest of the world. "I was putting in what seemed to be endless hours. In my 16 years on the job, I probably worked 30 year's worth of hours." In 1974, Mike suffered a serious accident on the job because of his old war injuries. He was hospitalized for four months and spent five days each week over the next two years in rehabilitation. "When I went back to work in 1976, I was popping Tylenol like candy and finally in 1985, when the pain was too much, I had to leave my job."

Disabled, with time on his hands, Mike developed a renewed interest in "things Vietnam." He started collecting paraphernalia relating to the war, storing it in boxes that have since taken over his entire house, two vans and a horse trailer. Three Purple Hearts, a Presidential Unit Citation, Vietnam Service Medal, Navy Unit Commendation, SVN Campaign Ribbon, Good Conduct Medal and Marine Corps Combat Action Ribbon—all honors he earned—fill one of Mike's many boxes. "Somehow the material things in the boxes have helped to fill a huge emptiness in my life." Mike's house is so cluttered with boxes that when his dog goes into the bedroom, he has to back out because there is not enough room to turn around.

Mike also began riding a Harley again, as he had before the war, and joined a group of Vietnam veteran bikers. In May 1985, they rode in the Vietnam Veterans Welcome Home Parade in New York City. "The parade sent my juices flowing on a roller coaster ride to hell and back. My rage started erupting sideways toward the people shouting 'I love you, welcome home.' I wondered if they were the same people who years earlier shouted 'baby killer.' Why do you love me now? Nothing's changed. I'm still the same person I was years ago. The same person you spit on." A volcano simmered inside Mike. A dried-up wound was opening at its seams. "I was sinking into a well. Sinking deeper and deeper. I needed help fast. I had stuffed Vietnam down so far, I couldn't tap into my feelings at all." Group therapy was not working, so after 28 months, he was referred to a veterans hospital, and there he worked intensely with a therapist five hours a day.

"In 1987, the Vietnam Veterans Moving Wall came to my county, and I decided to do a couple of hours of volunteer work. That couple of hours turned into four weeks straight. I literally lived at the Wall. I slept in my van and ate food people generously brought to me. The experience was like no other." Many times Mike connected with other veterans who came to the Wall to touch the names of their lost buddies. "Virtual strangers, we would hold each other and cry together into the wee hours of the dark night. This turned out to be a real turning point in my life and a true healing."

"But you know, it's a dozen years or so since then and I still don't have any answers," Mike says while staring downward. "I live my life day to day, not knowing if I'll be alive in the next hour and, sometimes, not caring."

Mike continues to live the war every day of his life, surrounding himself with war memorabilia to fill the void.

75

Bridges to Peace

Le Van Bang's life story sounds like a rags to riches fairy tale, but, nevertheless it is a true account. Born a poor country boy working in the fields near his small village in the war-torn north of Vietnam, he grew up to become an ambassador working in a modern office building in Washington. Along the way, this peasant boy received several college degrees, became fluent in English and advanced his career in diplomacy to become the highest-ranking Vietnamese man in America.

Bang was born in June 1947 during the Franco-Viet Minh War, while his father was away in the Army. His village was adjacent to Highway 1, and when the war got too close, everyone fled to safety into the nearby mountains. During the chaos of the evacuation, the frail, barefoot little boy was swept away with a crowd of people and became separated from his mother. "I remember sobbing in fear as I stood frozen at the edge of our village and looking at the only way out—the monkey bridge. A monkey bridge is a crude structure made from lengths of bamboo lashed together with vines. It's called a 'monkey bridge' because you need to have the agility of a monkey to cross over it." Old memories turn Bang's face colorless; he is a private man who rarely shares his emotions. "I had never crossed the bridge without my mother's help. And I couldn't find my mother among all the rushing people. Eventually, a woman swooped me up in her arms and carried me screaming across the bridge. I was petrified." As it turns out, his mother had stayed behind to help with the exodus, and they were not reunited for three terrifying days.

"We lived in the mountains for the next three years. I stayed with my sister all day, while my mother went out to find food. We returned to our village in 1954, when the war ended. But there was nothing left. Everything was burned to the ground. Even so, life did look better—the war was over, my father returned, we rebuilt our home and I was able to go to school." Along with studying, Bang helped his family survive. He planted rice and vegetables with his mother, and he fished in the river for crabs and sold them in the local marketplace.

Eventually, he finished high school, but not before his studies were interrupted

two more times. The first time was because his family did not have enough money to pay for lessons, and the second was in the mid-1960s because another round of bombing had begun. Despite all of his hardships, Bang graduated from high school, not only first in his class, but first in his province.

After graduation, in 1966, Bang joined the Revolutionary Youth Volunteer Brigade. "We repaired or rebuilt the roads and bridges that were damaged or destroyed from the American bombs." Bang, a wide-open smile on his face, chuckles as he talks

Ambassador Le Van Bang struggles to help Vietnam by building bridges between his country and America.

about those days. "Yeah, Peterson made the holes in the roads, and I had to repair them." (Bang is referring to Pete Peterson, the American ambassador to Vietnam, who, as an Air Force pilot, was shot down during the war and imprisoned for six-and-a-half years.) The two ambassadors, once enemies, are now friends.

Bang worked with the brigade until 1968, then he left for Cuba to obtain a bachelor's in translating and interpreting English. He returned to work in the foreign ministry in Hanoi in 1972, only to endure the infamous Christmas bombing, during which B-52s blasted the city for twelve straight days. "What a terrible time! The explosions from the bombs and the artillery kept us awake all night. We lay in our beds praying that we would not be hit! It was horrible to see the houses and the streets burning all around us." Small beads of perspiration appear on Bang's forehead as he remembers. Then, in a new tone of voice, he adds, "What it did to us in the North was to make us more determined to go on." Bang still has horrible nightmares and flashbacks from the terrors he endured almost 30 years ago.

After the Americans left and the bombs stopped, Bang married his high school sweetheart, had two children and continued to work as an official in the Foreign Ministry, which sent him to Australia to obtain a bachelor's degree in economics and history. He returned in 1977 and continued to advance up the diplomatic ladder, representing his country in Great Britain and at the United Nations in New York City. In 1995, he began work in Washington as chief of Vietnam's liaison office to the United States and was soon promoted to *charge d'affaires*. After serving as an assistant foreign minister in Vietnam, he was appointed the Ambassador of Vietnam to the United States in May 1997.

Loud chants of "Democracy for Vietnam," "Down with Hanoi Communists" and "Freedom for Vietnam" greeted Ambassador Le Van Bang when he first took office and made public appearances. "At first, almost everywhere I went to speak, I was received with anger and rage." The streets were filled with banner-waving Vietnamese-Americans, many of whom were re-education camp detainees, who were opposed to establishing any ties with the Vietnamese government until changes were made. "Gradually these protests have died down and relations are better now. The voices of Vietnam veterans, including Senators John McCain, John Kerry and Bob Kerrey, and many others in the business community have helped to ease the strains."

With an easy smile and knowing eyes, Bang tries not to focus on the past, but to look toward the future by fostering closer ties between his country and the rest of the world. "That old gutted road of my past is still bumpy. My job is to make the road ahead a little smoother." Ambassador Le Van Bang has crossed many bridges in his life; he tries not to look back as he crosses to a safer place.

The Invisible Ones

he Vietnam War was fought in humid rainforests and scorching rice paddies, in the cool highlands and on the unpredictable seas, in crowded cities and in dark, damp underground tunnels. More than a quarter of a century later, the Vietnam War is still being fought, not on land and sea, but in the souls of the soldiers and citizens whose lives were forever changed by it. Many of the American men and women who fought for their country sleep each night in vacant lots, behind thin cardboard walls, in doorways and in dim alleys all across their country. They left the battlefields of a foreign land only to do battle in their homeland. In a way, they still live in the field, surviving with limited food, clothing and medical rations, and living under dangerous conditions. They survive each day by their wits, carrying on through hopelessness and fear.

Many veterans who spent a year or more in the adrenalizing jungles of Vietnam found it difficult to return to the cadence of everyday civilian life; some found it completely impossible. Nearly one-third of the homeless in America are veterans. It is estimated that, on any given night in the United States, there are 275,000 veterans living on the streets. Over the course of a year, possibly twice that number experience homelessness at one time or another.

These veterans did not return from the war and immediately become homeless. Their fate usually came about gradually after unsuccessfully coping with alcoholism, drug addiction, mental illness, chronic health problems, physical disabilities, post-traumatic stress disorder, multiple divorces, unemployment and a lack of family understanding and support. Such veterans continue to fall between the cracks of a society that does not understand them or does not want them. They have become invisible; people pass them on the street and look away. This avoidance creates deeper feelings of low self-esteem and worthlessness. These veterans who gave their youth to Vietnam, now give their souls to the streets of America.

The forsaken faces of many veterans blend invisibly into the tapestry of dead-end alleys in America's cities and towns. José and Ernest are two of these faces. They both lived for too many years in a state of bankruptcy: bankrupt of money, of relationships,

> *It is estimated that, on any given night in the United States, there are 275,000 veterans living on the streets.*

and of dignity. Today, these former soldiers are on a different road—the road to recovery. José and Ernest live with similarly-troubled people in a drug-free, residential treatment center where they receive support through a variety of services, including counseling, education, medical and vocational assistance. José and Ernest will live in this facility until they are gainfully employed and able to live independently. Similar programs are offered throughout the country.

One-third of the homeless in America are veterans like José and Ernest. These former soldiers were just two of the war's invisible casualties. Here they are preparing to proudly march in New York City's Veterans Day Parade.

Twenty Bucks for Billy

On a sidewalk south of uptown, where losers line the street,
Billy's hunting for an iron grate to throw him up some heat.
He feels the threat of strangers and the fear of all alone,
And the war of Billy's yesterdays rages on and on.

He sits in a cold, dark doorway wearing someone else's shoes,
Looking up at the passersby through a cloud of pills and booze.
He holds a can of little flags and pencils and hopes you might take one,
And throw a little change to a patriotic son.

So here's twenty bucks for you, Billy, and "Thank you, Lord," for me.
Billy, you're my brother—but for the grace of God, there goes me.

It's a long way from the Heartland to the napalm and the pills,
Where shrapnel took his shinbone and whiskey took his will.
And when the war was over and the choppers flew away,
Home Sweet Home for Billy was a cardboard box on South Broadway.

Now it's twenty odd years later and the world is frozen still,
The cold just keeps on coming—soon there won't be no more Bill.
But in the meantime, Lord, he needs to drift away,
And hope the next life's better like the righteous people say.

So here's twenty bucks for you, Billy, and "Thank you, Lord," for me.
Billy, you're my brother—but for the grace of God, there goes me.

John Taylor
copyright 1997

I Don't Remember the Fear—Only the Numbness

> "*When my kids were young, they would always ask me questions about the war...*"

"*Too* many Americans were being killed in Vietnam and they desperately needed replacements, so before I finished my advanced training as a Marine, they sent me directly to 'Nam to a unit in the field." Jim spent his first three months in Vietnam in mundane routines as a grunt—a foot soldier. Once in a while though, the monotonous days and dreary nights were transformed into moments of complete terror. On the evening of January 30, 1968, the occasional terror unexpectedly changed into constant fear. As the Vietnamese celebrated Tet, the lunar new year, nearly 70,000 Communist soldiers launched a carefully coordinated series of attacks in over 100 separate cities and towns across South Vietnam. The battle was fiercest in Hue, the only city in South Vietnam held by the Communists for more than a few days. Jim was sent to fight there.

"Overnight, I went from working as a grunt, whose major problem was enduring marginal boredom, to being a radio operator dealing in total chaos." For the first time, the war was being fought as an open battle in the urban areas rather than as a guerrilla war in the rural arena. "The fighting was difficult for us because we were trained to fight in the jungles and rice paddies where we couldn't see the enemy. Now we were fighting in the street—house-by-house, bunker-by-bunker, eye-to-eye. To make the situation even more difficult, the heavens delivered clouds, rain and wind, making it nearly impossible for close air-support."

During the battle, the Communists rounded up thousands of so-called "cruel agents" during extensive house-to-house searches. The chosen were selected from a blacklist of civil servants, Catholic priests, Buddhist monks, teachers, intellectuals and those presumably connected to the American forces or the South Vietnamese government. Approximately 3,000 people were taken away to be executed, shot, clubbed, mutilated or buried alive in mass graves. Estimates of the final tally of casualties of the Tet Offensive are over 2,000 American soldiers, 11,000 ARVN troops, 37,000 Viet Cong and 165,000 civilians. Over two million others became refugees almost overnight.

"I'll never forget those days. The constant sound of gunfire. The sting in my eyes from the smoke of burnt-out tanks, trucks and cars. The clammy feel of my skin. The stench of decomposing bodies." Jim hesitates for a long time. "I don't remember the fear—only the numbness. Then it happened. On February 17, I was hit." Turning his head away, he continues, "I was read my last rites. Next thing I knew, it was March 3." Jim awoke two weeks later in a hospital in Philadelphia. "'Hey Stump, how ya feelin'?' another wounded soldier said to me."

"I was home. But what a homecoming!" As sadness consumes Jim's face, he explains. "I lost my leg and was told I would never walk again. My body was embedded with shrapnel. My father died. My kid brother hung himself in a hotel room." Years of painful operations and physical therapy allow Jim to walk today. Years of agonizing soul searching, a loving wife and four sons have enabled him to cope.

In 1996, Jim and his sons Brian and Jason traveled to Vietnam and went to the site where Jim lost his leg during the 1968 Tet Offensive. The trip was one of healing for the entire family.

"A year ago, I received a phone call from my old Marine lieutenant. He's a retired three-star general now. He raised the possibility of a return trip to Vietnam. A million questions rushed through my head. It was 28 years since the Tet Offensive. What would it be like to go back to the battlefields of Hue? To the place where I lost my leg? Could I handle it? After much deliberation, I decided to make the trip back to the place of my nightmares. Perhaps going back would finally let me put some of them to rest."

This trip to Vietnam was very different for Jim. He was not traveling with a bunch of Marines going to the battlefields of war, but on a vacation of sorts, with two of his sons, 25-year-old Brian and 21-year-old Jason. "When my kids were young, they would always ask me questions about the war. How could I tell them the stories of the bloody battles? How could I explain how scared I was in this far-away place? I was a boy, a boy younger than they are today." Being in Vietnam again, strolling among a myriad of Vietnamese people and seeing the unrepaired, bombed-out buildings of the past, made it easier for Jim to share his war stories with his sons. Going to Vietnam with their father has helped Brain and Jason to begin to understand their father's pain—the pain he buried so deeply for so many years. The trip allowed old walls of anguish to crumble and new pathways of communication and love to open.

There's No Cure

"When I was growing up, I didn't consider myself an American, yet on June 27, 1966, Uncle Sam sent me a draft notice, and eventually an invitation to the Vietnam War." Puerto Ricans were granted U.S. citizenship in 1917, just in time for them to be eligible for military service for World War I. Angel, a native-born Puerto Rican, was not allowed to vote in an American national election, but could be drafted into the American military from his Spanish-speaking country. "I was a Puerto Rican who spoke no English going to Vietnam to kill people for the United States. I went against my will, against my church, and against my upbringing."

Angel grew up dirt poor. He shared a bed with his five brothers and sisters and often had nothing to eat for days. He began working when he was very young, selling newspapers or shining shoes, while he did not even own a pair himself. "There was never any money for food, but always some for my father's booze. After disappearing for days at a time, Dad would come home and disrupt our lives with rage and a heavy fist. My mother did the best she could to protect us. In those days it was not acceptable for a woman to leave her husband, so we all stayed and suffered his violence. Those are the strongest memories I have of my childhood." A few years ago, in therapy, Angel was asked to draw a picture of his childhood. He drew his father in Puerto Rico and himself in combat fatigues ready to fight the enemy.

One month after graduating from high school wearing a cap and gown, Angel found himself in Fort Gordon wearing combat boots. "It was the 1960s and I was first sent to Georgia—enough said. Vietnam was a piece of cake next to my months in the South." Not speaking English compounded Angel's troubles. "They treated me like I was committing a crime. I was constantly punished for not following orders that had been given to me in a foreign language. I'd get double duty, extra KP, and more push-ups. Discrimination came from whites and blacks alike. The blacks took out on the Hispanics what the whites took out on them."

As bad as it was on the base, his experiences in town were worse. Angel remembers one incident in downtown Augusta. "Thinking nothing of it, a buddy and I went

to town to get a beer. Boy, were we in for the shock of our lives. We never got our beer because we never got into the bar. There was a sign on the door that read 'No Niggers, No Dogs, No Puerto Ricans.' I was devastated. That sign told me that in America I was worth less than a dog. My experiences in the South traumatized me long before I ever set foot on Vietnamese soil."

Stationed in Pleiku in the Highlands, Angel was assigned to the infantry. A soldier did not need to speak English to pull the trigger of an M-16. "I saw so many battles that after a while they all blended together. Killing people was the norm. As macho as you are when you got there, after watching your friends die, and knowing death awaits you behind any tree, macho means nothing. When I did guard duty at night, I would sit and cry from the fear that overcame me while I waited my turn."

Angel left the jungles a year later, but not before he contracted malaria and was wounded by a claymore mine. "I left the war in Vietnam and headed home to an-

Angel, a Spanish-speaking native-born Puerto Rican, was drafted to fight in Vietnam and then punished by the officers because he could not understand their orders. Today, he is a social worker and counsels other Hispanic vets who continue to suffer as a result of the war. Angel is shown here in the first row on the right.

other war in Puerto Rico. A war of horrible memories, sweating, screaming and even speaking Vietnamese in my sleep. Some nights were so bad, my mother would climb into my bed and rock me back to sleep." Like so many others, Angel hit the bottle to help deaden the pain.

Angel pulled it together enough to graduate from the Institute of Technology in chemistry, management and administration. He then began a thirteen-year stint as a chemical operator in a refinery. As good as he looked to the outside world, his personal life was a wreck. During the nine years after college, he went from one marriage to another, to another, to another, producing five children in all. With the alcohol, memories of Vietnam, and violent behavior at home, Angel had turned into his father. "At the time, I was wild. I know now that everything bad that happened was my fault." As he speaks, Angel lowers his head in shame.

One day, unexpectedly, the company where he worked went bankrupt, and he was out of a job. "There was nothing to do but drink and get rowdy with the guys. My life was falling apart—my world was spinning out of control. After too many run-ins with the police, I borrowed money from my sister and went to the States to begin a new life."

Nothing changed for Angel in the States, until he changed. After losing yet another job, a friend recommended that he go to a vet center for help. "I went there for help all right," Angel bellows loudly at himself. "I went in and asked the guy for a job. Instead of offering me a job, the counselor started talking about Vietnam and asked me if I had ever heard of post-traumatic stress disorder." He recommended a psychologist. "The first time I went to see her, I burst into tears and then exploded, 'I killed people. My friends were killed. I don't want to remember those things.'" That was in 1984. He is still seeing her today.

That visit changed the downward spiral of Angel's life. He eventually got a job doing bilingual work as a temp at the vet center, and one thing led to another. Angel is now a social worker at the same vet center and is working directly with vets and their families individually and in groups. "Once a week, I give back to my own by running a group for Hispanic veterans." Angel proudly adds, "What started out with three guys has grown to over 20."

His personal life has also turned around and flourished. He has now been married to the same woman for over 20 years, and they live contentedly with their two daughters. "In four years I will retire and go back to my roots, back to Puerto Rico where I belong." Suddenly, Angel's expression changes from one of softness to one of uneasiness. "If it wasn't for the war taking me on a major detour, I never would have left my homeland to begin with." Gritting his teeth, he continues, "I can't believe it—I still live with Vietnam in my gut, every day. It is a sickness that there's no cure for."

Vietnam: My Force, My Fuel

$\mathcal{A}$merican women played many roles in Vietnam during the war. They worked as translators, air traffic controllers, decoders, map-makers, photographers, clerks and nurses. Nursing was probably the most important and dangerous job they performed. Peggy was one of almost 10,000 nurses who served in Vietnam.

"I went to Vietnam for all the reasons someone else might choose to become a nun—to save lives and stamp out disease." Peggy graduated from Kings County Nursing School in 1966 and then joined the United States Army. Eight weeks after basic training, she was sent to the 24th Evacuation Hospital in Long Binh, South Vietnam. "When I arrived, the 24th Evac was a conglomeration of Quonset huts and four wood-and-screen buildings with tin roofs that made up the hospital. There wasn't even running water. How can you run a hospital without clean running water?"

Peggy worked in the pre-op ward. The casualties came in right off the helicopters. "I was responsible for choosing which of the wounded men we would take care of first, second or not at all. My first patient was a Vietnamese baby whose head was split open. I felt like someone had kicked me in the stomach. What was a baby doing there?" With disbelief in her voice she continues, "I went there to treat soldiers, not babies."

Seemingly endless streams of casualties followed. "During Tet, we worked nonstop. We treated 400 patients in the first 48 hours. I tried to remember each of their names and injuries—that was the least I could

Peggy helped to ease the suffering in this Vietnamese village in 1966, but she suffered herself when a fellow officer raped her and an Army doctor forced her to have an abortion. *(photo courtesy of Peggy)*

do. People back home were counting on me to take care of their loved ones. We tried to make sure no one died alone."

"We were young, far away from home and had so much to deal with. So very much. There were young soldiers, their bodies and spirits broken. The nurses couldn't help but assume some responsible role, taking the emotional place of a mother, sister or girlfriend. The conditions at the base camp were horrendous—mud, bugs, rats and enemy fire." Peggy lowers her head as she continues, "And, there were the parties."

"Commanding officers would regularly order the nurses to get dressed up and board helicopters that would drop them in the field where some general was hosting a party. It was humiliating. We were nurses, but we felt like cheap call-girls." One night, Peggy was exhausted and decided to leave the party early. "I crawled into bed and passed out." Her voice falters in a whisper of shame and horror, "I woke up to the pressure of someone climbing on top of me. He held his hand over my mouth as he raped me."

Another incident that will forever haunt Peggy: "I was dating an Air Force fighter pilot and became pregnant. The Army found out before I could decide what I wanted to do about the pregnancy. They ordered me to have an abortion. I was reluctant. Then one day a colonel came into the post-op ward, stuffed a rag in my mouth and said, 'I'm going to perform an abortion on you. If you tell anyone, I will deny it. If you persist with the accusations, you will be court-martialed.'" Tears form in Peggy's eyes, "These terrible memories will never go away."

Vietnam is always with Peggy. It has defined her life—even her reproductive life. She married in 1975 and two years later was due to give birth. "I had some tests when I was in my ninth month indicating that something in me appeared attached to my baby and could be a dead Siamese twin. I totally freaked out." Peggy gave birth to Daniel, a perfectly healthy baby boy, but six weeks later, at the age of 33, she had a hysterectomy to remove a large tumor. "My medical history is identical to that of Vietnamese women who were also exposed to massive amounts of Agent Orange." The herbicide Agent Orange was sprayed on and around bases to eliminate vegetation that might hide the enemy. It rained from the sky during the height of the war in 1967 to 1968, the same years Peggy served in Vietnam.

Peggy also suffered severely from post-traumatic stress disorder following her son's birth. "I never imagined my problems were related to Vietnam. I thought only soldiers got this. Once I realized what was going on, I went to the VA hospital to get help. They turned me away. There were no services available for women. We are truly the forgotten minority of war. I finally found a private therapist—I still see her to this day."

Since her discharge from the Army, Peggy has worked as a clinical nurse and counselor, a health-care administrator and program developer, a teacher and an advisor. In 1985, she attended the Women Veterans Working Conference that brought together women from all wars. This was the first time Peggy talked openly about her Vietnam experience. In 1990, she received her master's in counseling and recently attained her Ed.D. in counseling psychology. Her dissertation title was *Witness to the War—The War Stories of Women Vietnam Veterans*.

"When I left Vietnam in 1968, I thought I would never go back there or even think about it again—that it was a closed book. Instead, my experiences in Vietnam became my force, my fuel in life." Peggy speaks about the Vietnam War to a variety of groups, from kindergarten classes to gray panthers. She developed a school curriculum about war, has lobbied for veterans and works with a theater artist to put on performance pieces that tell her story. In 1988 and 1990, Peggy returned to Vietnam to help set up training centers for midwives. "Today, I work as a psychiatric clinical nurse specialist for child and family services. Most of my clients are Amerasians and Vietnamese refugees. Everything in life does come full circle."

Today Peggy believes that the nurses are the truly forgotten minority of the war.

Thu's Treasures

"I was born at a time that made me old enough to be involved in both the French and the American wars." From 1946 to 1953, Thu was a sergeant and male nurse in the Red Cross and took care of wounded Vietnamese soldiers and civilians in Dalat in the Central Highlands. By the time the Americans arrived, he had advanced to the rank of lieutenant. From 1956 to 1975, he again patched up the casualties—this time wounded American and South Vietnamese soldiers.

The war took its toll on Thu and his family. His wife and one of his daughters were killed in June 1973 by Viet Cong mortars. "After the war, I was sent to the Dien Khan prison for fifteen months of very hard labor. When I got out, I was forced to spend the next fifteen years working in the mountains as a farmer." Today, Thu works during the day at the Citadel in the Emperor's Library in Hue. He spends his evenings studying English. "My nights are awful. I get little rest. I can usually fall asleep quickly, but my sleep does not last long." During the drawn-out nights alive with the wind's sounds and whispers, terrifying nightmares consume and interrupt Thu's sleep. Both wars are still very much alive in his mind. "Maybe someday soon I will die and I will finally be at peace."

"My life, my hopes, my dreams are all in this bag." Thu proudly holds up a well-traveled, black plastic bag. Its contents—his treasures—have accompanied him through two of Vietnam's wars. Thu, like so many other Vietnamese whose lives were dictated by the wars that tore through their country, has many war stories to tell. Instead, he prefers to talk about the stories symbolized by the contents in his black plastic bag. "I carried these treasures with me through two wars. Whenever war comes close, I find a safe place, dig a hole in the ground and bury them. When the war ends, I go back and recover them."

Thu's valuables are not precious diamonds or jewels: they are precious photographs and mementos of his family and dearest friends. He takes them out, proudly sharing each image and the story attached to it with anyone willing to listen. "These pictures show all the fortunes I've had in my life." Sometimes, when Thu is sitting alone with his treasures, he imagines that all the world's greatest leaders have their own bags of treasures. He speculates that there might never be another war if these leaders would look into their own bags before deciding to engage in combat.

Thu keeps his valued treasures, the fortunes of his life, in a well-traveled, black, plastic bag, which he buried in the ground for safe-keeping during the French and American wars.

The Last Night of the War

"BLACK ANGUS, BLACK ANGUS, THIS IS WOLF MAN SEVEN ZERO."
"WOLF MAN, THIS IS BLACK ANGUS, WE'RE IN TROUBLE DOWN HERE."
"I'M WITH YOU, BLACK ANGUS."

> "I couldn't believe it. I started shouting, 'Holy sh-t!!! That was you?'"

Dennis, a Marine officer, was flying his OV-10 Bronco on a final mission on January 31, 1973, the last official night of America's involvement in the war; a cease-fire agreement had been signed and in two months all the Americans would be returning home. That night, however, Dennis was still flying combat duty because earlier that day another OV-10 Bronco aircraft had been blown out of the sky. Whenever an American pilot was shot down, a major operation went into effect to rescue him. "There still was no sign of him by the time I was assigned to fly. I remember we were up at 9,000 feet, over an area near the Cua Viet River, searching for him, when I thought, 'We are doomed.' Off to our left an anti-air missile was fast approaching our rear quarter. I saw another one approaching from the right. And another one in front." Dennis' palms are slick with sweat as he recalls that night. "In the next split second, I grabbed the control stick and turned the plane hard to the left. We escaped death by a hair." He takes a very deep breath before he continues, "I couldn't believe it. We made it through and then a few moments later, four more missiles were after us. Our aircraft shook violently and jumped about three feet when the next four warheads detonated right behind us. That was just the beginning of a very long night."

Under normal conditions, Dennis' and the other pilots' jobs were to execute air strikes and call artillery missions on the enemy while guiding ARVN ground troops and American advisors to safety. "That night, our hands were tied because of the missing American pilot. We couldn't call for artillery assistance to protect our men on the ground for fear of killing our own downed pilot."

Dennis vividly remembers communicating via radio with one of the men on the ground that night. "We spoke for three hours. His call name was Black Angus. His troop was trying to capture and hold a three-square-mile piece of land until the cease-fire took place. I could see the North Vietnamese artillery firing on the ARVN position. We were getting beaten up pretty bad. But all I was allowed to do was give Black Angus grid coordinates and offer moral support." By four the next morning Dennis had to leave the air. He never knew if those troops made it out okay and he continued to feel guilty about not being able to help Black Angus' troop or rescue that downed pilot.

Two weeks later, Dennis left Vietnam and started for home on one of the last planes out of Danang. He continued to serve as a major in the Marine Corps until 1979 and retired from the reserves in 1991. "Life was lousy after the war. I couldn't get it together." Dennis' face looks shattered with despair. "After coming home to a country that was torn apart—Watergate, hate, discontent, race riots—all I did was hang out and drink too much. Everything in my world was out of control."

Dennis, a retired Marine Corps major, was depressed and down on his luck in 1997 when serendipity brought him face-to-face with an anonymous soldier whose life he had saved in 1973.

By February 1997, Dennis was really down on his luck. He needed a car, but had no money. He tried to get a bank loan but was turned down because he did not have collateral or a job. "I didn't get it. I stuck out my neck in Vietnam, and nobody appreciated it. At that point, I truly thought there must have been something morally or ethically wrong with me. I didn't know where to turn." Weighed down with gloom, Dennis needed a place to think. He strolled into the bar at Clyde's Restaurant, a local hangout, and ordered a beer. Another retired Marine friend of his was there and introduced him to Walter, who had been in Vietnam too.

Dennis and Walter immediately started sharing and comparing war stories. It turned out that they had both been Marines and had both served until the very end of the war. "I started saying something like, 'Yeah, that was a real rough time. I almost got wasted the last night. Could you believe it, the last night! The Vietnamese Marines had grabbed this spit of land by the Cua Viet River and they were getting shot up bad.' Then Walter says to me, 'Hey, I was an advisor to the Vietnamese Marine Corps on the ground near the Cua Viet River. I was there that same night!'"

"I got really excited and said, 'No kidding? What was your call sign?' And he says, 'Black Angus.' I couldn't believe it. I started shouting, 'Holy sh-t!!! That was you?'" After a long disbelieving pause, silent tears and warm embraces, an immediate friendship was formed—a friendship that helped Dennis get his life back on track.

Twenty-four years after that last night of war, Walter and Dennis were destined to meet face-to-face, away from the background noise of gunfire. A lot has changed for Dennis since that February day in Clyde's Restaurant. He now has a job selling computer and data systems for the internet, owns a black Nissan and enjoys a supportive friendship with "Black Angus."

"Both Walter and I chose to go to Vietnam and do something important for a cause we believed in as young men. That choice made us separate from the rest of the world. Even though we may look like everyone else and move through crowds in the same way—we *are* different. That difference, that separateness, creates a deep-rooted bond few others can know or understand."

Closet of Secrecy

*G*ary speaks in a low, barely audible voice. "One sunny afternoon in 1967 my parents met me downtown at our local recruiter. I was only 17 and needed their permission to join the Marines. Shortly after that, my kid brother Howard did the same thing. We both served in Vietnam. We both returned to the States on April 18, 1969. I accompanied my brother's coffin."

"My brother's death devastated me, but I tried my best to get on with my life," Gary continues softly. "I took whatever jobs I could get, from a truck driver, fire alarm salesman and construction worker to a bartender and bouncer. Finally, in 1972, I landed a good job as a warehouse manager for a local beer distributor." A year later, he married and in the next few years the couple had two daughters. Memories of Howard's death began to fade. Life was good.

Then the worst happened. "Eleven years after burying my brother, I buried my wife. She died of an aneurysm." The wild look in Gary's eyes flares, gleams faintly and fades as he adds, "The only regret of my life is that I never told her I was a Vietnam veteran. She never knew why I was silent and moody. She never knew where my rage came from."

Gary was left a young widower with two daughters, aged three and five. "The first two years were unbearable. I totally shut down. I erased the world." He buried himself in a shroud of silence. "Looking back, I don't know how I survived. Even worse, I don't know how my little girls survived."

"It was a damp, drizzly day in November 1984 when I stood in front of the Wall—those massive tablets bearing the names of more than 58,000 Americans who died in Vietnam." A powerful emotion rushes through Gary's body as he remembers reaching out and touching, almost caressing, his brother's name. "My body shook as I gazed into the shiny reflecting surface and saw Howard's face looking back at me." Those few hours on a rainy November day at the Vietnam Veterans Memorial Wall in Washington gave Gary the permission he needed to walk out of his "closet of se-

> *"After three years, traveling to dozens of cities and hearing what feels like billions of stories, I still need my crying glasses."*

crecy." That same day, Gary met John Devitt, another veteran. They became fast friends as Gary shared some of his secrets for the first time.

John's and Gary's lives became significantly connected. John Devitt's friends and family had chipped in to buy him a plane ticket so he could attend the dedication ceremony of the Vietnam Veterans Memorial in November 1982. When John felt the energy and the healing power of the Wall, he vowed to take that healing to others who were not able to make the trip to Washington. His vow eventually resulted in the "Moving Wall," a half-size replica of Washington's Wall. John, Norris Shears, Gerry Haver and other Vietnam veteran volunteers helped to build the first Moving Wall, which went on display in Tyler, Texas in October 1984. Now there are three Wall replicas that travel throughout the country from March to December. John's first trip to the Wall not only changed his life, but allowed millions of others to begin healing as well.

In 1995, after retiring from the beer distributor, Gary decided to join John's crusade by taking one of the Moving Walls across America. Gary lives on the road from February to December and spends the winter months with his two grown daughters. "Traveling with the Wall opened my eyes and helped me realize that I'm not the only Vietnam combat vet out there," Gary says as he stares across at the black panels. "And it has allowed me to help others come out of their 'closet of secrecy.'"

The Wall, as much a shrine as a monument, has become a pilgrimage site, attracting people from all over the world. The miracles and mysteries of the Wall continue to overwhelm Gary. "Most times I wear dark glasses, even late at night. I call them my 'crying glasses.' After three years, traveling to dozens of cities and hearing what feels like billions of stories, I still need my crying glasses."

"One of the most memorable stories I heard was this one. It was two years ago in Billings, Montana. I watched as four couples slowly walked down the pathway to the monument. Their bodies were tight and the men's hands were all clasped in their wives' hands. Together, they visited different names inscribed on the wall. They rubbed their fingers over the names again and again and tears flowed down each of their faces."

Intrigued, Gary approached them. Bob, a tall distinguished man, began to tell their story. "My wife and I moved into a new neighborhood seven years ago. Shortly afterward, all eight of us here became steadfast friends." He looks at the others with appreciation. "Then last night something truly amazing happened. The guys and I were having our monthly card game in the kitchen. I got up in between hands to go into the living room to give my wife a kiss and froze in my tracks. An announcement that the 'Moving Wall' had arrived in a neighboring town was on the TV. I must have turned pale or something because when I went back to play cards one of the guys commented about my changed face. After all these years of friendship, my 'secret' was about to come out. I answered, not knowing what to expect. 'I'm a Vietnam veteran. I have to go to the Moving Wall tomorrow.'" Sighs, tears and embraces filled the room. It turned out that all four men were Vietnam veterans. All four men had lived in their own "closets of secrecy" all these years.

Upon hearing Bob's story, goose bumps rose on Gary's skin. His crying glasses hiding his pain, he embraced each man for a long moment and whispered into each one's ear, "Welcome home, brother."

Gary transports the Moving Wall across America. What fills Gary's heart most is seeing vets at the Wall with their wives' arms embracing them as they release a floodgate of tears from decades past. The one regret of his life—not telling his wife he was a Vietnam veteran. She died of an aneurysm in 1980.

2
MIAs/POWs

never forgotten

During Frank's five-year imprisonment, both friends and strangers alike wore POW bracelets bearing his name. Here, at a ceremony and parade in his honor, Frank's well-wishers bestow their POW bracelets on him. *(photo courtesy of* Burlington County Times*)*

We Left Them Behind

$\mathscr{S}$wallowed up beneath the thick canopy of bamboo where sunlight barely penetrates, existed a jungle prison camp—a place of hell that only those who survived it can possibly comprehend. The camp assaulted the senses with the smell of rotting flesh, the sound of gunfire and bombs and the taste of stale rice dotted with rat droppings. Of the 32 emaciated prisoners trapped in this prison, 20 lived to tell the story.

One of these survivors was Frank, an aircraft commander of a UH-1 Huey gunship. He was shot down on the moonlit night of January 5, 1968, while flying to the aid of an infantry company. The crash smashed his knees and compressed several vertebrae, and marked the beginning of an agonizing five-year odyssey fashioned by the devil himself. "My life and the lives of the other prisoners became one endless nightmare."

During the first three years of his captivity, Frank was entombed in four different jungle camps. "Our diet consisted of a small amount of low-grade rice—the kind usually fed to pigs. And it was infested with bugs and rat droppings. The rice was supplemented by manioc, a few greens and nuoc mam—smelly Asian fish sauce. The amount of food we were given was so little that we were slowly wasting away. Slowly starving." For more than a year the prisoners had no shoes, and once their original fatigues rotted off their bodies their captors gave them only flimsy black "pajamas" to wear. They did not even have blankets to ward off the chilly monsoon-season evenings. "We wrapped ourselves in old rice sacks that had the words 'Donated by the people of the United States of America' printed on them." Life in the prisoner of war camps debilitated the body, the mind and the spirit, and turned civilized human beings into primal animals whose only struggle was to simply stay alive.

Weighed down with despair and exhaustion, Frank and his fellow prisoners, many of whom were wounded, suffered dysentery, malnutrition, skin infections, scurvy,

> *"I am still haunted by dreams about the guys who died in the camps and about the guys I know we left behind."*

bleeding gums and edema. Their teeth rotted and fell out. They endured clouds of mosquitoes and suffered the sweats and chills of malaria. "When the men around me started to die, I fell into a deep depression and lost my will to live. I stopped eating regularly, and I stopped taking care of my daily hygiene. Finally, I stopped caring." Frank refused to get off his hard bamboo bed and found himself comforted by sitting for hours, days, and sometimes weeks in an almost catatonic state. "I thought I was going to die anyway, so what was the difference?"

When the prisoners moved to the third and fourth camps, their conditions improved a bit. They were given more food, which in turn made them stronger and better able to ward off infections and disease. "By early 1971, I was the weakest of the prisoners who were still alive. The guards forced me into an exercise program to build up my stamina and strength in preparation for yet another move. They made me walk 250 yards down to a stream and back carrying a pack loaded with rocks." This little jaunt took the guards five minutes, the other prisoners did it in fifteen, and Frank dragged himself there and back in just over an hour.

"As weak as we were, they expected us to walk from the South, along the Ho Chi Minh Trail, through Laos and into North Vietnam—about 500 miles in all." The prisoners and guards traveled along narrow jungle trails, trudged up and down steep hills, forged rivers with extremely swift currents and traipsed through slippery mud. Dozens of four-inch leeches clung to their bodies, sucking the blood out of them when they emerged from the muddy areas. With each step, pain shot up Frank's legs and back, making him even slower, and soon he fell behind the rest. "The pain was so bad and my spirits had sunk so low that I started to beg the guards to put me out of my misery. To kill me."

After six months of trekking, Frank and his fellow prisoners arrived at their new quarters, the Plantation Prison in Hanoi. "We were in heaven. We had new clothes, rubber shower sandals, a mosquito net, a blanket, and better food. My health improved a lot after five or six weeks, and we weren't worrying any more about dying of malnutrition or disease. But we had other problems. We were really isolated—we were crammed into small concrete cells and were so inactive that we found it difficult to keep our minds occupied."

In December 1972 when President Nixon ordered the unrelenting "Christmas bombing" of Hanoi, they were moved to Hoa Lo Prison, nicknamed the Hanoi Hilton, a place of barbed wire and concrete. About three months later, they got word that the war was over and they were going home. On March 13, they were lifted off the ground in a C-141. "When the pilot announced, 'Gentlemen, we have just left Vietnam's airspace,' our cheers were so loud that they must have been heard around the world."

"Home. What a wonderful word." For the first three weeks on American soil, Frank was checked out medically and debriefed. "During my debriefing, I was shown aerial photographs of the camps I was imprisoned in and a close-up of me stumbling along the Ho Chi Minh Trail toward Hanoi. I was shocked. I couldn't understand why I had to spend five years of my life wasting away when the government knew exactly where we all were!" This anger nagged at Frank's gut and years later motivated him to write the book, *Why Didn't You Get Me Out?*

Frank weighed only 110 pounds when he headed home to welcome parades and his family. On August 3, 1974, Frank married Jane. "She was, and remains, the best thing that ever happened to me." Frank chose to stay in the military and about a year later was piloting helicopters again. He remained in the Army until 1987, then worked as a commercial airline pilot until he retired in 1997. These days, Frank spends a lot of time speaking at various events describing his experiences in Vietnam.

"Spending five years as a prisoner changes a man profoundly, beyond all understanding. I am still haunted by dreams about the guys who died in the camps and about the guys I know we left behind." What Frank observed in Vietnam makes him certain there are still American soldiers, American POWs in Vietnam. "When I was walking on the Ho Chi Minh Trail in Laos, I came within ten feet of another prisoner, a warrant officer. This guy did not come home with the rest of us. In the Hanoi Hilton, the Vietnamese commander showed me a local newspaper with a photograph of twelve American crewmen in flight suits with no head gear. Almost all of these guys were bandaged. Three were missing arms and one had no leg. Of the hundreds of POWs who returned in 1973, none of them were missing limbs. These men and others are still unaccounted for. We left them behind. I know it."

"Spending five years as a prisoner changes a man profoundly, beyond all understanding," states Frank.

There Are
No More Words

*T*he relentless heat and humidity combined with the mass of humanity, no access to sunlight, insufficient diet and repulsive sanitation made the prisons in Vietnam harsh death traps. "There were about 35 of us crammed into a tiny space with no windows, a hard cement floor and walls, and an eight-foot tin ceiling. The days were unbearable. We could hardly breathe inside the darkness. Our clothing had been taken and in the heat of the day we stood, sweat pouring down our sore-ridden bodies." The moisture from their bodies rose, and the condensation, having no place to go, collected on the ceiling. "The days were filled with men screaming in pain as their own salty sweat fell from the roof and burned their eyes." With the backside of his hand, Binh wipes running sweat off his face as he sits in an air-conditioned room reliving the months he spent in this inferno.

Binh had been imprisoned in 1982 because the Communists thought he had tried to escape Vietnam by boat. They found him and a woman huddled together one morning on Long Hai Beach. "I told them over and over that I wasn't trying to escape. But they wouldn't believe me. In prison we were given one meal a day that consisted of a cup of rice, soup, a small fish and two cups of water for drinking. You can imagine how very hungry I was—I even ate rotten food. Many others died from dysentery and starvation." The prison was given eight cents a day per inmate for their food. But most of the food never reached them. "The police used the money to buy rice to feed their dogs."

"The only way we could sleep in the small room was to lie on our sides on the hard cement floor, side by side, body against body. Once, in the middle of the night, the police came in and climbed over and stepped on the prisoners to reach me. They came and dragged me into an interrogation room." Driving sheets of rain were falling the night Binh was interrogated. The police questioned his presence on the beach. They threatened him physically if he did not tell the truth. "I just went there

My life's story has been of war—one kind or another. War without an end," says Binh. Once a teacher and prisoner, he now drives a cyclo.

to rest and for my entertainment. I begged them to please believe me." They did not. "They beat me in my head and face with their guns. I was so weak, I thought they would kill me for sure. After tumbling to the floor, they kicked me in my stomach with their military boots." Binh finally blacked out.

Four months later, Binh was transferred to a re-education camp. "We spent our days building a dam under the grueling sun. Not a cement dam, but a clay dam. We gathered wood in the forest to support the clay, and inevitably, each day as the water in the river rose, the clay would break away. It was futile. I watched men drown as they attempted to build the unbuildable." Binh lived there four more months and was able to supplement his small food rations with snakes and crabs that he caught at the river's edge.

"There are many different ways a person can be considered a prisoner of war. For myself, my family and friends, we were prisoners of the American War in our own country. Our every day was affected by the bombings and missile attacks. And when the

American War was over, war wasn't over for us. There was the Cambodian Invasion, Pol Pot, the Killing Fields and the invasion from China. We lived our lives on the edge of fear and uncertainty, waiting. Waiting for the next reign of terror."

Born in 1953, Binh had grown up with war. Exploding bombs and gunfire were commonplace sounds of his youth. He was an excellent student and when he turned 18 he continued his studies in chemistry, physics and math at the university during the war. He worked as a teacher from 1976 to 1979, instructing teenagers in math and physics. "My career as an educator of children ended abruptly when I was ordered to teach the Communist police instead." The first day Binh came to the police camp to work, he was commanded to dig holes in the earth to be used as a latrine. "You have to understand, this hurt my pride. I was very angry. I was a teacher because I loved children. I told them I didn't want to build toilets or teach adults!"

Regardless of his feelings, for the next three years, Binh was told where he would teach and to whom. He was not earning enough to feed himself and his elderly mother, so he looked for another job to supplement his pay. "Because of my previous outspoken behavior, the Communists refused me any jobs. I had no choice. I had to be a cyclo driver."

Once out of prison, Binh went back to driving a cyclo. It was a bad time for the Vietnamese people. There was not enough food, and most subsisted on sweet potatoes and rice. "In my mind, I began to create a plan to leave Vietnam." Binh did try to escape, but failed. Again, he was caught and sent to prison.

"This time the prison had better living conditions, but we were forced to build roads and the manual work was grueling. I was poor and couldn't give the police anything of value, so I was especially mistreated." At one point, the police put Binh on trial for being a lazy worker. As his punishment, the other prisoners were ordered to beat him up. "After the beating and without any medical attention, I was sent to a dark room, my hands and feet chained by irons for three days and three nights. I was fed food and water through a hole. How I survived is still a mystery to me." Binh spent four months there, four more at the Vung Tau prison, then three more in a Mekong prison. Could things get any worse? "Because I was so poor I was made to clean the floor and work as a servant for other richer prisoners." With a faraway look in his eyes, Binh continues, "I don't know why I stayed alive."

Almost one year later, Binh was released. He went back to Saigon to drive a cyclo. "I have given up hope of ever teaching again and of a better life, for I see only darkness in my future. My life's story has been of war—one kind or another. War without an end." Binh's head is downcast. "There are no more words."

I Have No Life

*T*he air hangs hot and heavy over the streets of Saigon. Tho sits in Kim's Cafe with his back against the wall. His eyes search the streets as he sips lukewarm coffee. The habit of sitting with his back against the wall and his eyes gazing toward the entrance of the cafe began during the war. In 1968, when Tho was 20 years old, he volunteered to be a helicopter pilot in the South Vietnamese Army. The government sent him to Texas for training, and in 1969 he was assigned to an American "dust off" crew at an air base in Danang.

"When we weren't flying missions, we hung out in bars and shared stories of our lives before the war. One day, a buddy of mine was waiting for me to join him at a local bar. By the time I got there, he and the building were only charred remains. My dear friend and a five-year-old boy were burnt to cinders. I found out later that the innocent five-year-old had been booby-trapped with explosives. The booby-trap had been tied to his small body by the Viet Cong." Sadness consumes Tho's face, "The habit of sitting with my back to the wall began on that day in 1969 and has continued ever since."

"Six years after my friend was killed, the North Vietnamese captured Saigon. We hoped then that the country would finally be at peace. But the takeover of the South was anything but peaceful." Anyone who had ties with the Americans or the previous regime had their property confiscated and were imprisoned without a trial and sent to forced-labor camps, known euphemistically as re-education camps.

Tho and tens of thousands of others spent untold years suffering under horrendous conditions in these camps. Many of these re-education camps were built on land that was still covered with unexploded ordnance, as was much of the countryside. The most efficient way for the North to clear the mines was to use some of the inmates as human mine-detectors. Many were maimed for life, many others were killed. "As bad as the war was, being in the Army was still easier than being in prison."

When Tho was released from the camp, he tried to get a job and make a life for himself and his family. "People like me who were close to the Americans had it the hardest. There was no work for us." The Communist party had sent large numbers of

> *"As bad as imprisonment was, life today is worse . . ."*

Tho, a South Vietnamese helicopter pilot during the war, was a prisoner of war and now feels like a prisoner of peace.

northern cadres to the South to manage the transition, which created an enormous amount of resentment among the southerners, who now found themselves frozen out of positions of responsibility and power. If they could find work at all, it was in the form of a menial job.

"The only job I could get at first was to drive a cyclo around Saigon. Today I am a tour director. I work twelve hours a day and earn five dollars." Tho bows his head in shame. "But, this problem doesn't stop with me. When my children graduate from school and try to get a job, they will have to write on their application that their father fought on the side of the Americans. Their applications will then automatically be denied."

"As bad as imprisonment was, life today is worse," Tho believes. "The leaders of the Socialist Republic of Vietnam were proficient at war, yet unskilled at peace." Now, more than a quarter of a century since North Vietnamese troops captured Saigon, the struggle continues for the Vietnamese people who live south of the DMZ. "Today, I sit here in Kim's Cafe with my back to the wall watching those who watch me. All these years later, I am still not free." For just one moment, Tho breaks his eternal gaze outside the cafe. His eyes focus on the floor. "I try to make sense of my life as the war plays out in my mind. It's a funny thing—before 1975, when I was fighting in the war, I never smoked or drank alcohol. Today, I smoke and drink as much as I can. My wish is that someday soon I will get cancer and die. When that day comes, I know I will finally be at peace. I have no life now. We have no future."

Missing in Action

At the end of the Vietnam War, over 2,000 Americans were missing and unaccounted for. Barbara's husband was one of them. "I was just a young girl when I met Herbert. He was an Air Force man, the 'older man' who rescued me from my unhappy home." Barbara, 15, and Herbert, 19, were married June 30, 1956, eight months after they had met. In the following nine years, they had five children and made themselves a happy home as a military family.

Herbert had joined the United States Air Force in 1954, just out of high school. In 1966 he received orders to go to Southeast Asia. "Herbert was not required to go, because our youngest baby had a heart condition. But as a family we decided it was the right thing to do. So, on our tenth wedding anniversary, he left for Udon, Thailand, to work as a crew chief on C-47s."

Barbara was left behind to care for five children ranging in age from one to nine. "I was lost without him. The centerpiece of my family was missing." Holding back tears Barbara continues, "I was frightened and deeply lonely." Thirty days after leaving the States, Herbert phoned Barbara from Thailand. "We shared five minutes of everyday chitchat about

Shown here with his young family, Herbert was shot down over Laos only 30 days after saying goodbye to his wife Barbara and their children—for years no one knew if he was dead or alive. *(photo courtesy of Barbara)*

the kids, and then he said, 'I can't talk long, I've got to fly, I love you.' Then the phone went dead. Those were the last words I ever heard from him. Two hours later, while on its way to Vietnam, his plane was shot down over Laos."

"I couldn't sleep. I was haunted day and night by the uncertainty of what had happened to my husband. Was he alive? Was he captured and held prisoner? Was he being tortured?" Barbara lived on an emotional roller coaster, oscillating from hope to despair. "In spite of it all, I gathered up the strength to take care of my kids. They had their own problems dealing with the loss of their father, and I had to put their needs first."

With only a ninth-grade education and no job, Barbara had to find a way to feed and shelter her children. She took one job after another and had the perseverance to earn a high school GED. Eventually, she earned a bachelor's degree and then a master's degree in social work. Life went on, accompanied by uncertainty, anxiety, hope and despair.

When the last troops left Vietnam in March 1973, the American prisoners of war were released in Hanoi. Herbert was not one of them. Almost seven years after his disappearance, there was still no word of him. "I couldn't live in this state of limbo anymore," Barbara says with a face drawn and weary after years of stress. "I had to do something." On Father's Day 1974, Barbara, along with a grieving father whose son was also missing and the mayor of their town traveled to Laos to search for their loved ones.

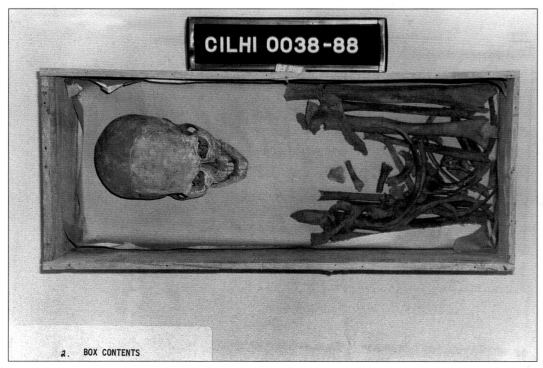

Twenty-two years after his plane went down, Herbert's remains came home, ending the uncertainty his family lived with day and night.
(photo courtesy of Barbara)

2. BOX CONTENTS

"We flew into Vientiane, the capital. It seemed like a really charming and sleepy kind of place. We went to the American Red Cross, but they couldn't help us." A friend suggested that Barbara speak to a monk who lived in Luang Phabang, a plane ride away from the capital. Monks can move more freely throughout the nation and might be able to help her. After coming this far, she could not let it rest. "I flew by myself to this ancient town to search for answers. It was at the junction of the Mekong and Nam Knan Rivers. I remember looking out the plane window at the suffering landscape

110

Barbara and her grown children
visited the Moving Wall in 1998 and
made an etching of Herbert's name.

111

below and wondering where Herbert was. My heart sort of cried out 'Where are you, Herbert'?" Laos is the most-bombed nation in history.

"I met the orange-cloaked monk in his temple. We exchanged greetings and I handed him a photo of Herbert. He went into a trance, and after a long time he said, 'I spoke to Herbert's spirit.' At first I was skeptical. But then he spoke of our five children, and he said that Herbert was concerned about our youngest son's heart condition. I was totally stunned." He also told Barbara that Herbert did not survive the plane crash. "For the first time in almost eight years, I realized Herbert was not coming home."

In 1975, the government declared Herbert legally dead. Now believing that Herbert was never coming home again, Barbara and the children attempted to get on with their lives. An underlying melancholy, however, weighed heavily on them. A person does not have to be a soldier to be a casualty of war.

"Fourteen years after Herbert was declared missing, I received a phone call from the Air Force mortuary service. 'Vietnam is returning eight sets of remains. Herbert is one of them.' My husband was finally coming home." Herbert was given a full military burial in his hometown on July 29, 1988. But instead of being able to put the anguish of the past to rest, Barbara's life came tumbling down again. "It was like a cloak of darkness had fallen over me. There was nothing left to fight for." Barbara fell into a severe depression and became suicidal. "I kept asking myself, 'What was it all for'?" Eventually the memory of Herbert's love for her and their five children enabled Barbara to finally say goodbye to the shadows of the past.

When Herbert was missing, Barbara dated very little. "When I did, I felt guilty, as if I was committing adultery." Two years after Herbert's funeral Barbara met Glen, with whom she shares her life today. "Glen gave me hope, he gave me love, he gave me back my life." Glen had served in Vietnam in 1969. Today, Barbara works for the Department of Veterans Affairs as a readjustment counselor for Vietnam veterans. With her life's experience, she can relate to these men as few others can.

In honor of the unaccounted-for Americans, the third Friday in September has been designated as National POW/MIA Recognition Day. Although Barbara and her children no longer live with uncertainty, some families, even after a quarter of a century, are still waiting for their loved ones to come home.

If Only
I Had Known

"*I* hated war. I was taught that civil war is for the uncivilized and I could never understand why we had to fight our own brothers." Despite this attitude, Tran advanced his career and eventually served as a lieutenant colonel working as a staff and training officer for the Central Training Command of the Armed Forces of South Vietnam. He stayed in this position, running two units, until the end of the war.

When South Vietnam collapsed in 1975, tens of thousands of former ARVN officers and civilians who had been "tainted" by their American connections were arrested and sent to labor camps for re-education. Tran was among them. "The Communists placed ads in all the local newspapers, announcing that all superior officers from major to general had to go to re-education training camp for one month. We did as we were told. I said goodbye to my wife and five children and told them I'd be back in a month." A forced grin forms on Tran's face. "How naive we were. If only I had known I would not return to my family for eight years, I would never have gone willingly to the camp. I would have tried to escape from Vietnam—by any means possible."

"The Communists treated us like animals. They tortured us physically, mentally, emotionally and morally." Day in and day out, the prisoners were fed mostly stale rice, manioc and cabbage, which gave them diarrhea. They supplemented their meager rations with anything they could find.

Tran, an American-trained South Vietnamese officer, was arrested after the war and sent to a re-education camp. He was told he would spend one month there— one month turned into eight years. *(photo courtesy of Tran)*

Tran tells just one story about how desperate they were for food. "I remember one Sunday morning, as I was staring at a picture of my family, I saw something move out of the corner of my right eye. It was a mouse. I protected my hand with a piece of cloth and grabbed it." Unable to kill the mouse himself, Tran asked a friend for help. "He killed it and we cooked it and ate that mouse together, licking our fingers to the very end."

Reliving the experience brings shivers to Tran's spine. Remembering his friend, a brave paratrooper during the war, Tran's face turns pale as he tries to hold back tears. "When he was sent to the camp, he got really sick. He used to weigh about 190 pounds. After six months he had shrunk to only half this. He died two years later. I really miss him." Tran himself was 144 pounds when he entered the camp and a mere 108 pounds when he went home to his family.

Detainees were forced to do hard labor. "In the beginning I had to go into the deep forest of the North Vietnamese highlands every day to cut down large trees that were used to make houses for the staff and ourselves." One day when he was carrying a huge tree up a rain-soaked hillside, Tran slipped. The tree fell, crushing his leg. "I laid there and cried like a small child." Picturing his wife and children, he felt a deep conviction that no matter how bad things got, he wanted to live. He had to go on. "I began praying to all the gods in all the heavens." Although raised in the Confucian religion, Tran even prayed to Jesus Christ, promising to become a Catholic if Jesus protected him. (A man of his word, today Tran is a practicing Catholic.)

After being injured, Tran, who had an artistic ability, was ordered to make memorial signs for the tombs of the dead. This job was much less taxing and surely helped Tran survive the camp. Even so, the days dragged into weeks, weeks into months, months into years, years into a seeming eternity. The prisoners believed they would never be given their freedom. Tran kept thinking, "I was born in wartime, I lived in wartime, maybe I will die in wartime." In 1979, China invaded Vietnam and the clashes continued into the 1980s. The Vietnamese Communists, needing more and more men to fight their latest war, drafted the men who ran the camps in the North as their chosen new soldiers. With no one left to run it, the camp where Tran was held closed down. Tran's voice becomes high-pitched while reliving his relief, "We were finally set free." Others were not as lucky as Tran. More than a decade after the war's end, an estimated 50,000 people were still being detained as political prisoners.

Tran, a mere skeleton of a man, returned to his family in March 1983. Two of his sisters and two of his brothers had already died during the war. He now learned that both his parents had died while he was away in the camp. His former life was shattered. "My wife and children survived my long absence by moving south to the Mekong Delta. They made a living by buying rice and other goods and taking them to Saigon to sell them for a profit." When Tran returned to his family, they were living hand to mouth. Guilt tinges Tran's voice as he explains, "We were always hungry. I did manage to earn some money by teaching English to people who were trying to escape from Vietnam. And I worked with a friend, painting banners." Now in a voice laced with pride Tran adds, "Things were not great, but it was going well enough that I was able to buy a used bicycle to travel to and from my jobs."

In 1989, the United States and the Vietnam governments mutually agreed that cur-rent and former detainees in re-education camps would be allowed to settle in America under the Humanitarian Operation, or HO, program. Tens of thousands of former detainees and their families have been admitted to the United States as a result. Tran, his wife and two of their children were among them, though they had to wait ten years from the time Tran was released from the camp until they could emigrate. Tran sadly adds, "My other three children didn't come because they were married and had established a life for themselves in Vietnam." Tran also left behind four grandchildren. "Reunification has no meaning for me. For me the war is always con-tinuing because we are always separated."

"I am grateful to be living in America, but life is not simple." When Tran and his family first arrived in the States, they lived on welfare for the first eight months. Tran worked at different jobs until he landed a position as a program director in a Vietnamese outreach center. Tran's wife who had been a nurse in Vietnam, and their children, did tailoring in their home to add to Tran's wages. "Financially we are okay today. But emotionally things are not good. We are always depressed. My wife cries all the time. Vietnam is forever in my mind. Maybe when things are peaceful, I will go back, reunite with my family and stay there forever. Maybe, someday."

Under the Humanitarian Operation program, tens of thousands of former detainees and their families were admitted to the United States. Tran and his family were among them.

3
REFUGEES

a life of impermanence

These two brothers lived in a Thai refugee camp for at least three years after escaping from Vietnam in a small boat. Here they are in 1992 still waiting to be told their fate.

Will I Be Forgotten?

*T*he Phanat Nikhom Refugee Camp in Thailand is a place unto itself. It is a place where long, dusty roads lead nowhere, a place of mindless wandering and make-shift hovels, a place where children and dogs compete for scraps as they pilfer through the trash. It is a place of restless, unfocused energy, of boredom, and compulsory routine. The steamy, hot days fade into black, hopeless nights, one after another. Confined to this land of limbo, 12,700 refugees from Vietnam, Laos and Cambodia share this cramped, dismal space.

The refugees' cultural traditions, once so important, change as they become assimilated into the camp culture. All around are the elderly without children and children without the elderly—all orphans in their own right. Many of the small children were born in this camp and have no homeland or even the memory of one. They have never walked barefoot in a rice paddy or swum in a river. They think that rice and water come to the world in the back of big black trucks.

Huynh, a slight, young Vietnamese man, walks as he talks. His history is much the same as the others. "My brother Quang and I escaped from Vietnam three years ago on a small boat. We were picked up at sea by an American Navy ship. They brought us to the Thai authorities, who then brought us here. I am now 21 years old. I try hard to make the best of living here, but the uncertainty of not knowing what tomorrow will bring is driving me crazy." His eyes reflect desperate loneliness; his feet kick the dry dirt as he drifts mindlessly toward his room.

"I keep wondering if I will ever see my family again. I miss them all so much. Will I be sent to America to start a new life? Or will I be sent back to Vietnam? I fear that the most. The Vietnamese government does not look too kindly on people who have escaped."

As Huynh enters the shadowy interior of his room, he stops to look at the memories hanging on the wall—nine photographs. Photographs of the family he left behind. He shares his tiny living space with a man from Cambodia. They do not speak

> *"My biggest fear is that I will have to stay here forever, that I will be forgotten. Forgotten by my family, my country and the world."*

119

the same language. He misses his brother, who is assigned a space in a different building. "I cannot plan a future," Huynh faintly mumbles, his posture dejected. "I live only in the moment. My biggest fear is that I will have to stay here forever, that I will be forgotten. Forgotten by my family, my country and the world."

According to the U.S. Department of State, there are approximately 19 million refugees and externally displaced persons worldwide. Included in this statistic are the more than two million refugees who fled Vietnam, Cambodia and Laos since the end of the Vietnam War. Some 1,200,000 have settled in the United States.

People began to escape war-torn Vietnam for a better life in the West when it became apparent the North Vietnamese would triumph over the South Vietnamese. Rumor suggested that South Vietnamese government officials, members of the Vietnamese elite, and anyone who had worked for the Americans would be executed. Fear of vengeance by the North spurred the initial flood of men and women to flee Vietnam. They escaped by land, sea and air—any way they could get out. By 1977, 130,000 refugees had been allowed to settle in America.

The second major exodus came in the late 1970s through the mid-1980s. Mostly Vietnamese political refugees or ethnic Chinese who had been persecuted by the Vietnamese government, these refugees collectively became known as "boat people." They departed from the coast of Vietnam in flimsy, ill-equipped, over-crowded, over-burdened vessels. An estimated one-third of these refugees perished at sea—by drowning, from dehydration or at the hand of pirates. Those who survived their escape were placed in camps throughout Southeast Asia and in Hong Kong. These camps offered the refugees the barest necessities for their physical survival. Many western countries, including the United States, Canada, European nations, Bermuda and Iceland opened their arms to these refugees, allowing them to emigrate.

The exodus slowed for a time, but surged again between 1988 and 1992 as more boat people headed out to sea. This new wave of Vietnamese refugees was not just politically oppressed Southerners, but economic refugees as well—factory workers and farmers from the South and the North. At this time, the average daily wage in Vietnam was 25 cents. These men and women, determined to leave behind the economic drought in Vietnam to begin a more lucrative life in the West, were willing to risk their lives in the process. When they reached a safe harbor, they were placed in refugee camps. These camps, although still crude, were an improvement upon earlier camps and offered rudimentary health care, education and counseling.

Huynh was still living in the refugee camp in 1992, three years after his "successful" escape. For him and thousands like him, the western world was no longer as sympathetic as it had been to the seemingly endless stream of refugees leaving Southeast Asia. The later arrivals who left Vietnam for economic reasons often faced repatriation; over 100,000 people were sent back to Vietnam. Today, all the Vietnamese refugee camps in Asia are empty.

The Girl
in the Picture

One of the most disturbing and enduring images from the Vietnam War was not of fiery bombs exploding, fierce soldiers in battle or foreign cities crumbling: it was the image blazoned across the world's newspapers of a nine-year-old girl running down a road naked and screaming in agony as napalm seared her body. Some people believe that Nick Ut's Pulitzer Prize-winning photograph changed history. Kim Phuc—the girl in the picture—knows how it changed her life.

In June 1972, as the war spread across Vietnam, it found its way to Trang Bang, Kim's village. "We were all so afraid when the Viet Cong invaded our village that we abandoned our homes and took sanctuary in a nearby pagoda." This holy place of sanctuary soon became the center of a storm of artillery, bombs and rocket fire as the Americans and the South Vietnamese attacked the VC. "I saw the plane coming down and four bombs landing. I didn't hear a big explosion, just bup, bup. Then suddenly it was as if hell was surrounding me." Two of Kim's brothers were killed instantly and Kim's skin was aflame with napalm, a jellied gasoline designed to sizzle through flesh and muscle, right down to the bone until it burns itself out.

She ran screaming in agony. "'Nong qua! Nong qua! (Too hot! Too hot!)' I tore off my burning clothes, but the burning didn't stop. I was running, running, running away." Soldiers and journalists poured water over her

This photograph of terrified children, including nine-year-old Kim Phuc in the center, as they run from an aerial napalm attack in June 1972, was published in newspapers worldwide. Some believe the horror it represented turned world opinion against the war. *(AP/Wide World Photos)*

back, neck and arms, which were already burnt black like charcoal. She lost consciousness. "I lost all my memory until I woke up a long time later in the hospital." With serious third-degree burns over a substantial portion of her back and arms, Kim spent the next fourteen months in hospitals.

By the time Kim was released from the hospital, her family had lost everything and was living in a tiny hut with barely enough money to feed themselves. Kim needed medicines and rehabilitation treatment in Saigon; she would surely have died without the help of a charitable foundation that paid for these medical necessities. "I was just a child and I cried a lot. Step by step, my mom encouraged me. She told me, 'Kim, I remember when you were born. You were a very beautiful baby. Now you suffer a lot from pain, but remember, everyone loves you.' I thank her love, because when you have love, you can recover from anything." Seventeen operations and years of therapy followed.

After high school, Kim's dream to become a doctor and help children was coming to fruition. "I was really happy in medical school. Then one day, a German film crew that wanted to do a story on the 'girl in the picture' changed everything." An international avalanche of endless interviews and photographs followed. Kim was forced by the Vietnamese government to quit school to become the "national symbol" of the war. Her dream ended. Again, she was a victim of the war. "'Why am I alive?' I kept asking myself. I wanted to die."

Then in 1986, Kim was offered an opportunity to go to Cuba to study and mount goodwill missions. She seized this chance to go back to school. In Cuba, she met and fell in love with Toan, a fellow Vietnamese student. They married six years later and honeymooned in Moscow. On their return to Cuba, when their plane stopped to refuel in Newfoundland, they got off and did not reboard. "I didn't know how to defect. I was so nervous. I closed my eyes and prayed for help." Kim opened her eyes and handed their passports to an officer. She simply said, "I want to stay." Their worldly possessions consisted of a camera, Kim's purse and the clothes on their backs. But Kim gratefully says, "At that point, we had everything. We had freedom!" Two years later, their son Thomas was born, and in 1997 they were blessed again by the birth of another son, Stephen. They now own a home in Toronto. Toan works with the disabled and attends Bible college where he is studying to become a Baptist minister.

Beneath Kim's wide-open, smooth face will always be the horrific, ravaged scars of war. The extensive areas of her body that were burnt still experience a hypersensitivity to heat and cold. "When the weather changes, the pain comes. It's like I am cut." Triumphing over her pain with dignity, she adds, "My character is not sad, not angry. In my house, I'm always laughing, smiling, smiling." Kim's Vietnamese name means golden happiness. "My life is now easy, and I live very happy."

Nearly a quarter of a century after her horrifying experience, Kim was invited to speak of her hopes for peace and reconciliation at the Vietnam Veterans Memorial Wall in Washington. She told the audience, "I have suffered a lot of physical and emotional pain. Sometimes I could not breathe. But God saved my life and gave me faith and hope." As Kim spoke, there were no dry eyes in the audience. "Even if I could talk face-to-face with the pilot who dropped the bombs, I would tell him, 'We cannot change history, but we should try to do good things for the present and for the future to promote peace.'"

As she spoke, Kim did not know that in the crowd of thousands sat John Plummer, the Army captain who ordered the bombers to drop the napalm canisters. Two failed marriages and years of trying to drink away the demons prove that Plummer was yet another victim of that unforgettable day. Eventually he gave up the alcohol, married a third time and became a Methodist minister. Plummer approached Kim after her speech. He fell into her arms sobbing and repeating, "I'm sorry, I'm just so sorry." Kim patted Plummer's back. "It's all right. I forgive, I forgive." They talked and prayed together for hours. Now they are friends and speak to each other on the phone regularly.

The famous photograph and the real-life "girl in the picture," have been an inspiration to many. A non-profit group, the Kim Foundation, provides free medical assistance to children around the world who are victims of terrorism and war. In 1996, a documentary, *Kim's Story—The Road From Vietnam*, was aired. Kim was named a Goodwill Ambassador for Peace by UNESCO (United Nations Educational, Scientific and Cultural Organization) in November 1997, and her life story, *The Kim Phuc Story—The Girl in the Picture* by Denise Chong, was published in 1999.

Here, her body still in pain, Kim receives kisses from her five-year-old son, Thomas.

"My life has been full of miracles," Kim concludes with a serene smile. "The fire of bombs burned my body, the skill of doctors mended my skin, but it took the power of God's love to heal my heart."

Giving Back

*J*uliette's family—her grandfather (a French-Vietnamese doctor) and both her mother and father, who were educated in France—hid the unpleasant side of life in Saigon from their children. "I grew up vaguely aware of the war and of poverty, but I was not a part of it. Then one day, when I was fourteen, something happened that changed the course of my life. Something I'll never forget."

Juliette attended the Conservatory of Music, which was located in an exclusive area of Saigon, right behind the Presidential Palace. "One day, across the street from my school, I saw a small boy dressed only in short, blue pajama pants scaling a barbed wire fence. Moments later, a gate opened and some nuns and a guard came running out after him. They caught him and dragged him back inside. I heard him cry out, 'I want my Mommy. I want my Daddy.' When the gate closed behind them I ran over and peeked inside." What Juliette saw was nothing her sheltered life could appreciate or begin to understand: There was a little house with a hundred or so babies crawling on the courtyard floor. It was a Vietnamese war orphanage.

Weeks later, Juliette's Girl Scout troop leader made arrangements for the troop to help care for the babies. The babies were either Vietnamese who had lost their parents in the

Juliette is shown here at 19 surrounded by two very famous Vietnamese musicians—Mr. Chinh-Trich on the left and Mr. Nam-Co on the right. *(photo courtesy of Juliette)*

war or Amerasians who had been abandoned. "Only four of us worked at a time caring for all those little babies. We were always feeding, changing, or holding and rocking them. We had to hang bottles from the ceiling to make it easier to feed so many babies at the same time." Because of this experience at the orphanage, Juliette, born into a privileged family, later chose to spend her life helping the less fortunate.

Juliette graduated from the Conservatory of Music in Saigon in 1968 with two degrees—one in Asian music history and another in the *dantranh*, an ancient instrument similar to a 16-string zither. "I taught music for the next year. But I felt so disillusioned. I saw so much injustice around me. Not just the war, but there was a tremendous disrespect for women's opinions and talents." Juliette decided to leave Vietnam and head to America as a foreign exchange student. The year was 1970 and the war was still raging.

Before leaving for America, Juliette went to say goodbye to her grandfather in the countryside. The bus ride was uneventful until the sound of gunfire rang out over the rumble of the bus. It was the Viet Cong. "They stopped the bus, made everyone get off and lined up the passengers shoulder to shoulder. They made us empty our pockets, and place our jewelry and shoes on the ground in front of us. The VC then shouted at us, 'Do not look around! Look down at your feet or you will be killed!' We were all so scared."

"The war was so crazy, so out of control, that anything could have happened next. The VC shouted again, 'Hold up your pants!' They went down the line of people and looked at everyone's feet. The Viet Cong were looking for the feet of soldiers. Locals wear sandals and have tanned feet, but soldiers wear combat boots and don't have tanned feet. They have blisters instead. They yanked two men out of the line-up. 'Open your mouth. Open wider!' They shouted and then shoved a lemon in each man's mouth to stop him from screaming. They took them away and I heard two pops." The sound went straight through Juliette's already trembling body.

The remaining passengers were then ushered back onto the bus to leave the horrible event behind. "The visit with my grandfather was brief. All I wanted to do was leave the violence of Vietnam and to go to safety in America."

Juliette went to America and moved in with Patrick, an American soldier she had met in Vietnam and his family. Though she saw no war in America, she felt her own kind of war churning inside. Patrick was as confused as Juliette about life and its pathways. In 1971, both poor and jobless, they decided to marry. Patrick eventually joined the police force, and so went from one potentially violent job to another. The couple had a daughter, Chrystina, and a son, Patrick Michael. Juliette, who felt thankful to American servicemen for sacrificing their lives for her people, joined the American Red Cross as a volunteer, hoping to give a little back. She went to veterans hospitals and spent time visiting with veterans who had no families.

> "I saw people walking around with no skin color, like dead bodies. It haunted me for years."

Juliette, who endured many difficulties in Vietnam and America, is now the commissioner of the Massachusetts Office for Refugees and Immigrants. In a moment of peace, she is seen here playing the *dantranh*.

In those days, there was no support system for veterans returning to civilian life. Patrick had a difficult time dealing with his own issues and with the responsibility of a wife and two children. Juliette was also confused, living between two cultures. "I didn't want to live or bring up a child in war-torn Vietnam, but in America I was so lonely. I missed my family and friends." Slowly things between Patrick and Juliette deteriorated, and they divorced in 1976.

With two children, no job or financial support (Patrick had quit the police force and skipped town), Juliette had to choose between welfare or some other way to survive. "I knew the path I chose would be hard, but I would never go on welfare. Instead, I went back to school and sold shoes to feed my kids." Juliette got her bachelor's degree in social work, her master's in teaching, and by 1981 she had a permanent position with the Massachusetts welfare department. Pretty much everyone in her life had a hand at raising her children. "My poor kids had a real rough life. I still feel bad—they really suffered." Today, Chrystina works in movie production and Patrick Michael is a college student.

Juliette stayed in America and married a Vietnamese man in 1987. Together they raised three children, Chrystina, Patrick Michael and Larry, her stepson. As the years passed, she began spending more time in the Vietnamese communities of her home state. In 1992, she helped found the Vietnamese-American Civic Association and became its executive director in 1996. The governor of her state was so impressed with the job she was doing that he recently honored her with the New American Appreciation Award, an award given to immigrants whose contributions to their new homeland have merited recognition. Presently, Juliette is on the board of directors for the American Red Cross and was appointed as the commissioner of the Massachusetts Office for Refugees and Immigrants by Governor Argeo Paul Cellucci. She helps refugees from all over the world with resettlement, education, job placement, housing and health care.

"I did journey back to my homeland twice since relocating to America. The first time, in 1987, created such conflict for me that I suffered from severe nightmares. I saw people walking around with no skin color, like dead bodies. It haunted me for years. The last time, in 1998, I witnessed too many Vietnamese still suffering. The donations of money from the West have not reached their villages." Juliette's anguish shows on her face. "Before the end of my life, I would like to go back to Vietnam to work with the poor again, to finish the work I started when I was a Girl Scout. I need to give back."

Haunted Memories

> *"Still, when I am near the ocean and smell the saltwater, a lonely feeling takes over my soul."*

Only thirteen years old and without his family, Dave fled Vietnam on a fifteen-foot river boat with eleven strangers. He wore a loose-fitting shirt, tattered sandals and long pants with an American ten-dollar bill sewn into their seam. "My dad escaped in 1975. He was an officer in the South Vietnamese Army and would have been imprisoned if he stayed. My mom followed him in 1980 with my sister and brother." Dave lived with his grandmother and aunt until 1984, when his parents, then living in Texas, sent him money for his escape. Each family member had to wait his or her turn. The trip cost three ounces of gold, a tremendous amount in a time of such great poverty.

"A small boat came to the shoreline in Rach Gia, where the twelve of us waited. We boarded and headed to where the river meets the ocean to meet our escape boat and navigator." Expressing their outrage when only a small boat and no navigator awaited them, they were forced at gun point onto the boat and sent out to sea.

"We left in the darkness of night. I'll never forget the smell of the saltwater, the slight wind on my face and the feeling of peace." By the second night, Dave's serenity was soon shattered when, in the fading light, a ship of Thai fishermen approached their tiny craft. "Naively, I expected these men to be our knights in shining armor. Instead, they were the devil himself. After climbing on board our small, crowded boat, they threatened us with knives, stole our belongings and raped one of the women." This was only the beginning of the outrage and horror that was repeated many times over. "We were stopped more times than I could count during our nine days at sea, and each time the atrocity committed was more horrid than the last, from robbery to repeated mob rapes, and finally . . . ." After a long stretch of silence Dave continues, "The three women traveling with us were taken away by these renegades of the sea—we never saw them again."

On the third day, the boat's engine was destroyed, and the destiny of this small group of strangers was left to the currents of the sea. "We had enough rice, dried fish and water to last us, but on the fifth day more pirates came and threw all of our provisions overboard. When one of the passengers tried to rescue our food, a pirate stabbed him and threw him into the ocean." The pirates then rammed the boat, leav-

ing holes in the bow, trying to sink it so there would be no witnesses to their crimes. "As the sharks circled, we pulled the bleeding man out of the water. We bailed and plugged the holes with clothing mixed with grease and oil from the engine to make it waterproof." While everyone was praying and crying, Dave, who had never before seen sharks, stared with excited fascination.

A good-looking young boy with longish hair, Dave was too young to appreciate the great peril he was in until the next ship approached and the fishermen on board yanked him onto their boat. They roughly stripped him down. "After discovering I wasn't a girl, they threw me back onto my boat. Chills run up and down my spine when I think of all the possibilities that day could have presented."

On their ninth day at sea, one exhausted refugee began to shout, pointing to the sky, where a lone seagull circled. Everyone joined in screaming and cheering. Where there was a seagull, there was land. The currents had carried them to the safety of

When he was thirteen, Dave escaped from Vietnam by boat. The cost— three ounces of gold and years of nightmares. Today, he is a sergeant in the United States Army.

Thailand. They were taken by local police to the nearest refugee camp and fed three meals a day. "Once my father was notified of my whereabouts, he began sending me 50 dollars a month, a fortune in this place of no rules and regulations. I was king of the world, having the greatest adventure of my young life. I couldn't wait to see my family and go to America where the streets were lined with gold and money falls from the sky." Dave's boyish giggles over his past beliefs are overshadowed on this day by a deep sadness in his eyes.

A little over a year after reaching the refugee camp, Dave was reunited with his parents. "My dream had finally come true. But where were the gold-lined streets and the picture-perfect life?" The dream that kept him alive and made him invincible at sea slowly became a waking nightmare. "Shortly after I arrived in Texas, my dad moved out. My mom was always in tears. Our family was shattered." Dave's English was poor, making him feel even more alienated from his new life. Needing a sense of belonging, he joined a street gang. "Luckily, I never got too caught up with it. I guess I wanted the glorious bad guy image, but deep down inside I was a total chicken and didn't really participate in the drugs or any bad activities."

Dave graduated from high school and then joined the United States Army, realizing that if he continued to hang out on the streets, he would surely die in the streets. He trained in jump school, then served in Saudi Arabia, and is now a sergeant classified as a specialist dealing with nuclear, biological and chemical warfare. He married in 1996, the same year he was sent to Korea to work as an advising commander for preparation of nuclear/biological warfare.

In 1998, Dave was given a special assignment to work at the Pentagon. During the war, the United States government had trained hundreds of South Vietnamese to infiltrate the North and gather information. During these assignments, many of the men were caught by the enemy, imprisoned and lived in extremely harsh conditions. Today, Dave works as an interpreter to help determine which of these claimants legitimately deserves financial reimbursement for their work in war time.

In the early evening, as a mass of white clouds turns gray and the rain begins to fall, Dave sits on his back porch pondering his life. "The days of my escape have traveled with me throughout my life, and until now, I have shared them only with my wife. Still, when I am near the ocean and smell the saltwater, a lonely feeling takes over my soul. I am again a boy of thirteen, in a small boat afloat on the endless sea. And my mind wonders to the three young women who were abducted from our boat and stolen away." Dave's haunted boyhood memories bring tears to the grown man's eyes.

Soaked, Frightened, But Free

*H*ong grew up in Saigon with twelve brothers and sisters. "We all felt safe during war time, until the last weeks before the end, when everything went crazy," Hong says, her eyes enormous. "The entire city became obsessed with escape." Her father thought they did not need to flee because he had not been a soldier or a direct enemy of the Communists during the war. He had been a car dealer. Unfortunately, the Communists thought otherwise. "In 1978, they spotted a few American cars among his fleet of automobiles and assumed he had some connection to the United States. So they threw him in jail."

"Our family was devastated. Not only did they take him away, but they didn't tell us where he was going. We were sick with worry. We did not know if he was being tortured, or worse yet, if he was dead." The agonies of those days are still etched on Hong's face. "We were desperate to find out what happened, so we paid someone to go to the prisons to find him. Finally, one day we received a message. My dad was so clever. He wrapped a paper note around a lemon and tied it with a rubber band. He threw this out a prison window and someone brought it to us. At last we knew where he was. At last we knew he was alive."

After eight months, Hong's father was

Hong and her brother Thong sit by the South China Sea in Malaysia in May 1983 after escaping by boat from Vietnam. *(photo courtesy of Hong)*

Years after her ordeal, Hong still wakes up five minutes after falling asleep at night, her heart racing and "her face soaked with memories."

finally released from jail. In the meantime, the Communist authorities had confiscated his business and the family's house. With no home and very little money, their family unit was shattered. Hong stayed in Saigon with a friend while the rest of her family lived with various relatives throughout the countryside.

Their situation had changed so dramatically that one day Hong's exhausted father gathered his children together, "You know how I have always told you that an education is the most important thing in the whole world. Unfortunately, there is no longer any money to pay for school." With tears in his eyes, he encouraged them to leave, to escape to a place where they would have a chance to learn and have a better life.

With her father's blessings, Hong attempted to escape from Vietnam. Each time was more harrowing than the last. "The worst was the time I escaped the authorities by running barefoot up a mountain in the middle of the night. I didn't make it down the other side until six in the morning. I thought I was going to die. My skin and clothes were all torn up. I had nothing to eat or drink." Tears of joy overwhelm Hong's memories of that day. "I was found exhausted and bleeding by an old woman. She was wonderfully kind. She sewed my ripped clothes. She even fixed her only tong for me to wear and she gave me money so I could get back to Saigon. It was her whole life's savings."

Hong finally escaped in 1983, on her sixth attempt. "My thirteen-year-old brother and my sister and her three-year-old daughter were with me on a big boat. We left out of Vung Tau and landed on Pulau Bidong, a small island off the mainland of Malaysia. The crew turned the boat toward the shore, but anchored in water too deep to wade in. I jumped off the side of the boat and used a plastic oil can with a towel tied to its handle as a life raft. We all managed to get to shore—soaked, frightened, but free."

It would be two years longer before Hong was sent to the Philippines where she learned English, and met Quan, the man she would marry. Eventually, they were transported to the United States. "I'll never forget the plane ride to America. They gave us food that included two packets of butter. It seemed so extravagant." She saved the butter packets in case she did not get more to eat. "I kept on thinking how much these precious packets would cost in Vietnam. I kept wishing there was some way I could give them to my dad."

Hong has not only mastered English since her arrival in America, she has received a bachelor's in public health and a master's in counseling and psychology. She now works as a counselor with other Asian refugees. Her husband, Quan, works as an inspector in an aerospace plant, and their son, now twelve, is growing up a typical American kid. Yet Hong has never left her past behind her. "I still suffer from serious post-traumatic stress disorder." As did many Asian immigrants, Hong arrived in America with experiences of past violence and tragedy seared into her memory. "I wake up five minutes after falling asleep at night, my heart racing and my face soaked from the memories."

Hong has returned three times to her Vietnamese homeland since her escape, each time searching for the woman who saved her life. "She moved six times since she rescued me. I finally found her in 1996. At first, she didn't recognize me, but when I reminded her of our past meeting, she started to shake. We cried together for a long time. She's still poor, of course, and lives in a small village in the South. I send her money from the States, but it is only a token. There isn't any amount of money that could repay this woman for my life."

> "I was found exhausted and bleeding by an old woman . . . she gave me money so I could get back to Saigon. It was her whole life's savings."

Clusters of Bamboo

*L*ucy's life did not start out with grief and tragedy. As the story goes, her mother was trying to reach the hospital to give birth, but the eager baby Lucy would not wait. So she was born on a small boat surrounded by a myriad of fireflies under a dark sky full of stars on the Dakbla River. Her memories of a childhood in Kontum, a little town in the central part of Vietnam, are mostly of beauty and peace. Tall trees that produced delicious, sweet, purple fruit lined the street, and pink bougainvillea and golden trumpet flowers surrounded her house. Her father worked hard and was able to buy land and own numerous rice fields. Many workers toiled in the fields and servants took care of the house.

"My childhood was happy," Lucy stops mid-sentence, "but before long, it was interrupted by war." The Japanese bombs are Lucy's first memory of war—only one of many. "I was only six and too young to really understand what was happening." But by the age of fifteen, when she was living at a French boarding school, Lucy was not allowed to go home to her family—the Viet Minh had taken over—and she and her classmates were interred in a refugee camp until the Geneva Accord was signed and they were allowed to return to their homes. "The other girls and I used to watch the black crows appear from nowhere, circle and drop onto the French soldiers' corpses."

Lucy married a year after graduating from high school. She and her husband soon had four daughters. She later resumed her education, and in 1963 became a French teacher in a public high school, and later the deputy director of studies. By this time, the American War was escalating, and life in Vietnam was becoming increasingly difficult.

When Tet of 1968 came, so too came panic. "The Viet Cong had infiltrated our neighborhood. There

Shown here with teachers and students at a high school near Saigon in 1974, Lucy (second from right) escaped Vietnam a year later with her four children. Her husband had intended to follow his family, but the Communists detained him in a re-education camp for seven years.
(photo courtesy of Lucy)

were many casualties. When the fighting stopped, and things calmed down, we tried to get back to some semblance of normalcy." Classes resumed and Lucy took some of her students on field trips to visit the wounded Vietnamese and American soldiers. "The sidewalks around the military hospital were filled with young American GIs, 19 or 20 years old, with their blue eyes and blond hair. They were in wheelchairs. Some had no arms, others no legs. On their faces we saw their youth, on their limbs the mutilating effects of the war. I kept asking myself, 'Why did they have to suffer? What would happen with their lives now?'"

"One evening while I was visiting a wounded friend in a military hospital, I heard a helicopter land and then a series of thuds. My friend reluctantly told me, 'The helicopter has just returned from a battle zone. The thuds are the sounds of body bags being unloaded.'" Living with the possibility of sudden death forced Lucy to live her life deliberately and to take nothing for granted. "Every night, with the sound of bombs dropping in the background, I would go to bed and say the Act of Contrition, ask forgiveness for my sins and prepare to die."

In April 1975, just before the war's end, Lucy's husband made special arrangements with American officials for her and their four children to be transported out of Vietnam to the United States by an American military plane. "My mother had died the year before, and I didn't want to leave my 87-year-old father behind. I begged him to come with us. His answer was simple, 'Your mother's grave is not yet covered over with grass. How can I leave it?' Then my father began to cry." Lucy also cries as she retells this story. "His parting wish was for us to be safe and to get a good education. I never saw him again. He died two years later." Lucy's husband had intended to follow his family shortly after they left, but the Communists detained him in a re-education camp from the war's end until 1982.

"My journey to America began when the door of the airplane closed behind me, severing the physical connection to my homeland. As the wheels of the plane left the ground, I was struck with emotion, and a strong sense of loss. I had left my family, never to see them again. I had left my country, never to return. I am now a refugee."

Lucy has met many demanding challenges since first landing on American soil in 1975. Far surpassing her father's dreams, Lucy obtained her Ph.D. in francophone literature and became the director of the United Asia Learning Resource Center at the University of Massachusetts at Amherst. Her daughters are highly educated too. "Every day was a day of struggle, perseverance and hard work to get to where I am today. For years I lived a nomad's life. I moved from house to house, my belongings packed in suitcases and cartons." Lucy has finally settled into a beautiful home, decorated with everything Vietnamese. Even her yard has clusters of bamboo, which represents integrity.

Still, Lucy is torn, reflecting on her past while wrestling with her future. "Being a

> *"I begged him to come with us. His answer was simple, 'Your mother's grave is not yet covered over with grass. How can I leave it?' Then my father began to cry."*

refugee means I have lived with war, loss, killing and death. It means having to leave everything and everyone behind in search of freedom. A refugee is not a status. It is a permanent state within a soul that has no permanence. I live in a world of impermanence. I keep myself busy, trying not to think about Vietnam. Yet, I do. I fill my time with books about my country and create its presence here in America by taking imaginary trips there." Lucy organizes cultural activities and re-creates familiar festivities for her Vietnamese community in America. "I am hopeful that someday, by bringing home the sounds and smells known to me since birth, I will be able to soothe the burning pain I feel deep inside."

Lucy spent much of her life as a refugee and feels that her soul exists forever in a state of impermanence. She grows bamboo in her backyard in America to create the feel of her homeland that she misses very much.

A Bitter Peace

or many Vietnamese, the suffering began anew on April 30, 1975, the day the world was told that the war had officially ended.

Born in the Khanh-Hoa Province of South Vietnam in 1948, Hoa was the seventh of eleven children. "My dad was an honest man who bought buffalo at auction and sold them to companies who processed them into food. We weren't rich, but we were happy." By her teen years, life was changing. The bombs of war had arrived. "I was very, very frightened. The Viet Cong raided our villages at night." Hoa never slept. Worry and fear kept her awake all night.

Hoa married an officer for the ARVN in 1971. They had four children, one after the other. When the war was over, her husband was sent to a re-education camp, leaving her with the children. "He was told he would be there for ten days, but he did not come back. We did not hear from him."

Hoa, sick with worry, did the best she could to care for her children. Six months after her husband had left, a letter from him finally arrived. He wrote that the Communists were not letting him out and that he was sick and desperately needed medicine. Hoa tried to buy some, but no one was allowed to sell medicine at that time. Her cousin managed to get a small amount. She was allowed to send a three-kilo package to the camp, so she hid the medicine among candy, sugar and a jacket. To this day Hoa is regretful, "I should have sent more sugar—that is what he really needed."

Ten months later, Hoa was finally allowed to

An Army officer during the war, Hoa's husband spent three years in a re-education camp, which broke his spirit and left him physically disabled. Hoa, her husband and their four children spent twelve years after the war hauling goods on this *ba gat*, because they could find no other work. *(photo courtesy of Hoa)*

The aftermath of the war took a major toll on Hoa's life, and although peace was welcome, it was a very bitter peace.

visit her husband at the camp. "Transportation to the camp was very poor and dangerous." One way or another, Hoa made the trip every three months for the next three years of her husband's imprisonment. "I had to sit on the floor in the back of a truck. We traveled day and night, without windshield wipers or lights." On one trip, the tires exploded four different times. "I felt so terrible for my husband. He had dysentery, and couldn't walk without a friend to help him. Each time, before I reached the camp, I prayed he was still alive."

Hoa's husband was set free in 1978. He had survived the physical atrocities and horrors of the re-education camp, but came home emotionally and mentally changed. "They stripped him of his dignity. Our lives were never the same again."

For the next twelve years, Hoa and her husband barely made ends meet. They hired themselves out to carry goods of any kind and worked around the clock carrying products on a *ba gat* (a cart attached to a bicycle). When their children were not in school, they also helped. "Those were the hardest days of my life. Whenever the train came into the station, we had to load the goods on our *ba gat* and then, no matter how heavy or awkward, run two to three kilometers to deliver the load." Hoa stares blankly into the distance, tears silently streaming down her face. "One day we had to carry wrought-iron fencing posts. They were weighty and cumbersome. The cart took a bad turn and the entire thing, posts and all, fell on my husband. Somehow, he survived the accident, but how much more could his tired body take?"

Hoa's sister escaped by boat from Vietnam in 1975 and made it to the United States. "As soon as she could, she sent papers to sponsor me and my family." In 1989, word finally came saying they could go to America, but Hoa's husband was too sick to travel and they had to abort their plans. "We were so unlucky. But my brother and mother were able to go at that time. Sadly, my father died just before the journey." Finally, in 1993, Hoa and her children did come to the United States, but her husband had to be left behind since he still needed medical treatment. He arrived two years later and now lives with Hoa and their children in Massachusetts.

Hoa works as a community relations specialist at a Vietnamese-American civic association. "I miss Vietnam, but I don't want to go back because there is still too much suffering." She worries about keeping her family safe. "I work to provide my children with the best education so they should graduate from college and have a good life." Her youngest is in twelfth grade and the other three are in college. One is studying chemical engineering, another technical engineering and another accounting.

"The aftermath of the war took a major toll on our lives. It left my husband disabled, both physically and emotionally. He spends his days alone in the house. Our lives will never be as they were, once upon a time." For Hoa and her family, the war's end brought such a bitter peace.

> "The aftermath of the war took a major toll on our lives. . . . Our lives will never be as they were, once upon a time."

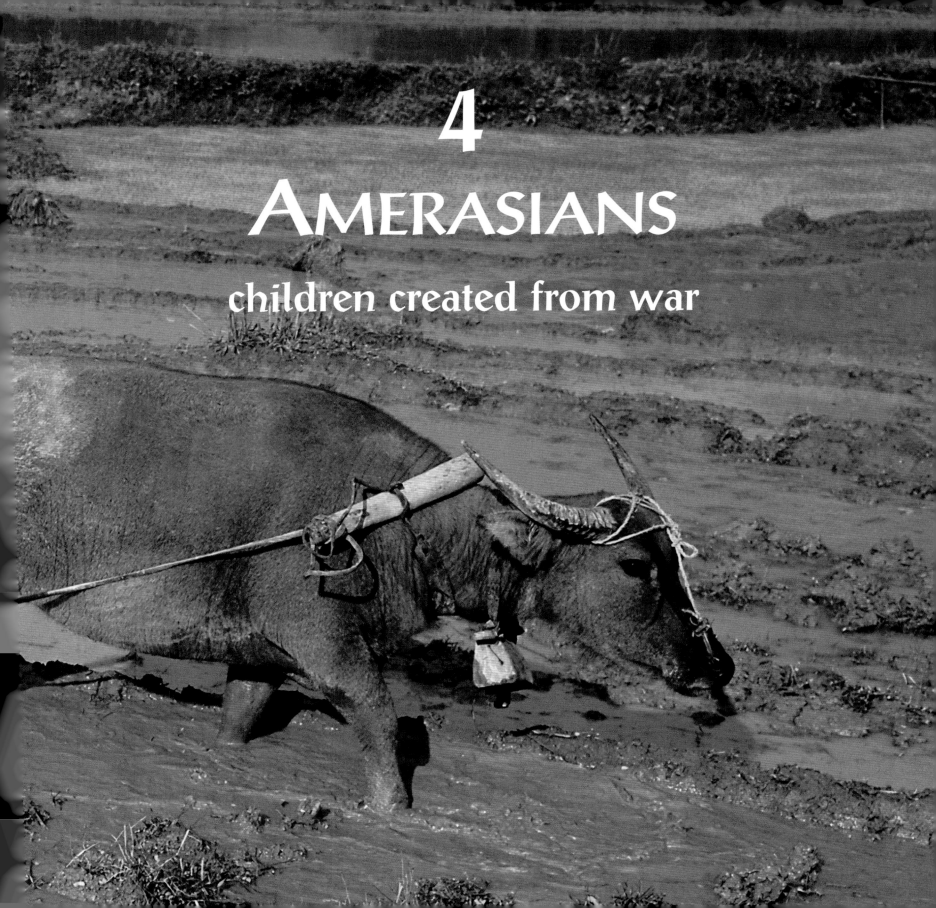

4
AMERASIANS
children created from war

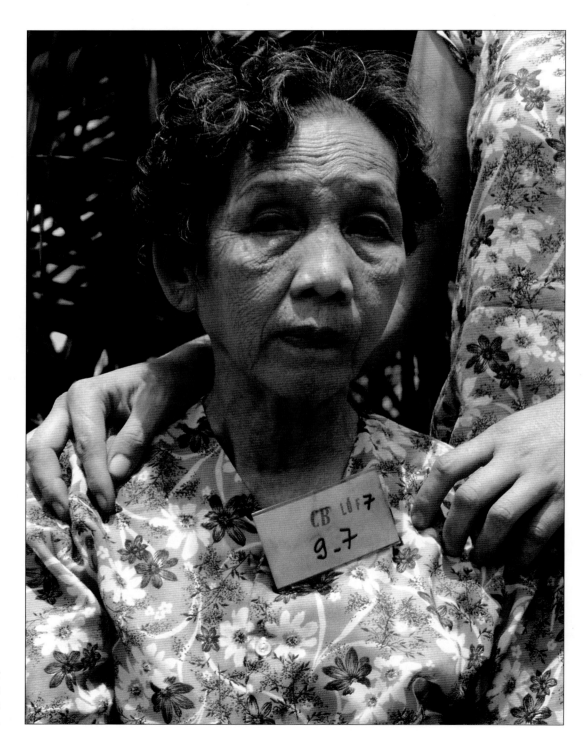

A Vietnamese woman and her
half-American daughter wait in a
relocation camp in Saigon before
being placed in a Western country.

Children of War

The Vietnam War left many tragedies in its wake, but one of the saddest and most easily overlooked legacies is the approximately 35,000 children fathered by American soldiers with Vietnamese women. When their tour of duty ended, most of these soldiers left Vietnam and these children behind. For years, these children were caught between two countries and two identities, barely acknowledged by either.

Many Vietnamese consider anyone born of mixed blood to be socially inferior. They scorn the Amerasians and refer to them as "*bui doi*" (dust of life), or "*con lai*" (half-breed). The children whose fathers were African-American suffer the most persecution, because in Asia dark skin is considered a sign of peasantry. While the few Amerasians who come from more affluent families are treated with less disdain, too many others face terrible ostracism and discrimination, and are often forced to turn to the streets for survival.

At first, the United States government made no provisions for these children of war, but then a law was passed in 1982 allowing those Amerasians who were born after 1950 in Thailand, Korea and the countries of Indochina to come to America as immigrants. Under the law, children were expected to come alone and Asian mothers or other siblings were not allowed to join them. Only nine thousand took advantage of this opportunity.

Five years later, the Amerasian Homecoming Act was passed into law. This new legislation allowed the Amerasian children and their immediate families or guardians to emigrate to the West together. For some Amerasians, the Homecoming Act created a new set of problems. Some unscrupulous or desperate Vietnamese went into the remote interior areas of the country looking to purchase or marry innocent Amerasians—all for a free ticket out.

The first step of the Amerasians' journey took them to the Philippines. There, they entered a comprehensive training program where they learned about Western culture and were taught English as a second language. Six months later, they were sent to the United States, Australia, New Zealand, Canada or one of many European countries.

> *When they first arrived, many Amerasians had one fervent hope—that they might be reunited with their American fathers.*

The transition period to their new country was difficult for most of these new immigrants. In America they were given food and shelter, although without their neighbors and family support system to bolster them, they felt alien in a foreign culture. So, "Amerasian Clusters" were created in about 50 designated sites throughout the United States, where newly arriving Amerasians could receive the support of others like themselves and of the Vietnamese community already living in America. This helped to ease the sense of isolation many encountered when they came to live in the countries of their respective fathers.

When they first arrived, many Amerasians had one fervent hope—that they might be reunited with their American fathers. Actually finding their fathers was an overwhelming, if not impossible task. More often than not, a child of war knows only his or her father's first name and maybe an old address. The last name, branch of service or social security number of the father was usually lost to the confusion of war and language, even if the mother knew it at one time. What made it even harder to find these men was that many of them did not even know they were fathers. They were long gone by the time their Vietnamese girlfriends knew of their pregnancy. Many others who knew of the existence of their son or daughter had little interest in developing a relationship with them after all these years. Still others, who had tried for years to bring their children back to the States, gave up after dealing with reams of governmental red tape. Only about two percent of Amerasians have ever been reunited with their birth fathers.

Many Amerasians bear emotional scars—scars

Life in Vietnam is difficult for Amerasians and their families, but when they traveled to the West hoping to leave their troubles behind, they often discovered that the streets were not paved with gold.

much deeper than the usual scars left by having been born in a war-torn country. They grew up as victims of cruel attitudes, ostracism and even violence. Some were abandoned by their ashamed or desperate mothers. The "children of the dust" carry the burden of these experiences all their lives. Now as adults, Amerasians are bringing a third generation of mixed-blood children into the world. Perhaps, these children will not have to bear the scars of their inheritance.

Children of the Dust

CHORUS:
Papa, you must be big
Papa, you must be tall
Do you wonder who I am at all?
Papa, you're in my dreams
Papa, you're in my heart
Do you want to keep our lives apart?

Mama said you came with war,
with uniform and gun
To help us win a desperate fight
that never should have begun
Did you look with pride into the blue eyes
of your newborn son?
Did I make you feel, no matter what, you'd won?

CHORUS

Then one day you went away
with the bombs and battlesongs
And I grew up just like you,
though probably not as strong
And Papa, people spit at me
and say I don't belong
Did you mean to take me with you, all along?

Mama said she's sending me
to a strange and far-off land
She wiped her tears with a cloth;
for mine, she used her hand
"Son, keep this cloth until the day
you die American
They won't refuse you in your fatherland."

CHORUS

Oh, Papa, it's so hard to wait,
although I know I must
I know that you will claim me still,
for you are great and wise and just
There's so many others like me,
we're called children of the dust
Still waiting on the promise that we trust

CHORUS

Do you want to keep our lives apart?

Patricia Shih
copyright 1986

145

Until Tomorrow

*M*ai's childhood memories are very different from those of her American friends. "They reminisce about playing with Barbie dolls and visiting the zoo. I recall the Viet Cong raiding our village every month or so and stealing everything in sight. And I describe how I hid in the oil tank so the Viet Cong would not find me. My mother said that if the Viet Cong found me, they would take me away from my family to be either sold or killed." That was because Mai was not pure Vietnamese, though she did not know this at the time. "And then I tell them about the night that separated me from my family for many years."

As she grew older, Mai's dark baby hair began turning light blond, and her skin color changed from ethnic Vietnamese to a much paler version. Because of the discrimination in Vietnam regarding mixed ancestry, Mai's mother Van dyed her daughter's hair black and rubbed dirt on her arms, legs and face in an effort to make her skin look darker. "I spent most of my life thinking that my mother's husband Hung was my father. We loved each other and I did not question that I looked different or that my mother dyed my hair."

But the older Mai got the harder it was to pretend she was pure Vietnamese. By 1981, Hung and Van decided the family should flee Vietnam and take their chances elsewhere for a safer, better life. "I was about seven—too young to understand what was happening. My mother told me to go shopping with Hao, my older brother." Hao took Mai to a small boat instead of to the shops and there they waited for the rest of the family to arrive. But something went terribly wrong, and the rest of the family did not arrive. This night would separate them for many years to come.

"The boat left for sea crammed with 20 grown men, my fifteen-year-old brother and me, the only girl. I sobbed for my mom for hours, until I finally passed out." After a few days, an oil

Mai's childhood memories revolve around her simple village life in Vietnam and of the times she hid in the oil tank so the Viet Cong would not find her and take her away or kill her because she was part American.

(photo courtesy of Mai)

tanker picked them up and they were sent to a Thai refugee camp. Six months later, Mai and Hao were flown to New York's JFK Airport. "Talk about culture shock, I went from the lush, green rice paddies of Vietnam to the loud, bright lights of America."

Mai and her brother were both placed in a foster care home on Long Island. "I was really scared, but my foster mother made everything all right and has been like a second mom to me ever since." Hao stayed in the foster home for only a short time before he left for college. He later married and had two children of his own.

Mai began the second grade and excelled in school. With her vibrant personality, she made a place for herself almost immediately. Mai had always been told she was full-blooded Vietnamese. "At some point in high school, I looked hard into the mirror and realized deep inside I wasn't. Somehow my blood was mixed. But how? Both my parents were Vietnamese."

After finishing college and working for several years, Mai felt compelled to return to Vietnam to see her estranged family for the first time since her escape. "It was such a grand adventure. The gummy heat of Saigon brought back a flood of memories. I got to see my whole family again. We held each other for so long, it was like a 'Kodak moment.'"

"One day—it was a cool morning well before sunrise—I was sitting in the yard with my mother. Somehow, I got up the courage and asked her straight out why I looked different." After a long pause, and between heavy sobs, the story of Mai's birth father, Jimmy McDonald, unfolded. "My life started because two people fell in love."

Mai did not realize until she was grown that her birth father was not the Vietnamese man she called Dad.

During the war, Hung and Van lived at Camp Holloway, an American base in Pleiku, with their three children. Hung worked as a driver and guide for the soldiers; Van worked as an interpreter. Life was good. They had more than most during the war. Then, the North Vietnamese captured Hung and took him away.

> *"I spent most of my life thinking Hung was my dad, not knowing I had another father. I do love Hung very much. But part of me still wants to know my birth father."*

Van was devastated. She did not know what to do, or where to turn. Not knowing if her husband was dead or alive, she tried desperately to find him. Her resources and connections were limited, making the search difficult. Jimmy, an American helicopter pilot stationed at the base, offered his help. Even with all the means available, the search proved hopeless. For almost three years, no word of Hung's whereabouts came.

Jimmy and Van spent a lot of time together; they became friends and eventually fell in love. Their love produced a child, Mai. When Van was in her sixth month of pregnancy, Jimmy was sent home to the States. Jimmy promised he would return and take Van and all the kids to the States as soon as he could get the paperwork in order.

At the same time Jimmy was saying goodbye, Hung was making his escape from prison. He had spent the past three years living in a muddy cell. One very dark night, he took an opportunity to escape. Bullets whizzed past Hung's head as he ran into the thick forest. He felt a warm wetness dripping down his face, but continued running, regardless of the pain from the bullet wound. Hung knew that if he stopped, he would surely die. He slept during the day and when the darkness of the night took hold, he ran. One night, he tripped a mine and badly injured his hand. Wounds and all, Hung traversed many hills and mountains attempting to reach his home.

Meanwhile Pleiku was becoming unsafe. The bombs were getting too close and too regular. Van picked up and moved her children further south. She sold clothing, candy and bananas—anything to support and provide for them. Hung searched for his wife and children and eventually found them, and to his great surprise, discovered a new addition—three-month-old Mai. Once over the shock of the events that happened in his absence, Hung took in Mai as his own. She was told he was her father.

"I wasn't shocked, I really knew all along. What I didn't know was how strong my birth father's love was for my mom. He kept his promise to her and he did return to Vietnam to take us home with him. But, when he went to Pleiku to get us, my grandmother told him our house was bombed and we had all died. She felt, at the time, that telling this lie was best for everyone. This was the last anyone has heard of my father."

"I spent most of my life thinking Hung was my dad, not knowing I had another father. I do love Hung very much. But part of me still wants to know my birth father. My mom and Jimmy named me Mai which means 'tomorrow' in Vietnamese. I hope someday I will meet my birth father, Jimmy McDonald, but for now, I must wait until tomorrow."

Tell Him We Are Still Waiting

"*W*hen I was little, my mother used to tell me this story," says Bich, sorrow emanating from behind her beautiful, dark brown eyes. "'Johnny had a three-day pass in January 1973. He had been in Vietnam for seven months and was deeply dreading the remaining five. Lonely and homesick, he longed for the comforting arms of someone. Anyone. While walking the back streets of Saigon, his eyes fell upon a young woman whose beauty struck him. They spent time together, laughing, crying, holding, loving. After three days, Johnny returned to his unit with warm memories in his heart. Two months later, when the United States military role in Vietnam had officially come to an end, Johnny was sent home to America. Seven months later, a beautiful, freckle-faced, baby girl was born to the woman who had laughed with him.' That baby was me."

In July 1992, at a relocation camp on the edge of Saigon, hundreds of frightened first- and second-generation Amerasians, holding onto the sleeves of their loved ones, waited to be relocated. Bich was there with her mother who, like other Vietnamese mothers, had no choice but to raise her child in a society that treated Amerasians as racial outcasts, as *bui doi*—the dust of life. Bich, a lonely, wide-eyed young girl, stood shyly behind the others, her arms wrapped around her thin waist. "My body shook as I whispered to every foreigner I encountered, 'Bich. My name is Bich. Can you please help me and my mother?' I would reach out and touch my mother's shoulder. She was so fragile, so slight. She looked more like my grandmother than my mother."

"I would tell my story to anyone who would listen—'My father was an American GI. He and my mother knew each other during the war. He told my mother that he would return to Vietnam when the war ended and take us back to America with him.' I was so shy. I looked at the ground when I talked and I know my voice quivered. 'He has not come.' And often tears formed in my eyes. 'We are afraid now that

Bich, in 1992, waits in Saigon to be transported to the West. Born of an American soldier and a Vietnamese woman, she asked everyone she saw to tell her father that she and her mother were still waiting for him. His name was Johnny and he lived in Oklahoma.

Grown-up with two children of her own, Bich and her sons, four-year-old Trinh and three-year-old Johnny, live in Springfield, Massachusetts.

he cannot find us. Can you search for him in America and tell him we are still waiting? His name is Johnny and he lives in Oklahoma.'"

Bich left the relocation camp and arrived in the Philippines on July 30, where she and her mother were educated in the ways of the Western world. Eight months later, she traveled to the United States. Bich now lives in Springfield, Massachusetts, with her two sons, Trinh, four, and Johnny, three.

150

I Just Know Today

She is not sure when she was born. Her given birthday is August 15, 1967. Thoa, like many other Amerasians, has no way of proving her birth date. There are no records in Vietnam, and usually no one knows or cares. "I do know that I was born in Bien Hoa. And I know that when I was one month old, my mother left me."

Thoa's mother gave her to the child's grandmother to raise. Her mother subsequently had two other children by two different American soldiers. The next born, a boy, was sent to an orphanage and has since disappeared. The third born, also a boy, was raised by his mother and now lives in Georgia with his American father.

Thoa was fortunate in one sense. A faint smile emerges from her usually expressionless face, "My grandmother loved me very much and would do anything for me." Believing that an education was the only way her granddaughter could ever emerge from the depths of poverty and discrimination, she insisted that Thoa attend school. Thoa was only able to finish the fifth grade. "That was all my grandmother could afford."

Unlike so many others, Thoa married a Vietnamese man who truly loved her. Like so many others, she moved in with his family and became her in-laws' submissive servant. Thoa was able to escape from virtual enslavement in Vietnam and come to America with her husband and their three children through the Amerasian Homecoming Act. Since arriving in the States, she has given birth to two more children.

Thoa's life in America did not turn into the American dream, however. She suffers from many medical problems and raises her five children mostly alone. Thoa's husband abandoned her and their children for more than a year—his abandonment brought to the surface old wounds of her childhood that have never healed. He is back now, but things are not good. "I felt so disturbed when my husband left me and the kids that I didn't know how to care for them alone." Thoa sits back in her chair and stares blankly into space. "I miss my grandmother very much. I wish she were here with me now." Thoa's grandmother still lives in her tiny village in Vietnam. "She would know what to do. She would be able to help me and my children."

> "I miss my grandmother very much. I wish she were here with me now . . . She would know what to do. She would be able to help me and my children."

Thoa's mother left her to be reared by her grandmother when she was only one month old. Today in America, often separated from her husband, she wishes she had her grandmother to help raise her five children.

Does Thoa feel safe and is America now her home? "I just know today." Eyes downcast, a veiled darkness settles over her face. Thoa believes she is the "dust of life."

I Love Her to Pieces

"*I* guess you could say I was a juvenile delinquent when I was growing up," admits Bob. "I spent four years of my childhood in and out of reform schools. When I wasn't locked up, I was out committing petty crimes that always seemed to land me back there." When Bob was 17, his grandmother and legal guardian gladly signed his Army induction papers. She thought the Army was the only chance she had to save her grandson from a life in prison.

"When I joined the Army in 1956, my plan was to stay in for three years. My strategy was to use the Army to get a new start in life on the right side of the law. I didn't retire until 22 years later." When Bob was just getting out of his first tour in the Army, he met Pauline through mutual friends. They married in 1961 and had three children.

In 1967, Bob was sent to Vietnam and stationed in Long Bien where he worked as a supervisor in a teletype relay station for a year and a half. "I was real lucky. Most of the time I didn't even carry a weapon, never mind using one. Once in a while we experienced rocket attacks, but I was never wounded or even shot at." His time in Vietnam was divided between the relay station and a nearby orphanage. "Some of the guys and I ran activities for the Vietnamese and Amerasian kids in the orphanage. We showed them movies and gave them parties." Their involvement in the orphanage was a great distraction from the war and gave both the soldiers and the children a different perspective and much needed warmth and affection.

Bob retired from the Army at the age of 39 and started searching for a career to fill the second half of his working life. Army training had not given him skills that seemed marketable in civilian life. "I wound up doing a bunch of odd jobs until I found out I had a real aptitude with computers." For the past ten years, Bob has been doing computer work for a law firm and has been very involved in a local chapter of the Vietnam Veterans of America.

Bob and his family shared their home and their hearts with a homeless Amerasian girl. *(photo courtesy of Bob)*

153

> *"My heart breaks when I look back on all she has had to endure. Sometimes life is too cruel and unfair."*

In 1992, Bob met a Vietnamese woman at a fireside chat held by Senator John Kerry. They became friends and decided to join forces to help bring the Vietnamese community and the American Vietnam veterans together. "It was a very difficult task to pull off. We started by attending each other's meetings. The dialogue between the two factions was uneasy and real slow at the beginning. But we eventually formed a strong bond. Today, we never miss each other's events and celebrations."

Bob met Anne Marie, a teenage Amerasian girl at a Tet celebration in 1993. He learned that Anne Marie had begun her life just like many other Amerasians had—abandoned. Her Vietnamese mother had placed her in a basket and left her at birth. A stranger, a woman whom Anne Marie later called grandma, took her in. The woman came to love Anne Marie very much, but her husband was a cruel man. As soon as she was old enough, Anne Marie was working in the fields tending the buffalo and in the kitchen fixing meals and scrubbing pots. When the Amerasian Homecoming Act was passed, the woman's husband seized the opportunity to make a profit and he sold the Amerasian girl to a Vietnamese woman, who adopted her with the thought of a free ticket to America in her mind.

When Anne Marie landed on American soil with her new mother and five brothers and sisters, the family used her like a servant and refused to allow her to go to school. More than anything, Anne Marie wanted an education. Feeling desperate and alone, she left her new family and, unaccompanied, took a bus to Massachusetts where a friend had agreed to help her. Anne Marie did not speak a word of English. She had a note to show people as she traveled that read, "I don't speak English, will you help me?" Once at her friend's home in Massachusetts, she went on welfare and began school. But the friend's welcome was short-lived and Anne Marie felt compelled to leave. After being homeless, she eventually found a Vietnamese social worker who gave her temporary shelter in her basement, and finally Anne Marie found Bob. "My heart breaks when I look back on all she has had to endure. Sometimes life is too cruel and unfair."

"After the Tet celebration, I went home to my family and told them about Anne Marie. I asked them how they would feel about having a guest in our home." This was not the first time Bob had called upon his family's generosity. They had sponsored a seven-member Cambodian family in 1983, sharing their home and food with them for three months. "After a unanimous vote, I approached Anne Marie with a proposition she couldn't refuse. She could come and live with us until she felt it was time to move on."

"The first few days were really trying. She ate almost nothing. On the third day we were standing in the kitchen talking when all of a sudden she passed out." Bob carried her slight body into the living room and placed her on the couch. When she came to, he started asking her questions. "It turned out that she didn't want to be a burden on us by eating our food." Bob lost it. He began yelling at Anne Marie. "In this house you have the same rights as my own children. That includes eating as much food as you

want. If you don't eat, you'll have to leave!" Anne Marie slowly picked herself up off the couch, went into the kitchen, and ate enough to make everyone happy.

When she first came to Bob and Pauline's house, Anne Marie spoke very little English and was learning at a fourth-grade level. Once settled into this loving atmosphere, she excelled at school and graduated from high school as an honor student. Anne Marie stayed with Bob's family for four years, then felt it was time to leave the nest after she finished high school. She went to California to attend a beauty school. She did so well in school and worked so hard that she now owns her own manicure shop in a Detroit suburb.

Bob speaks fondly of Anne Marie. "Anne Marie is one of my children. I introduce her as my daughter and she calls me Daddy." Bob chokes up as he continues, "I love her to pieces, and someday when she finds 'Mr. Right,' I will be there to walk her down the aisle."

Bob considers Anne Marie to be one of his many children. "I love her to pieces, and someday when she finds 'Mr. Right,' I will be there to walk her down the aisle."

Mixed Blood

Mai Ly, a beautiful baby girl of mixed blood, was born sometime in 1973 in Saigon, after most Americans had already pulled out of Vietnam. Born an Amerasian, and fatherless, her life was destined to be difficult.

Mai Ly and her family stayed behind in Saigon and struggled to make a living. No longer able to afford city life, they moved to the countryside near Can Tho when Mai Ly was six. At seven, Mai Ly worked with her mother in the rice fields and together they sold and bartered fruit, vegetables and peanuts at the central outdoor market. They lived without electricity in a house made of straw and bamboo. A monotonous diet of rice, combined with sweet potatoes and manioc, sustained them.

"When I was eight, I went to school for the first time. The other kids were really mean to me because I had mixed blood." They constantly teased and even beat her. She takes a deep breath, "I wished my dad could have been there to protect me." No longer able to deal with the persecution, Mai Ly dropped out of school after only one year.

She continued to work the fields with her mother and to sell goods at the marketplace. When her mother's boyfriend moved in with them, life got even more difficult for Mai Ly, who was now a budding young woman; the boyfriend attempted to rape her. Her mother then realized it was no longer safe for her daughter to live in their house. Thinking to keep her safe from harm, she arranged a marriage for fifteen-year-old Mai Ly to a Vietnamese man she did not know.

Mai Ly married the man and moved in with him and her new in-laws. They soon had a son. Unfortunately, the abuse she hoped to leave behind simply manifested itself in another way. "I had to clean the house, wash the clothes, feed the animals, take care of my son, find wood to build a fire and cook all the meals," she remembers wearily. This slave treatment went on for three years until she was notified that the Amerasian Homecoming Act made her and her family eligible to go to America. "I was so happy when we left Vietnam. I felt a great relief to escape all the abuse."

Mai Ly now has four children ranging in age from one month to eight years, but her marriage has deteriorated since arriving in America. "It is a burden to be born

half-American and half-Vietnamese. It has made my life so hard." Deep in her soul, Mai Ly feels deserving of all the abuse she has endured. Still blaming herself for the attempted rape by her mother's boyfriend, she has not been able to leave the pain and guilt of her youth behind. "I miss my mother very much. I write and call her and send her a little bit of money every month."

"I wish a good life for my children, that their lives will be better than mine." After a long silence, she says in a low voice, "I hope someday they will be able to meet Peter, their grandfather, my American dad. And I hope someday he will hold them and tell them how much he loves them."

Mai Ly knows the burden and guilt of being born half-American and half-Vietnamese, and was happy to come to America.

Family Secrets

*M*ost Amerasians who left Vietnam escaped by sea or were sponsored through official channels such as the Amerasian Homecoming Act. Maura was one of the very few who was brought to America by her parents. She came to the United States in 1970 as an infant with her Vietnamese mother, Mai, and her American father, Brian. The young family had a difficult time at first. No one wanted to rent an apartment to an interracial couple, especially when one half of the couple was Vietnamese. Eventually, they settled in Rhode Island, and tried to have a normal life. Brian worked as a financial consultant and his career thrived. In the next seven years, Mai and Brian had five more children, who were all tormented by the other kids in their all-white, upper middle-class neighborhood.

"The kids used to call me names. 'Hey, Chink . . . Hey, Chinky girl . . . Yeah, you!' I hated it. I would go home and look in the mirror. I didn't get it. I didn't look Chinese—why were they calling me a Chink? When I told them I was part Vietnamese, not Chinese, they would say, 'Look kid, a slope is a slope, so why don't you just get back on that boat and go back to your own damn country.'" Maura never understood these remarks and would always explode in a hurricane of anger when she heard them. "I would yell back at them, 'This is my country! And I didn't come on a boat. I came on a plane with my mom and dad.'" Then in a flood of soft tears she would go on to explain, "I wear Jordache jeans and alligator shirts. I have braces and a perm. I'm not any different from anybody else. Can't you see that?" Most did not. "I remember when I was seven or eight and I invited some classmates over for lunch. They giggled as their answers cut straight through my heart. They said, 'Oh no, we won't eat at your house. We heard your mother serves cat for lunch.'"

"As a child, I was very high-strung and very angry." Dance became a healthy outlet for these emotions. Unlike many young girls who dream of becoming ballerinas, Maura was different because she had talent. She attended ballet school six days a week between the ages of eight and sixteen and continued to study dance and the performance arts in college. After college, the tiny dynamo moved to Seattle and began a fledgling career as a dancer and choreographer. She spent the first year and

Mai and Brian were determined to raise their interracial children to be all-American kids. The children were teased by their classmates however, because they looked different. This family photograph was taken in 1978. Maura is the first on the right.
(photo courtesy of Maura)

a half there doing childrens' theater. "I was a dancer in *Dragon Wings*, a show about Chinese immigrants in the early 1800s. I wish I could say that the pay was enough to cover my rent, but it wasn't. I had to clean houses and work at a driving school to supplement my meager income from dancing. But it was worth it. I had the opportunity to present my own choreography and dance for two other companies."

Maura's career was on the upswing when something happened that turned her life upside-down. "It was July 4, 1992. I remember it so clearly. I was on the phone with my mother and we were arguing about my boyfriend. He moved out to Seattle too, and was living with me. My father was so angry that he practically disowned me. My mother began shouting at me, 'You must do what your parents want! I had to do what my mother made me do! I had to marry a man I didn't want to and have a baby with him.' I was so shocked. What was she talking about?" Mai did not elaborate then, but Maura learned the details of her mother's past—her secret life—over the following months and years.

Maura's mother had been born in the southern Vietnamese province of Quang Ngai in 1945. When Mai was barely a year old, Viet Minh soldiers raided her home and killed her father, grandfather and two uncles, leaving her mother to raise four children alone. At age thirteen, Mai was forced into an arranged marriage to an older man. He beat her repeatedly. After two miserable years, Mai fled with her infant son to her mother's house. The husband went after her, so Mai fled again and lived on the run trying to earn a living while caring for her young child. Unable to survive this way, Mai brought her son back to her mother to take care of him while she went to work. But to Mai's horror, her husband snatched her son away. Mai worked in Saigon for the next ten years. She met Brian, a U.S. Naval officer, fell in love, got married, and had Maura. Brian resigned his commission in the Navy and stayed on as a civilian advisor to the South Vietnamese Navy until, with the government's permission, the young family left Vietnam for the States.

This information alone was enough to start Maura's head spinning, but then she learned several more life-shattering facts from her sister, who had been pumping her mother to tell all. Mai had been pregnant with Maura when she and Brain got married. "My father came from a strict Navy and Catholic background. When he came home from work it was like in the *Sound of Music*—the house was spotless, dinner was on the table and all the kids would line up for inspection. Throughout our lives my dad always yelled at us kids to behave. My mom, being pregnant when they married, went against the strict Catholic upbringing I was fighting against my whole life. They had no right to criticize me now. My dad had been bad, too, when he was young."

"There was another part of my mother's story that really took me by storm." Anh, a young man who had lived with the family for a year in Rhode Island when Maura was young, had been introduced as a distant relative. He was really her mother's son from her arranged marriage in Vietnam. "Looking back to when Anh was living with us, I should have realized something was wrong. My mother, who usually got along with everyone, fought with Anh all the time. She and my father had kept this secret from the entire family. How could they have done that?"

"Learning all these secrets caused me to question my entire relationship with my parents, with myself and with my Vietnamese heritage—the part of myself that I'd denied while growing up in suburbia." The turmoil in her heart sent Maura into the dance studio, where she spewed out what became the first three minutes of her hour-long solo show *When You're Old Enough*. "I consider this to be a pivotal period of my life. Hearing those secrets opened up floodgates like nothing else." Maura directed the furious feelings unleashed by the secrets into her creative energy. Her choreography bloomed and developed into her signature style of using multimedia effects to create a performance that incorporates poetry, live and recorded music, singing, spoken text and drumming into a dance whose storyline focuses on issues now close to her heart—issues such as her childhood, her feelings about being an Amerasian and her feelings about her own parents.

Another life-changing event was a 1997 trip to Vietnam that Maura took with her mother to meet their relatives. "It was overwhelming to say the least. A combination of incredible and bizarre." Everywhere Maura went, the locals touched her hair, her skin and her clothing. "I felt like a rock star." Meeting and getting to know her Vietnamese family helped Maura come to terms with her own life. "I learned how very complicated everything was in Vietnam, especially during war time. My trip there had an amazing calming effect on my life. Before the trip I never knew where I fit in. All my life, when I had to fill out those awful forms that wanted to know what race you were, I had always answered 'other.' Irish-Vietnamese. After going to my homeland, I was now finally comfortable using the word Amerasian. I was an Amerasian." In May 1999, Maura completed her ethnic circle when she and her parents traced her father's roots on a trip to Ireland.

One more healing event took place in 1998, during the premiere of Maura's *SKINning the SurFACE,* a historical piece about Amerasians that dealt with the themes of home, father and skin color within the context of Vietnam and the war. In the performance, Maura is a traveler caught in a space where Amerasians exist between Vietnam and America. At the end of the performance, Maura leaves this limbo when her mother and father take her away. In the premiere performance, Mai and Brian actually came up on stage to free her.

Maura married Perry, a Chinese-American actor and musician, in 2000. "We ended up having four ceremonies, each celebrating different parts of our collective heritages." The first one was in Vietnam at her mother's family home. "It was hot as hell and a blast. The women wore *ao dais* and there was a beautiful procession through the rice paddies, we bowed and lit incense before our ancestors and toasted everyone." The second was a Chinese tea ceremony and banquet in California with both Perry's and Maura's

families, including Maura's half-brother Anh and his family. The third was the legal one—on December 21 at City Hall in New York City. The fourth was on December 28 in a heated tent in her parent's backyard. "All my dad's family was in attendance. We finally recited vows at this one. Four weddings—a karmic joke on a woman who swore she'd never marry." Maura and Perry now perform throughout the world in her dance company, *Maura Nguyen Donohue—In Mixed Company.*

Maura is a very different person today than the hurt, angry girl of her childhood. "We are now years past the family turmoil, and reconciled in so many ways. I was able to forgive my parents for making the choices they thought would keep me safe." Maura turns to stare out a picture window before calmly finishing, "I now feel less angry and more at peace. I realize now that I have the best of both worlds. I truly love my life and my diversified family—I love all of that which makes me one."

Today Maura is a dancer and choreographer whose performances are powered by the pain and confusion she felt upon discovering the family secrets.

5
HIGHLANDERS

the struggling ethnic minorities

Like most youngsters in Vietnam, the older siblings of an ethnic minority family share the responsibility of caring for their younger sisters and brothers. These sisters live in a remote village on the road from Hanoi to China. They are on their way to bathe at the local stream.

People of
the Highlands

The Highland areas of Vietnam are among the most culturally and linguistically diverse in all the world. Fifty-three ethnic minority groups, making up thirteen percent of the country's population, live mainly in the sparsely-populated mountainous areas and highlands that account for three-quarters of Vietnam's total land. Some Highlander groups have lived in the region for thousands of years, while others migrated from neighboring countries to Vietnam during the last few centuries. The largest concentrations of ethnic minorities live in the North, and in some parts they actually outnumber the ethnic Vietnamese (known as the Viet).

The French colonialists who came to this region in the 1800s pressed these ethnic minorities into labor forces, employing them especially on rubber plantations. They called these ethnic peoples "Montagnards," which means "mountain people" or "highlander." "Yards," a shortened version of the French term, was used by the American soldiers when they occupied the area. Many of the lowland Viet majority tend to discriminate against the Highlanders, and often refer to them as "moi," meaning savages. The current government favors the term "national minorities," while the Highland people prefer to be identified with their village and tribal group, since each has developed their own unique art, dance, music, dress and architecture.

Historically, the Highland life has revolved around small villages where kinship plays an important role. The people share resources and live a simple life. Their homes are usually either com-

With breathtaking panoramic vistas as their backdrop, this family treks toward the rustic livestock market in Can Cau. Everything from horses, water buffalo, medicinal herbs, ice pops and hand-made tapestries are for sale at the market. Traders come from as far away as China in search of bargains.

munal longhouses made of thatched roofs and woven bamboo wall panels, sometimes raised on stilts to avoid floodwaters, or simple wooden houses built on the ground. Many of these ethnic people are semi-nomadic and practice the ancient slash-and-burn form of agriculture, where a plot of land is cleared and farmed until the soil is exhausted. Their livelihoods are based on agriculture with rice as their staple crop. To supplement their food supply, they fish and hunt and forage the jungles for game, wild fruits and vegetables. Many also raise chickens, buffalo, goats and pigs.

The Highlanders observe diverse religions including the practice of ancestor worship—the belief that the soul lives on after death and becomes the protector of its descendants, and animism—the belief that powerful spirits dwell in animals, trees, rocks, wind and rain. These powers must be appeased by gifts of food, incense, flowers and prayers. In recent decades, as a result of outside influences, many have become Protestants or Catholics.

Throughout history, war played a pivotal part in the lives of the Highlanders, who have had to fight not only foreign enemies, but often each other to retain their cultural identity and territories. The American war was one of the worst. Bombs, rockets and long-range artillery spread across the land like wildfire, devastating their villages and disrupting their way of life. Their life-long struggle for autonomy took second place to their struggle for survival during the war. All told, more than half of the villages were abandoned or destroyed, and their casualties numbered about 200,000.

During the war, both the northern and southern forces tried aggressively to recruit the Highlanders in the Central Highlands as warriors and scouts in order to benefit from

This Koho grandmother shares her home—a stark, one-room wooden house with a corrugated roof, a bare, cold, dirt floor and one small bed—with her grown daughter and five grandchildren. Her son-in-law was killed when a tree fell and crushed him to death.

their intimate knowledge of the rugged mountains. Many Highlanders joined the American side and have paid dearly for their decision since the end of the war. The government conscripted them into re-education camps, where they endured years of hard labor and were reportedly tortured. Many reports indicate that the Highlanders, who today continue to resist the Communist government, are still persecuted, while those who live within the parameters of the government are generally left alone.

The current government policy toward the Highlanders include: populating the

166

Highlands with Viet settlers; discouraging the traditional slash-and-burn agriculture, which is destroying the ever-dwindling forests, and replacing it with sedentary farming; and promoting Vietnamization (Vietnamese language and culture). When instituted, these policies will have an everlasting effect on the ethnic minorities in Vietnam. Possibly the more serious threat to the Highlanders' ethnic existence is not the wars, the government or its new regulations, but the infringement of tourism on the fragile balance of the land and the erosion of the local lifestyle. By allowing themselves to become a tourist attraction, the Highlanders can earn more money, but in return they lose their traditional ways of sustaining a living.

There are many opinions on the current conditions and the future of the Highlanders. Rumors of unrest and uprisings against the ruling Communist Party and strong subsequent retaliation abound. One thing, though, is for sure: In Vietnam, cultural change is forever ongoing and inevitable.

Nearly two-thirds of all Vietnam's minority people live in the northern uplands, which are similar to the steep, terraced hillsides of the Hoang Lien Son Mountains, shown here. These three young boys travel with their family's buffalo.

Victims of Peace

"Moscow collapsed. That means anything can happen. Maybe even someday, there will be a change in the Vietnamese Constitution." After a long pause, Pierre continues, "America is my home now, but if I had the chance I would go back to Vietnam tomorrow. I miss the rest of my family, my friends and my life in Vietnam much more than I can say. But I believe if we were to go there now, we would be killed."

Born near Dalat in the mid-1930s, Pierre was raised to be a farmer. As a child, he went to school and worked in the rice fields during the day and spent the nights with his family in their bamboo-and-straw longhouse. When the days became too hot and sticky, he played in the stream at the bottom of the rice field. His life was simple.

An excellent student, Pierre was awarded a scholarship to attend Dalat University. He smiles, "I went to school with all rich kids, the children of kings." Pierre majored in French literature and graduated with a bachelor's degree. In his third year at the university, he married, and the year he graduated, he started his family of eight children. At the beginning of the American War, Pierre taught French for a few years in a public high school and then was offered the opportunity to attend Southern Illinois University. There he acquired a second bachelor's, this one was in elementary education. In 1968, he returned to Vietnam and worked as the Director General for Operations and later the Secretary General with the Ministry for the Development of Ethnic Minorities. He also belonged to the Ethnic Minority Counsel, whose responsibility was to advise the President and the Congress about laws pertaining to Highlanders. Pierre's career ended at the end of the war when the new government sent him to prison.

"I spent my first year in a camp in the South, and the next three years in the North. By nine in the morning, I was already so hungry my whole body would shake." There is an obvious nervousness in Pierre as he relives his many months in the re-education camps. "Each day we were given only four bowls of rice mixed with manioc. There was enough water, but the water was no good and made us deathly ill. The quinine tablets we had to take to deal with the malaria carried by the incessant mosquitoes destroyed our bladders, so many of the prisoners didn't take them. They died of malaria instead." Pierre worked all day and some-times into the darkness, planting tea. Desperately hungry, he ate anything that he could catch: frogs, grasshoppers, snakes, and one day, even a rat. "I cooked that skinny old rat in a newspaper in the bathroom in the quiet of the night." Pierre constantly worried about his wife and children and how they could survive without him supplying money and food. "The Communist Vietnamese had taken away our land and all of our valuables. I guess my wife and I were both in a prison camp of sorts. The one dif-ference—the walls of her cell were invisible."

After four years, Pierre—although released from prison—was still a prisoner. He was on parole, but was not given his ID papers and was not allowed to go anywhere. "I was told, if I tried to escape I would be sent away again for ten more years. None of this was acceptable to me. I wanted to live as a free man." Pierre knew this would not happen if he stayed in Vietnam. After his third attempt to leave by sea, and enduring one week "squashed like sardines with 22 others" on a tiny boat that fled from Vung Tau, he made it to safety and freedom. "On our first day at sea, we got caught up in a big wind that broke off one of our two propellers. Then we ran out of drinking water. We were desperate and thought we were going to die, so we prayed a lot." After taking a vote to return to Vietnam and face ten more years in prison, the suffering escapees were unexpectedly plucked from the vast China Sea by a French freighter.

"We reached Singapore on July 3, 1983, a day I will never forget." Because of his education and knowledge of languages (he was fluent in English, French, Viet-namese and eight Highlander dialects), Pierre was allowed to work as an interpreter for the embassies during the day, but returned to the refugee camp each night. A much-desired commodity, Pierre was offered asylum in Canada, Australia and France. He chose America.

Three months after his rescue at sea, Pierre settled into his new home in Sacramento, California. In 1987, with the help of the American Green Berets, he relocated to Greens-

This photo of Pierre (second from left) and his family was taken on September 11, 1957. (photo courtesy of Pierre)

169

boro, North Carolina, where he became the director of the Montagnard Settlement Program. He also worked with limited-English-proficiency students at a local high school. He received his citizenship in 1989, and his wife and children joined him in 1992.

Today, Pierre works for the Catholic Church helping Highlander refugees assimilate to the American culture and teaches English as a second language, citizenship and vocational classes. Pierre is also studying to become a deacon.

"Life in America is good, but never smooth. We have more than enough to eat, a good house and plenty of cars. My kids are happy here. They don't know of war, they only know of money. But my wife and I miss our home and our family we left behind in the Highlands. We would move back in a minute, but fear we would be killed. Just last week, I was in touch with my family in Vietnam. They told me that the authorities are still asking about me." Pierre's focus turns to the ground, where he stares for a long time. "We were victims of the war while the bombs and napalm were being dropped, and today, so many years later, we are still victims of the war. There may be 'peace' in our country, but there is no peace in our hearts."

After years in re-education camps, Pierre escaped from Vietnam by boat. Today, he works for the Catholic Church helping Highlander refugees assimilate to the American culture and teaches English as a second language, citizenship and vocational classes.

Life on the Run

"**W**hen the Communists took over in 1975, my whole life changed," declares Y Hin. "The Communists retaliated against anyone who had worked for and fought with the Americans." One of the groups they chose to punish most severely was the FULRO (United Front for the Struggle of the Oppressed Races), a group of Highlanders that Y Hin represented. He worked during the war as a diplomat and liaison between the Vice President of the FULRO, Kpa Koi, and the American Embassy in Saigon.

The United States Special Forces, known as the Green Berets, singled out the FULRO for their valuable skills and abilities as both faithful and fierce fighters. The Green Berets organized them into defense groups, trained them in military tactics and armed them with modern weapons. Invaluable to the Americans, these Highlanders fought to prevent Communist infiltration from the North into the Central Highlands. The Communists soon discovered that trying to punish the FULRO was fruitless because most of them refused to lay down their weapons and submit to re-education camps or an even worse fate. Instead, they fought or fled to seeming safety.

Y Hin led 10,000 Highlanders —members of the FULRO and their families—into exile in the jungles of Vietnam, Cambodia and

Ten thousand Highlanders escaped persecution in 1975 by fleeing into the jungles of Vietnam, Cambodia and Laos. Only 398 had survived. Some of the group is shown here in 1992, when they were finally rescued. *(photo courtesy of Y Hin)*

Laos, where they lived on the run for almost a decade to escape Communist retribution. In the jungle, Y Hin and his people defended themselves not only from the Vietnamese Communists, but from tigers, poisonous snakes, extreme conditions and the Khmer Rouge. "The Khmer Rouge controlled the land in Cambodia and periodically required payment of many kilos of elephant ivory, deer horns and tiger bone if we wanted to stay there. Life was incredibly hard. I had known nothing of living on the run, of using a weapon of war or of scavenging for forest food. But I soon learned."

Y Hin had grown up in a farming community where fruit trees, rice and beans were cultivated, a community where families hunted, fished and raised livestock for food. He unexpectedly had to learn to eat, sleep and live on the run. "From June to April we had to dig up poisonous roots in the jungle and make them edible. After removing the skin and cutting the roots into pieces, we dried them in the sun for three days, then put them in the river to soak for three nights—a time-consuming process that removed all the poison. From April to June, we could eat other jungle roots without this preparation." The refugees supplemented this mainstay with frogs that they caught in the stream and with roasted termites, seasonal fruits and honey that they gathered in the forest. Sometimes they were able to kill jungle cow, deer and even elephants. "We lived from meal to meal and were always hungry."

One scarce item, precious to their survival, was simple sea salt. "We didn't have any salt at all for the first five years. Then a brave group took on the dangerous job of going to the sea. We used the salt they brought back as sparingly as possible from 1981 until 1990, when we ran out."

In the jungle, tragedy repeated itself many times over. Exposure to danger became routine and began to wear down the people. The chilly wet season alternated with the oppressive dry season. These extremes occurred over and over, year after year. Y Hin's head is downcast as he says, "Nights came fast. We had very little clothing and no blankets. Many children died of exposure." Others died from illness and disease, food poisoning and attacks from human enemies, tigers and elephants. "We always lived on the jagged edge of fear."

Within four years, the group of 10,000 people diminished to 2,000. Weighed down with sorrow, Y Hin finishes telling his story, "In the end, only 398 of us were rescued and flown under U.N. supervision to the United States. Our nine-month-old son died a few weeks before we were saved." After their 17 years in the jungle, Y Hin, his wife and their three surviving children were brought to America in 1992.

Today approximately 4,000 Highlanders live in a community in North Carolina where everyone helps each other. No one needs welfare. Within only a few years after he and his family arrived in America, Y Hin earned a master's in business and acquired a pilot's license. He worked hard and has been able to buy a car and a beautiful home.

Y Hin became an assistant pastor of his community's church, just as his father was pastor of the Evangelical church in his Vietnamese village. Wanting to continue his father's good works, he is also the President of the Montagnard/Dega Association, a non-profit corporation dedicated to assisting Highland refugees.

Despite his success and the important work he is doing, Y Hin sometimes feels like an orphan in America. "How can I be happy with all my wealth when the rest of my family is struggling back in Vietnam? When my own father has no food and continues to be persecuted." After a long pause, Y Hin continues, "Maybe someday when the Vietnamese learn to treat people with equal rights for equal life, I will go back to my homeland." Y Hin takes a deep breath. "We have a hard life in this world until we go to Heaven."

Y Hin was the organizer of the exiled Highlanders. He is now a pastor and community leader in North Carolina, where approximately 4,000 Highlanders live and work together in a supportive environment.

Charcoal Makers

For an exhausting day's work, each person will receive about six cents—very little pay for such great effort, even by Vietnamese standards.

Approximately 6,000 ethnic Lat, Ma, Chill and Koho people populate the nine hamlets of Lat Village, an area about seven miles or a 30-minute car ride from the city of Dalat. The four tribes each speak a different dialect, and they all live a humble and simple life. These agrarian people grow rice, black beans, corn, pumpkin, squash, sweet potatoes and coffee for sale and subsistence, but barely make a living off the land. The picturesque village houses are constructed from rough plank walls and thatched roofs that stand above the ground on piles to protect them from the floods that regularly inundate the area. The children can attend both primary and secondary school, and on weekends most villagers attend either the single Catholic church or the single Protestant church in the region.

Lat Village lies in a beautiful mist-shrouded region of valleys, cascading waterfalls, fast-flowing rivers and life-filled lakes set against the Lang Bian Mountains, a series of five volcanic peaks ranging from 6,900 to 8,000 feet in elevation. Once used as an American base during the war, the upper regions of the forest are still rich in lumber, medicinal plants, and animal and bird life. The foothills, however, are now heavily defoliated, although only a half century ago they teemed with lush vegetation and sheltered an abundance of tigers, oxen, deer, rhinos, boars and elephants.

Since the end of the war in 1975, times have been exceptionally hard on these people. Due to a strain on food supplies, multiplied by the daily loss of acres of forests, some of the Lat people find it necessary to leave their fields, hike north up the Lang Bian Mountains and apply themselves to the difficult task of making charcoal. Every family member is involved, including children, the elderly and even pregnant women. After the daily steep three-to-four hour climb up the mountains, the villagers immediately begin making charcoal. First, they cut down trees with a simple hand saw, and then cut the wood into four-foot lengths. They dig a pit in the lush soil and then pile the logs, along with leaves and moss, on top of each other. They cover the logs with shovelfuls of soil, then dig four airholes, one on each side, and set the buried wood on fire.

After many hours the Lat removed the dirt covering from the pit, and recovered the wood transformed into lightweight, low-energy charcoal. The family then carries the charcoal down the mountainside to sell in their village or in Dalat. For an exhausting day's work, each person will receive about six cents—very little pay for such great effort, even by Vietnamese standards.

Eight-and-a-half months pregnant, this Lat woman climbs the Lang Bian Mountains each day with her family. There, they cut down trees and make charcoal to sell in and near her village.

175

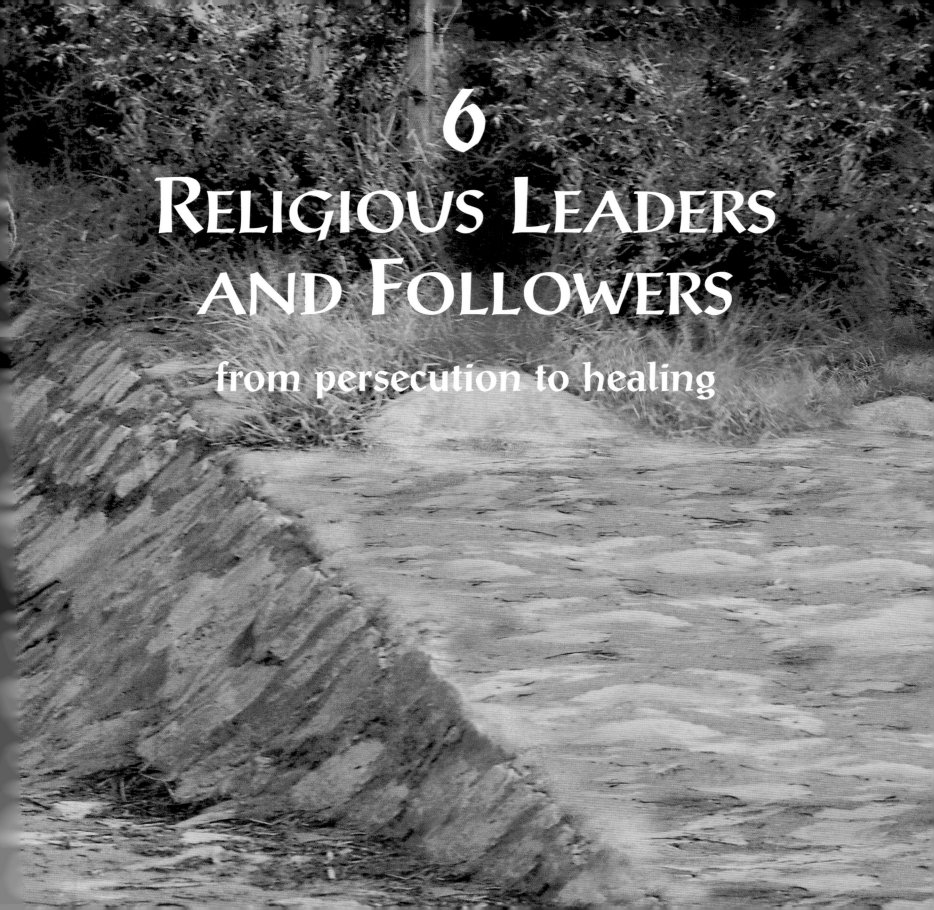

6
RELIGIOUS LEADERS AND FOLLOWERS
from persecution to healing

The Cao Dai religion, founded in 1926 in Vietnam, synthesizes the world's great religions and preaches world unity and peace. During the war, Caodaists refused to support the Viet Cong, and today they continue to pay for that decision.

Cao Daism

For about four years during the 1920s, visions of the "Supreme Being" or "Cao Dai" appeared to Ngo Van Chieu, a lowly Vietnamese bureaucrat in the French administration. This middle-aged man interpreted these visions into the tenets of a new religion. Chieu began to preach his spiritual discoveries and soon had a small group of 247 followers, who together founded the Cao Dai religion in 1926. Four years later, a half million people were converts.

Cao Daism (meaning "high palace") attempts to create a perfect synthesis of world religions by combining the philosophies of Christianity, Buddhism, Islam, Confucianism, Hinduism, Geniism and Taoism. Today, Cao Daism is the third most followed religion in Vietnam, after Buddhism and Catholicism. The sect's colorful headquarters are located in the Tay Ninh province, 60 miles northwest of Saigon.

To perfect their spiritual life, Cao Dai followers pray at least once a day.

Ngo Van Chieu received a vision of the Divine Eye, which is now the symbol for Cao Dai and adorns all Cao Dai altars. The eye represents the spiritual heart. Emanating from the eye is the light of the universe, or the spirit—a part of God. At the altar, along with the Divine Eye, followers also worship Lao Tse, who represents Taoism, Jesus Christ, who represents Christianity, Confucius, who represents Confucianism, Sakyamuni, who represents Buddhism, and Khuong Thai Cong, who represents Geniism. Caodaists recognize various saints, including prominent international figures such as Trang Trinh (1492-1587)—a Vietnamese poet and prophet, Victor Hugo (1802-1885)—a

French author, and Sun-Yat-Sen (1866–1925)—the leader of the Chinese Revolution of 1911. In the temple, dignitaries wear ceremonial dress and hats. Worshippers make offerings of incense, tea, alcohol, fruit and flowers, sing chants and pray at the beginning and end of each ceremony.

Followers of Cao Daism observe three rules to perfect their spiritual lives. They pray at least once a day, either at an altar in the temple or in the home, at six o'clock in the morning, midday, six o'clock at night or midnight. They eat a vegetarian diet at least ten days each month. And they follow five disciplines: Do not kill; Do not steal; Do not commit lewd acts; Do not indulge in the use of alcohol and a luxurious lifestyle; Do not lie. Followers also believe in the spirit world and use a mechanical device, such as a Ouija board, to communicate between spiritual beings and humans. During a seance, a small moveable platform, when touched lightly by two or more mediums, moves around the board, pointing to various numbers, letters and words, thus receiving messages from the spirit world. A long quill pen may also be used to transcribe messages received while in a trance during a seance. Caodaists also believe in reincarnation, where a person experiences a series of lives, and Karma, in which one's future lives are dependent upon good and bad deeds in the present life.

The central philosophy of Cao Daism preaches that the faithful have a duty toward themselves, their family, their society and all humanity. By fulfilling these duties, one is led to full spiritual completeness. A Cao Dai priest preaches world unity between the great cultures of the East and the West. Both men and women play an essential part in the administration and the priesthood of this religion, although the temple entrances and seating are separated by gender. Women enter from the left door, walk clockwise

This temple elder stands next to a dragon, a vital temple feature which symbolizes the force of intellect.

around the hall, then congregate on the left side for worship, and men enter from the right and walk counter-clockwise, congregating on the right.

The Cao Dai sect has been nationalistic from the start. Followers were politically active in protesting French rule in Vietnam, and during the French occupation in the 1930s and 1940s the Caodaists' private army amounted to 20,000 soldiers. The Tay Ninh region was the scene of brutal fighting during the Franco-Viet Minh War. The first Cao Dai pope, Ngo Van Chieu, died in 1943 and his successor, Pham Cong Tac, was deported to the Comoros Islands under the French rule. Later, the Cao Dai Army slowly integrated with the South Vietnamese Army.

During the Vietnam War, Cao Dai followers refused to support the Viet Cong and feared the worst after reunification. Not surprisingly, soon after its takeover in 1975, the Communist government of the newly formed Socialist Republic of Vietnam tried to officially disband the sect. They seized all Cao Dai lands, including the Cao Dai Holy Place in Tay Ninh, and broke up the sect's leadership. The *Cuu Trung Dai* (executive body) and *Hiep Thein Dai* (legislative body) were replaced with a governing council under the direct control of the new government. It is reported that four leading members of the sect were executed in 1979. Then in 1985, many of the temples were returned to the Cao Dais, and since the late 1980s the official stance has softened, allowing more freedom of worship. But persecution of religious groups still continues, according to the Puebla Institute, a human rights organization based in Washington. More than 4,000 Cao Dai members were arrested as reactionaries and counter-revolutionaries as recently as the early 1990s.

The Vietnamese government requires religious groups to be registered, and reportedly uses this information to control and monitor their operations, hierarchy and clergy. The authorities also employ administrative detention as a means of controlling the religious leaders and followers they believe hold dissident opinions. Cao Dai leaders regularly report that undercover government observers attend services and monitor the activities of the congregation and clergy. The parishioners are incensed about these tactics because they feel that the Cao Dai principles and traditions are not being respected and observed. To this day, the Cao Dai sect has left many of its top-level positions vacant because it does not want to expose its leaders to more government persecution.

Despite the government restrictions intended to suppress religions in Vietnam, people still pour into the temples, churches, pagodas and mosques all over the country. Today, Cao Daism has several million followers and hundreds of Cao Dai temples are scattered throughout Vietnam and Cambodia, as well as the United States, Canada, England, France, Germany, Japan, Australia and other countries where Vietnamese refugees have settled.

> *Despite the government restrictions intended to suppress religions in Vietnam, people still pour into the temples, churches, pagodas and mosques all over the country.*

From Fatigues to Collar

Today, he wears black and a white collar, but not so long ago he wore green jungle fatigues and combat boots. Today, he prays for others' souls, but not so long ago he prayed for his own life. Today, his name is Monsignor Fink, but not so long ago it was Charlie.

Charlie grew up a happy-go-lucky kid on Long Island, in New York. He attended public school, ran cross-country and track, dated and was an altar boy in a local Episcopal church. He always took religion seriously and began studying the Catholic religion while majoring in philosophy at St. John's University. "Two things dominated my college life—my decision to become a Catholic and my hopes that the Vietnam War, looming on the horizon, would end before I graduated."

Charlie graduated from college shortly after the Tet Offensive and went to his local draft board, expecting to get a deferment to attend graduate school. "I'll never forget the surprising response I received from the woman sitting behind the desk. In between laughs, she said to me—'You must be kidding! I suspect you'll be in the army within the next six months.'" One month later, Charlie enlisted. By March

Charlie holds an AK-47, the primary rifle used by the Viet Cong and the North Vietnamese. *(photo courtesy of Charlie)*

1969, this happy-go-lucky kid was a shaken, scared boy on his way to war.

"I'll never forget my first night at the 199th in Vietnam, this awful place on a river's edge. I was sleeping on the ground and woke up when I felt something walking on me. I was really stunned and confused. I whispered in the darkness, 'Hey Haines, Nolan—what's this crawling on me?' Through their hysterical laughter, they choked out, 'Them's rats—welcome to Vietnam.'" Within a few weeks, a safety switch of sorts went off inside Charlie. "The heat, the rats, the jungle rot, the gunfire—all became mundane events in my day."

Never considering himself a great soldier, Charlie had to find ways to simply keep himself alive. "I chose to keep a clear head by not getting involved with drugs or alcohol. That was one way I felt I could give myself better odds." The other was the deal he made with God. "I prayed the rosary every day. I promised that if I left that place alive, I'd pray the rosary every day until the day I died. I'll never know whether I survived my tour because of this, but I do know it certainly helped to keep my sanity while I was there."

In late May, the character of war changed for Charlie when he was reassigned. "I went from booby traps, oppressive heat and dry rice paddies to snipers and swampy jungles. I became point man and had to machete my way through the thickness of the hot, steamy

jungle. One day, my squad leader, Claude, a blue-eyed, blond kid from Nebraska with 50 days left in 'Nam, came up from behind. He good-naturedly offered, 'Give me that machete, you look beat.' I was exhausted, so I gladly handed it over to him, and dropped back to third man."

Less than 100 yards later, Charlie heard an ear-splitting explosion. "The sound from the blast hit me hard. I was totally dazed, enough so that I didn't realize I had been hit."

Charlie once wore green jungle fatigues and combat boots. Today, he wears a monsignor's robe. For some soldiers, their perceptions of God never failed while in Vietnam. Many others lost their faith. Still others found God in the midst of gunfire.

> *"I remember thinking to myself as I passed the duck pond near my house, 'I can't believe this duck pond exists on the same planet as the battlefields of Vietnam.'"*

He looked down, and saw red wetness seeping through his pant leg. Then he felt a burning sensation. A couple of pieces of shrapnel from a claymore were imbedded in his leg. "I looked in front and saw Claude lying on the ground, yellow smoke rising from his body. A few moments later, Dave, our radio operator, ran forward to help Claude. Dave was struck by enemy gunfire and mortally wounded." Many years later, Charlie learned that one reason Jan Scruggs—who was also a member of their company—fought so hard to have the Vietnam Veterans Memorial Wall built, was because of Claude and David's untimely deaths.

Charlie was evacuated, patched up in a field hospital in Xuan Loc and sent to the rear, where he trained as a radar specialist. Eventually, he was set up near a river with a radar screen where he was to pan the horizon and send information back to the base. "This turned out to be a good deal. We actually had a TV and a stove that ran off a generator. Of course, we still had the rats. We never seemed to get rid of the rats."

After having been terrified and wounded, and living in awful conditions for a year, Charlie left the combat zones of Vietnam. Thirty-six hours later, he found himself walking toward his home in America. "It was about eleven at night and I remember thinking to myself as I passed the duck pond near my house, 'I can't believe this duck pond exists on the same planet as the battlefields of Vietnam.' When I reached my home, I rang the door bell. My dad, a tough old soul, was so happy to see me that he stood there speechless and then absolutely dissolved into tears. This was the first time I ever saw him cry."

For the next two years, the accumulated effect of being scared and tense for 365 days almost overwhelmed Charlie. "The adjustment to home life was difficult. I felt nauseous all the time." But the strength of his faith got him through. He eventually enrolled in graduate school at the Catholic University of America, intending to pursue an advanced degree in philosophy. "At first I didn't have a clue what I wanted to do with my life, but by the end of the year, I decided to join the seminary." Charlie was ordained a priest in April 1976, and a monsignor in 1996.

"My days in Vietnam taught me a lot. I am forever grateful to be alive. And to this day, it doesn't take a whole lot to make me happy. A long, hot shower can be a religious experience." Monsignor Fink learned about toughness, but also about how fragile we all really are. "I don't regret being a soldier. You couldn't pay me to give up that part of my life. Actually, the two things that symbolize the most treasured experiences of my life are the collar I wear as a priest and my combat infantry badge." As promised, he still prays the rosary every day.

Bury Me with Soldiers

I've played a lot of roles in life;
I've met a lot of men.
I've done some things I'd like to think
I wouldn't do again.
And though I'm young, I'm old enough
To know someday I'll die,
And think about what lies beyond,
Beside whom I would lie.

Perhaps it doesn't matter much;
Still, if I had my choice,
I'd want a grave 'mongst soldiers when
At last death quells my voice.
I'm sick of the hypocrisy
Of lectures by the wise.
I'll take the man, with all his flaws,
Who goes, though scared, and dies.

The troops I knew were commonplace
They didn't want the war;
They fought because their fathers and
Their fathers had before.
They cursed and killed and wept—
God knows
They're easy to deride—
But bury me with men like these;
They faced the guns and died.

It's funny when you think of it,
The way we got along.
We'd come from different worlds
To live in one no one belongs.
I didn't even like them all;
I'm sure they'd all agree.
Yet I would give my life for them,
I hope; some did for me.

So bury me with soldiers, please,
Though much maligned they be.
Yes, bury me with soldiers, for
I miss their company.
We'll not soon see their like again;
We've had our fill of war.
But bury me with men like them
Till someone else does more.

Charles R. Fink
copyright 1980

In a Blaze of Honor

> ### *"Let them burn, and we shall clap our hands!"*

A photograph of Thich Quang Duc, a 66-year-old Buddhist monk from Hue, blazed across the front pages of newspapers worldwide on June 11, 1963. The photograph shocked the world and was a wake-up call that all was not right in Vietnam. Thich Quang Duc sacrificed his life in a flash of publicity to draw attention to the plight of persecuted people everywhere, and the Buddhists of South Vietnam in particular.

President Ngo Dinh Diem's dictatorial regime in South Vietnam had always tried to keep the Buddhists in check, but in the early 1960s, it stepped up its repression. President Diem, a devout Roman Catholic, refused the Buddhists permission to fly their multicolored flags and to gather on the anniversary of Buddha's birthday. Despite the order, on May 8, 1963, more than 20,000 Buddhists gathered in Hue, Vietnam's ancient capital city, to celebrate the 2,527th birthday of the Buddha. Their peaceful march unexpectedly turned violent when, upon orders from one of President Diem's local officials, the South Vietnamese Army opened fire on the crowd.

Thich Quang Duc, a 66-year-old Buddhist monk sacrificed his life at a busy street intersection in Saigon to protest religious repression.
(AP/Wide World Photos)

This monument in Thich Quang Duc's honor stands at the street corner where he died. His martyrdom inspired 30 other monks and nuns to follow in his example.

Confusion and chaos broke out as everyone ran for cover. When the panic was over, one woman and eight children were dead, either from bullets or from the stampede, and another 20 were wounded. The South Vietnamese government tried to blame the Viet Cong for the deaths.

In protest against the government's actions, Buddhists throughout the land held rallies and carried out hunger strikes. As a plea for compassion and charity toward all religions, a procession of monks, including Thich Quang Duc, traveled many miles from Hue to Saigon to protest Diem's anti-Buddhist campaign. When they arrived in Saigon, Thich Quang Duc stepped from the car and sat on the asphalt, curling himself into the lotus position at the busy intersection of Nguyen Dinh Chieu and Cach Mang Thang Tam streets. His fellow monks and nuns encircled him. One of the monks drenched Thich Quang Duc with gasoline. Another lit a match. The gasoline ignited instantly. Without uttering a word, without making any movement, Thich Quang Duc was engulfed and burned to death by the ensuing flames. His dramatic death inspired some 30 other monks and nuns to soon follow in his example.

The world was shocked by the images they saw of this scene, but most people were even more appalled and enraged by statements made by Madame Nhu, the President's notorious, much-hated sister-in-law. She made callous jokes about barbecued monks and said, "Let them burn, and we shall clap our hands!" The American press nicknamed Madame Nhu the "Iron Butterfly" and "Dragon Lady." Her statements accelerated the already strong disgust the public had with Diem's regime. In November 1963, both President Diem and his brother Ngo Dinh Nhu (Madame Nhu's husband) were murdered by Diem's own officers following an American-backed *coup d'état*. At the time, Madame Nhu was outside the country and was last reported to be living in Rome.

The gray-green sedan used to drive Thich Quang Duc to the immolation site is on display on the grounds of the Thien Mu Pagoda in Hue. A shrine to his memory stands in Saigon at the site of his death. Buddhists in Vietnam today still remember their turbulent history as they continue to struggle for freedom to practice their faith.

I Was Never a Hero

*I*n 1965, the Third Marine Division was the first American combat division sent into Vietnam. Chaplain John O'Connor, who Pope John Paul II would later name to be the sixth cardinal archbishop to the city of New York, accompanied those troops. For the better part of a year, he celebrated mass every day with the American soldiers and the Vietnamese, sometimes from a make-shift altar and sometimes while under fire.

O'Connor did not choose to go to war. "I had no desire to enter, none whatsoever." A kid from a working-class neighborhood in southwest Philly, O'Connor was ordained a priest one month before his 26th birthday. He had been content teaching, working in hospital psychiatric wards and assisting in a parish. In 1952, when the United States military needed more chaplains to serve in Korea, his superior suggested that he join up. What was supposed to be a short tour of duty in the Navy ended 27 years later, when O'Connor left military service as the chief of Navy chaplains with rear admiral stripes on his uniform.

Chaplain John O'Connor served with the first American combat division sent into Vietnam in 1965. Here he converses with the bishops of Danang and Hue. *(photo courtesy of* Chaplains with Marines in Vietnam 1962–1971)

"I spent my first night in Vietnam in a hole in the ground. At two in the morning when the rains came, we were floating in mud and scared. Every time a twig cracked, it was a potential enemy. My job there was to provide morally and spiritually for the troops. As a priest I didn't think much about what might happen to me. It wasn't easy for the men. I had to keep them calm and prepare them for death—or whatever might happen. It was a very hard challenge."

O'Connor's voice deepens, "I was never a hero. I'm a natural-born coward." Father O'Connor spent much of his time counseling Marines who were in trouble; he tried to teach them how to love even if they had to kill. "The commandment 'Thou Shalt Not Kill' means you should never take an innocent human life." He continues, "There are two dimensions at work here. One, presumably people armed against you are not innocent. Second, if you accept your own government's assessment of the situation that those that are armed against you are persecutors of their own people—that the Viet Cong and the North Vietnamese are persecutors of the South Vietnamese—then your moral position is that you are trying to defend the innocent by warding off the guilty. You didn't have American soldiers or sailors or Marines who were killing out of hatred. They were killing out of self-defense. It is a very difficult distinction to make. All war is very difficult."

Remembering one of his more memorable days in Vietnam, an easy smile forms on Cardinal O'Connor's face as he shares, "Perhaps the funniest thing that happened to me, the most humbling experience, was up in the DMZ." After a day of comforting men in the thick of heavy fighting, he and his helicopter crew were headed back to Danang. "There I am, in all my glory, sitting in the back of the helicopter, smoking away on a fat cigar, thinking I was Wild Bill Patton. Unexpectedly, the skies darkened, the fog and rains rolled in, and suddenly there's a warning signal that we're running out of fuel." The pilot turned to ask O'Connor's advice—should he attempt going through the mountain pass or head out to sea to fly around the mountain? In other words, should he risk crashing into the mountains or into the sea? Sitting there with this big old cigar hanging from his lips, O'Connor told him he would pray that the pilot made the right decision. "Very privately though, I felt the only contribution I could make to this situation was to tell God that if we landed safely, I would never smoke anything again." He kept that promise.

After tours of duty that included the Destroyer Force with the Atlantic Fleet; the USS Canberra, a guided missile cruiser; the Third Marine Division in Okinawa; Vietnam; Parris Island; Quantico; and the Cruiser-Destroyer Force with the Atlantic Fleet, O'Connor retired from military service in 1979. Although an admiral in the Navy, he was only a monsignor to the church. And at this point in his life, all he wanted to do was go home and work again as a teacher. Instead, on May 27, 1979, O'Connor stood before Pope John Paul II in Rome and was consecrated a bishop. He was assigned to assist Cardinal Terence Cooke in New York until May 1983, when he was appointed the Bishop of Scranton, Pennsylvania. Before his arrival in Scranton, most people had never heard of him; by the time he left to become New York's eighth archbishop, less than a year later, the *Scranton Times* had designated him "Man of the Year."

When O'Connor came to St. Patrick's Cathedral, the largest Gothic-style Roman Catholic Church in America, the archdiocese spread over 1,400 square miles with a membership of a few million Catholics. During his orientation, he was presented with a small silver tray that contained a statue of St. Patrick, the keys to the front door of the cathedral, a glass of water and a bottle of aspirins. Just over a year later, Archbishop O'Connor officially became the Cardinal of New York at an elaborate ceremony in St.

Peter's Square in Rome. John Cardinal O'Connor, a man of young spirit and energy, continued to confront the issues of the current times. He was rarely asked about, or volunteered to talk about, Vietnam, although he did bear strong feelings about his time there. "I don't know anyone who has ever been in a combat situation who wasn't changed in some way. I don't know how I would define it. I was never wounded, but I saw many men bloodied—I saw men killed." He stares off into the distance for some time, then finishes by saying, "It's the kind of thing that you think about, and cry about."

After battling cancer for months, John Cardinal O'Connor died Wednesday evening, May 3, 2000, in his Manhattan residence. Deeply saddened, thousands gathered to say farewell, to mourn his passing, and to celebrate his life.

Cardinal O'Connor was head of the most prominent archdiocese in the United States and served two tours in Vietnam. He eventually achieved the rank of rear admiral during his 27 years in the Navy.

Healing Powers

"My childhood memories are mostly of happy and peaceful times. I attended a French-run school and then became a farmer and tended silkworms." All that changed in 1946 when Lang joined the revolution against the French and fought with Ho Chi Minh for Vietnam's independence. "I worked in the forest with a medical unit and later attended a course to become a medical officer." Once the Vietnam War started, Lang joined the South Vietnamese Army and worked with American advisors in Danang while studying law at the university.

Lang, a South Vietnamese Army soldier, was diagnosed with cancer in 1969. Here, he stands in his one-room home.

In 1969, he became profoundly ill and was subsequently diagnosed with rectal cancer. "Treatment at the United States military hospital in Danang was unsuccessful." Lang turns his head wearily away and says in a low voice, "They sent me home to die."

Lang's health continued to deteriorate. One hot and tense evening in 1970, he wrote a suicide note and ingested many drugs. "When my suicide attempt failed, I needed to find a way to keep my mind from plunging again into the blackness of despair." Lang had heard about the healing powers of Transcendental Meditation. He heard that the mind can go deep enough to change the energy patterns that course through the body and can thus destroy any disease that has disturbed its harmony. Having no other alternative, he decided to study TM.

"For the next three years I expended all my energies on practicing meditation." With a reserved smile, Lang happily adds, "By 1973, I was completely free of cancer. Now I meditate every moment, even when I talk, even when I walk," Lang says with a faraway look. "I know meditation cured me of cancer." He goes on to explain, "I was a medical officer so I understand modern medicine. Oriental medicine has been the same for thousands of years and is already proven. Western medicine did not help me. If I knew nothing of Buddhism and meditation, I would have died."

Lang married twice and raised nine children during his younger years. Today, at the age of 74, he lives alone as a vegetarian in a one-room house surrounded by his private garden. He walks more than a mile each day in Hue's thick, gummy heat to the Thein Mu Pagoda, where he spends his time as a Mahayana Buddhist monk in prayer.

After leaving the Army, Lang cured himself of the cancer by practicing Buddhism and meditation.

> "When my suicide attempt failed, I needed to find a way to keep my mind from plunging again into the blackness of despair"

7
FAMILIES

voices of the aftermath

This family photo of Bobbie with her father was taken before he left for Vietnam, a trip from which he never returned. *(photo courtesy of Bobbie)*

Do You Know My Dad?

"If a genie appeared and granted me one wish, I would wish for just five minutes more with my dad. I miss him so much. I would love to know him now that I'm a grown woman." Today, Bobbie is eleven years older than her father Frank was when he died at 5:02 on the morning of June 6, 1965. Frank was a helicopter pilot stationed off the coast of Vietnam on the aircraft carrier USS Iwo Jima. He lost his life during a search-and-rescue mission when his helicopter collided into another chopper and plummeted into the ocean. He left behind six-year-old Bobbie, her three younger brothers and his wife, who was seven months pregnant.

"My doll arrived in the mail after my dad died. I remember thinking that she was the most beautiful doll in all the world." Frank had sent the doll from Vietnam only a few days before his helicopter crashed. "I was enchanted by her and spent hours searching through her hair, shoes and the hem of her *ao dai*. I took off her arms, her legs and even her head. I thought if I looked long and hard enough I would find the secret, hidden message my dad had sent me." The light and shadows breaking through the blinds play on the underlying melancholy in Bobbie's eyes. "I kept on thinking, if only I could find his message, maybe then I would know why my daddy left me."

Bobbie's life has not been easy. Losing her father at such a young age left her devastated. For years she used alcohol as a teenager and as an adult to drown away her life's suffering. Thankfully, today she is in a much better place. "At the age of 38, I have finally begun to grieve. After all these years, I can finally say out loud, 'My father is dead.'"

Many children who lost their parents to the Vietnam War in the 1960s and 1970s were told at the time not to tell anyone how their parents died because others might taunt them or call their fathers "baby killers." The nation was torn apart by the chanting of angry protesters by day and body bag counts by night. It seemed so

> *"I always know when I am at the Wall I can count on at least one pair of strong shoulders to catch the falling tears of my dad's memory."*

Bobbie lost her father to the war in Vietnam when she was only six. She did not really begin to confront her grief until she was well into her thirties.

many people were enraged and ready to retaliate, even against the innocent. Today, many of these faultless children continue to live as silent adults in the dark, shadowy grip of the past. Thankfully, Bobbie was not one of those who was shamed by her father's death.

One of the things that has helped Bobbie cope with her broken heart is an organization called Sons and Daughters in Touch. They locate, unite and provide support to sons, daughters and other family members of people who died or remain missing as a result of the Vietnam War. "The bond with other people who carry the same hollow feelings of loss that I do has allowed me to get through many a troublesome night. With their emotional support, I have started collecting letters my father had sent from Vietnam to my mom and other family members. These letters are priceless to me, and I know if my house were burning to the ground, I would race through the smoke and flames to rescue them." Someday Bobbie wants to write a book in memory of the man who once called her 'Skinny-mini-bean-pole.'

Another place where Bobbie embraces solace from the empty hole in her heart is at the Wall. Wearing her T-shirt with the words 'Do you know my Dad?' gives her hope of finding someone who can answer questions about his untimely death. "When I go to the Wall, I am never alone. I am with my dad, of course, but I am also with some of my new-found uncles." Many men who fought in Vietnam have emotionally adopted these fatherless children of the war and have become an integral part of their lives. Bobbie has been fortunate enough to meet two of the men who served with her father. These two men, who watched as her father's helicopter crashed into the sea, still have a difficult time talking about it. "I always know when I am at the Wall I can count on at least one pair of strong shoulders to catch the falling tears of my dad's memory."

Gold Star Scars

The grenade that took young Garfield Jr.'s life left the scars of war on the hearts of those who loved him. Garfield Sr.'s words are muffled and indistinguishable through heavy sobs as he struggles to recount his son's heroic act. Mary, more able to talk about her son, says, "We'll never forget the day a dark gray government sedan pulled into the driveway . . . I never imagined the war's tragedy would darken our door. I thought there was some mistake. The Army always makes mistakes." When, ten days later, a coffin containing their son's body arrived home in Riverhead, New York, Mary could no longer hope for a mistake. Struggling with the anguish of losing his only son, Garfield Sr. finally finds his voice. "It's hard to explain. My son was one of a kind. His nickname was 'Brother,' for he was a brother to all who knew him, a brother who was always there to take care of everyone."

Garfield Jr. graduated from high school in 1968. Less than a year later, he died in Vietnam. *(photo courtesy of Mary)*

Garfield Jr., a private first class, served as a radio operator for his Army unit in the rugged, jungle-covered Central Highlands of South Vietnam. On January 15, 1969, he and his troop were sent on a mission to find a downed helicopter and recover its two dead pilots. As the squad worked to extract the two bodies from the wreckage, and the daylight began to fade into darkness, they were suddenly surrounded by heavy enemy fire. The fighting continued throughout the night, at times coming terrifyingly close. Suddenly an enemy hand grenade, thrown through the bush, rolled into the center of their ranks. And just as suddenly, in an extraordinary act of courage and without concern for his own life, Garfield Jr. threw himself on the grenade, muffling its force and absorbing the blast to shield his comrades from the explosion. He gave his life, unconditionally, so his buddies could live.

As tears fall silently, scars of the Vietnam War continue to mark Mary and Garfield Sr.'s lives. How does a parent bury a child? Over 30 years later, deep tracks of pain—but also a deep pride—cut across their hearts. "That church simply overflowed with people coming to say goodbye to our son," Mary

> " Oh, people tried to console us, telling us that in time our heartache would lessen and our wounds would heal. But, how can you heal a wound larger than yourself?"

reminisces. "Oh, people tried to console us, telling us that in time our heartache would lessen and our wounds would heal. But, how can you heal a wound larger than yourself? In the natural order of life, parents grow old and die before their children die. That's the way life's supposed to be. When a child's life ends before a parent's, it is a true travesty. A travesty that can never be healed. Never."

One way the family found to grieve the loss of their child was through the Gold Star Mothers organization. On June 4, 1928, American Gold Star Mothers was organized as a nonprofit, non-denominational, non-political organization of mothers whose children served and died in the line of duty. In 1940, President Franklin D. Roosevelt issued a proclamation designating the last Sunday in September as Gold Star Mothers Day. "The gathering of people who experience the same dreadful pain we do has helped all of us to work through the grieving process. Whenever we go to meetings, we see our son's tragedy repeated in the eyes of the other parents many times over. It somehow helps to know others who share the same pain."

The family has also helped to heal its wounds, not by forgetting, but by keeping their son's memory alive in many other ways. In 1972, the church where Garfield Jr. was baptized created a space for a library in his honor. Riverhead's Disabled American Veterans Post was named in his honor, and in 1993 a bronze bust on a marble stand depicting their son in his dress uniform and wearing the Medal of Honor was dedicated to young Garfield's bravery. "The face is the noblest part of the body, it's where the good spirits live," says his mother. Under rich blue skies, the streets of Riverhead were jammed with an emotional audience of about 600, attending the dedication outside the town hall. They came to honor Mary and Garfield Sr.'s fallen son with proclamations, hymns, prayers, performances, a salute by a formation of helicopters and a second by an honor squad. They came to honor him with love.

The dedication on the bust reads:

P.F.C. GARFIELD M. LANGHORN
1948–1969
MEDAL OF HONOR
"THERE IS NO GREATER LOVE THAN THIS,
THAT A MAN LAY DOWN HIS LIFE
FOR HIS FRIENDS."
GOD • FAMILY • DUTY • HONOR • COUNTRY

During an act of noble heroism many lives are saved, and one life is lost. On January 15, 1969, in an extraordinary feat of bravery, Garfield gave freely of his twenty-year-old life so others could live.

In 1998, Garfield was posthumously inducted into the Army Aviation Hall of Fame in Charlotte, North Carolina, and the Army Aviation Association of America established a scholarship in his honor.

Mary slowly turns the pages of a worn scrapbook that she created over many years. Mixed emotions flood her eyes as she stares at a photograph of Garfield Jr. when he was young, beaming with boyish pleasure. "If our son had lived, he would be in his fifties today, but because he didn't survive, he will always be 20 to us."

On January 15, 1969, in an extraordinary act of bravery, Garfield Jr., gave freely of his 20-year-old life so his buddies could live. His memory is kept alive each day that his father goes to the cemetery to cut the grass and rake the leaves around the gray headstone, and each day that his mother goes to the town hall to polish the bust of her son. Parents who bury a child never stop grieving.

Grandma Hien

*T*he life expectancy of a Vietnamese woman born today is 70 years. Hien is 91. Today, as she sifts through her life's journey, a few events stand out vividly as defining moments in her collection of memories. "In the 1940s, we were living in Thai Binh, one of the poorest places in northern Vietnam. It was a very difficult time." Hien turns her head away. Tears fall softly. "Probably the saddest time of my life."

Japan invaded Vietnam in 1940. A catastrophic famine occurred during their rule because of floods, breached dikes and the forced exportation of agricultural products such as rice, the Vietnamese staple. Two million of North Vietnam's ten million people starved to death. "I lost many of my family and friends to the hunger." One windy monsoon evening, Hien lost her son. He was seven months old.

"Years later, when the Americans were in Vietnam, I lived through the worst fear of my whole life." Hien wipes her eyes with her trembling hands. "There was no safe place from the bombs." On December 18, 1972, at 7:43 P.M. Hanoi time, American bombs began falling on North Vietnam. This time of year was usually a time of peace and holiday celebrations, but became known as the "twelve days of Christmas bombing" in Hanoi and the port city of Haiphong, which were the targets of the bombs.

As Hien speaks, her right hand nervously taps at the table's edge. "I can still envision that Christmas week as if it were yesterday." She helped make helmets of rice stalks and strips of bamboo cane for protection from the bombs. When the public radio announced that the planes were coming, she hid in a shelter or in a small underground room. "If I wasn't near a shelter at the time of the bomb attack, I would dig a hole in the ground and sit in it. Protected by my helmet, I would wait—wait for the loud explosions of the bombs as they burst all around me." Hien glances away. Her bottom lip quivers, "I was very scared. I prayed all the time. I knew I could die at any moment."

"I worried the most about my poor daughter. She couldn't work at her regular job during those twelve days because of the bombing. Instead, she had to pick up the body parts of family, friends and strangers." Hien stares across the table as she recalls the horror. For that one instant, as she looks into the eyes of her 49-year-old daughter, the two women are connected by this gruesome memory and become the only two people in the world. "I still worry today. I hear my daughter late at night when she screams out in her sleep about the remembrances of yesterday."

"I will remember, until the day I go to my grave, the hunger, the fear and the nightmares of the past." When Hien was young, she was not free because there was always war. Now that there is no war, she again cannot be free. "I am too old. My body is tired and crippled. And there are too many memories." After a long silence, Hien concludes, "If I could live my life over again, I would choose to be born today. Today, without those memories of the past. Today, when everything is good."

> *"If I could live my life over again, I would choose to be born today. Today, without those memories of the past."*

These aged hands tell the story of Grandma Hien's difficult life.

Cu Chi Tunnels

> *"Now, 20 years later, I work in these same Cu Chi Tunnels, the place where I played when I was a boy. The place where my father died."*

Sau was a small child when the Americans arrived in his country to fight alongside the South Vietnamese. His father and uncles were soldiers allied with the North; they lived and fought in the South using the Cu Chi Tunnels as their home base. The Cu Chi Tunnels, with secret entrances only 20 miles or so from Saigon, were a network of underground tunnels and villages more than 150 miles long. "I spent my childhood playing during the day with my friends in and around the entrances to those tunnels. At night I would wait at the edge of my village and look out into the darkness hoping for my father to come home, to emerge from one of the tunnels and come home. I was ten years old. I called my father 'Daddy'—the Americans called him 'VC,' 'Gook,' 'Slope' or 'Charlie.'"

Sau's father was using tunnels that were built originally by the peasants and Viet Minh to fight the French colonialists. These extensive tunnels were excavated one trowel of dirt at a time, mostly at night, over two-and-a-half decades. The tunnels fell into disrepair after the Franco-Viet Minh War, but around 1960 the Viet Cong guerrillas restored them and used them to communicate from village to village in American-controlled areas. In some places, the tunnels were several stories deep. During the war with America, they contained weapons factories, command centers, classrooms, storage facilities, and living areas that included field hospitals and kitchens. From the secret tunnels, the Viet Cong were able to mount surprise attacks on the enemy, then mysteriously disappear without a trace through hidden trapdoors.

Baffled by the Viet Cong activities in the area and fearful of the enemy controlling an area so close to Saigon, the American's plan for defense began by setting up a large military base in the Cu Chi district. Unbeknownst to them, the U.S. Army's 25th Division was located right on top of the elaborate maze of tunnels. It took months for the Americans to discover how their soldiers were being murdered in their tents at night without a sign of the enemy's presence.

Once the Americans learned about the tunnels, tens of thousands of American and South Vietnamese troops devoted all their energies toward finding and destroying them. In the process, they destroyed most of the countryside, first by bulldozing the jungles and razing the villages, then by spraying massive amounts of defoliants, and finally by igniting the dead vegetation with napalm and gasoline. But throughout all of this, the VC remained unscathed, safely tucked underground. Frustrated with their mostly failed attempts, the Americans even used Alsatian dogs to sniff out the tunnels' entrances, and solders nicknamed "tunnel rats" descended deep into the ground armed with flashlights and pistols to ferret out and fight one-on-one with the VC. After trying everything else, in the late 1960s, the Americans carpet-bombed the now barren area with B-52s to destroy the tunnels. Some historians say Cu Chi's 260 square-mile area is the most devastated area in the history of warfare.

The Viet Cong guerrillas who served in the oxygen-deprived tunnels sometimes stayed underground for weeks or months at a time. They withstood extremely difficult conditions and were exposed to toxic quantities of Agent Orange. Only about 6,000 of the 16,000 who lived and fought in the tunnels survived the terrible conditions they were made to endure. "The war killed most of my family," Sau says softly. "My father was one of its casualties."

"Now, 20 years later, I work in these same Cu Chi Tunnels, the place where I played when I was a boy. The place where my father died. My job is to take the people, once called 'the enemy,' on guided tours." Today, as Sau enters the tunnels, his senses trigger powerful, unforgettable memories. Memories of the claustrophobic darkness, the echoing silence and the smell of the damp earth, "but mostly, memories of my father."

Sau works as a guide in the Cu Chi Tunnels, taking people he once called "the enemy" through the claustrophobic place where his father died during the war.

205

She Shimmered in Time

"She shimmered in time." Lana's poetic words describe her adopted Vietnamese daughter, Heather, whose short life ended 24 years ago. "I'm sorry we couldn't save her, but I'm so very glad we had the opportunity to love her."

In 1973, after five years of marriage, Lana and Byron faced up to the realization that they had little hope of having children of their own. So they chose adoption. "We soon found out how futile an American adoption would be and instead we decided to look outside this country." They got in touch with Friends of Children of Vietnam and began a long, tedious adoption process. "Page after page after page of application papers, hours of home study and interminable interviews—we thought it would never end. We were even fingerprinted. Almost an entire year after we began the process, we finally received our approval. Then we had to wait. Wait for our baby."

It was early 1975 and the tension in Saigon was rising. The Viet Cong were closing in on the city. President Ford announced that Operation Babylift would be set in motion using American military transport aircraft. Other countries around the world joined in the effort, and on April 3, 1975, the evacuation of Vietnamese and Amerasian orphans began. On the second day of the airlift, a C5-A cargo jet carrying 228 orphans crashed into a rice paddy 20 minutes into its flight from Tan Son Nhut Air Base. Forty-nine adults and 78 orphans died.

Lana, Byron and an entire community of potential adoptee parents on Long Island were devastated. No one knew whose children were on the plane, and fear showed on their weary faces as they waited to hear the names of those who perished. "Without question, it was one of the worst days of my life." Lana, still visibly upset, tells the story of that day as she strokes Heather's face in one of the few photographs she has of her child. "Thank God, Heather wasn't on that downed plane."

From April 3 to April 19, 1975, Operation Babylift flew more than 3,000 children to new homes in America, Europe, Canada and Australia. Heather was one of these children. She left Vietnam on April 11 and was twice hospitalized—for pneumonia, malnutrition, anemia, scabies, salmonella and a cough—before reaching New York on April 23. "Heather only stayed home with us until April 29, when we had no choice but to take her to the hospital. We stayed there with her day and night. I remember sitting at her bedside watching the television report that the North Vietnamese were taking over Saigon." As the South lost ground, so too did Heather. "I remember thinking, God didn't bring her all this way here, so many thousands of miles, to have her die on us. But she did." Heather struggled to hold on, but she was too ill. "Our tiny miracle baby, Heather Constance, smiled at us twice before she died on May 17."

"The trauma of her death was such a shock that it followed us forever. We were never the same again." Heather's funeral was on May 20. "That night, in one of the darkest moments of our lives, the phone rang. It was Friends of Children of Vietnam. They had three more babies to place. They wanted us to take one. Our minds raced. We had just buried our daughter—we couldn't go through it again. We needed time for silence and tears. I said I'd call them back the next day." Without barely a pause to grieve, Lana called the next day and opened her heart to yet another life.

Evacuated when she was three months old, Jennifer was the very last baby placed from Operation Babylift. "She came home on June 5, 1975, and was ours the minute we saw her, shaved head and all. There was no sleeping her first nights home. We hovered over her day and night, constantly checking to make sure she was alive." Jennifer flourished and grew bright and confident. Piano, flute, soccer, gymnastics and dance lessons filled her childhood. "Jenny is so gifted and talented. And very much her own person. Her first sentence was, 'I do it!'"

Jennifer earned many achievements. She won a good citizenship award, was named sportswoman of the year, and graduated an honor student from high school. She graduated from Drew University *cum laude* with a bachelor's in psychology and from Columbia University with a master's in social work. She now works as a social worker with underprivileged, low-income families. Jennifer's interest in her heritage has grown stronger as she matured. She would like to visit Vietnam someday soon.

Lana and Byron did not want Jennifer to

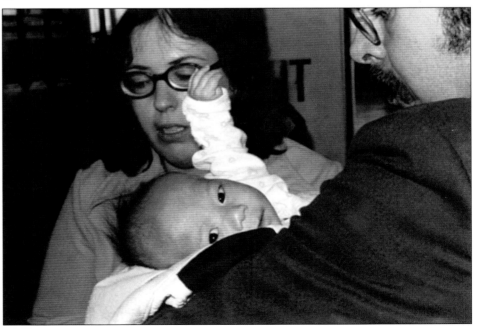

Lana and Byron with their adopted daughter Heather in 1975. *(photo courtesy of Lana)*

grow up as an only child, so on December 11, 1979, Jason, an abandoned child from an orphanage in Seoul, South Korea, became her new brother. He graduated from Hofstra University and is presently working as a social studies teacher. "We are so proud of both our children. Our lives have been transformed by them. We are truly blessed."

Even so, each and every spring, when the earth stirs, Lana remembers her lost child. "I loved her so much—she was my baby. She was a gift to us all. Not a day goes by that I don't think of her and talk to her. I am so thankful that she died being loved. I wake early every morning from April 23 to May 17 and ponder what I can do in Heather's memory. It's as if I'm on a mission, and for those 25 days that mark the anniversary of Heather's life with us, I donate money and try to help increase awareness of the tragedy of her death."

Heather is buried far from Vietnam, near a bench, a lovely dogwood tree and a globe of the world. Lying in the earth next to her is a young corporal. She died in his country. He died in hers.

Lana, Byron and their adopted children, Jennifer and Jason, visit the gravesite of Heather, an infant rescued during "Operation Babylift." Lana, still visibly sad over their loss says, "Our tiny miracle baby, Heather Constance, smiled at us twice before she died on May 17."

She's Lost Forever

*N*ights are always agonizing for Vien; they offer too much time for too many memories to replay in her mind. "When I was young, I married the man I loved, had a child and mourned my husband's death, all in one very short year." Vien struggles to keep the tears inside as she tells her story. Her young husband had been a soldier, fighting for the freedom of the South. A Viet Cong's bullet shattered the back of his head and ended his life as he parachuted into enemy territory.

"I was left homeless and penniless. I had a beautiful eleven-month-old baby girl and a broken heart. After three very hungry years, I finally got a job working on an American Army base in Nha Trang. As happens during war-time, I met an American GI, fell in love, and had his child." Vien stares vacantly into space as she continues, "Billy was sent home to Kansas, and he never looked back. I was alone again, now with *two* children to feed."

"After Billy left, I met a Vietnamese man who asked for my hand in marriage. My hand and my first-born Vietnamese child—not my half-breed baby. He told me, 'That child has got to go. She is nothing, *bui doi*—the dust of life. Get rid of her. Do you hear me? Get rid of her or the marriage is off!'" Vien's hands shake as she attempts to cover the sorrow on her face.

"I had no choice. The Americans were leaving the base in a few months. I wouldn't have a job or any money to buy food to feed my children. If we didn't have someone to take care of us, what would we do? I couldn't see any other way out."

On a dreary, fog-covered morning, Vien carried her seven-month-old Amerasian baby to an orphanage in the mountains just west of the city. "The nuns told me it didn't matter that my child was not purebred. They promised that they would treat her like all the other children. I was assured that she would be protected from the war, and that they would find her a good home." Those words have haunted Vien ever since.

"I couldn't do it. The next morning I ran back to the orphanage. I wanted my baby back. Somehow I thought we would survive without a man in our life. We had to!" But when Vien returned to the orphanage to get her child, she was met with the

> **"My prayers are for my children's health and prosperity. And for my lost baby girl. I pray that someday, she will forgive me for giving her away."**

209

shock of her life. Her baby was gone. "The nuns told me they didn't know what had happened to her." At this news, Vien started to shout frantically, "She's gone? What do you mean? I only left her here yesterday. You gave your word that you would protect her. Where did she go? Where is she?" Thirty-three years later, tight rage consumes Vien's body, while tears flood her face. "My little innocent baby was lost, lost forever."

Vien did marry her suitor, and had three more children, two girls and a boy. Then one morning, seven years later, her husband kissed her and the four children goodbye, left for work, and never returned.

Today, life is as hard as ever. Vien scrapes together a living by selling papayas, mangos and cigarettes, and by giving massages to tourists on the beach. "I do anything I have to so my children will have food." Vien also spends her days staring deeply into the eyes of each person as they pass, hoping that one day she will see the eyes of her lost baby looking back at her from a grown woman's face. As the night puts the shadows of the day to sleep, Vien prays silently at the water's edge. "My prayers are for my children's health and prosperity. And for my lost baby girl. I pray that someday, she will forgive me for giving her away."

To marry a man to support her, Vien gave away her seven-month-old, half-American baby girl. Today, while she earns a living by selling produce and giving massages on the beach, she stares longingly into the eyes of each person passing, hoping one day she will see the eyes of her lost baby looking back.

Love at First Sight

"*I* never believed in the adage 'love at first sight' until I met Kenny." Almost 30 years later, Dorothy still has a smitten look on her face as she reminisces. "I was only 18 in December 1972 when I went into a local bar and met Kenny and his two inseparable sidekicks, Neil and Kenneth. By the end of the evening, all three of them had asked me out. But, in my mind, there was never a question about who I would say yes to."

Dorothy's love for Kenny was tested early on. "We were on our first date when Kenny shared two things about his life. First, that he was a Vietnam veteran. Second, that he had five years to live. I know it sounds crazy, but if he had told me he was going to die in a motorcycle accident the next day, I would have said, 'Let's get married tonight!' I loved him so much, so fast."

Kenny had been told that if he enlisted in the Army for three years instead of two, he would not have to go to Vietnam, so he joined up in 1967. They lied. He was sent to the war in 1969. Eleven months later, this once healthy young man returned to the States near death's door. Diagnosed with chronic hepatitis and cirrhosis of the liver, Kenny was told by his staff sergeant to prepare himself because he was going home in a pine box. His body was so jaundiced, they nicknamed him "Golden Boy." Kenny's parents were called into the hospital to say goodbye to their son. "But my Kenny fooled them all—18 months later he was released. It was then that the doctors told him he had five years to live."

Despite this death sentence, Dorothy and Kenny married on December 18, 1974. Kenny had regular check-ups and his health was stable for almost two years. He was working for the phone company in a manhole when he had a grand mal seizure. Dorothy stares into the distance, "They raced him to the hospital and discovered he had a brain tumor. The neurologist said that because the Vietnam War was a part of Kenny's recent past, he suspected that Agent Orange caused the brain tumor, but they can't prove that it did—or that it didn't. He was operated on in November, but because

> "*Every day, there are moments from our lives that trickle back into my memory. Kenny will always be a part of me.*"

the tumor was too close to the optic nerve and they couldn't remove all of it, I was now told, at best, my husband had just one year to live."

"We did a lot of soul searching. And we shocked a lot of people when we decided to have a child." Dorothy and Kenny spoke to the neurologist, to make sure this would not be a problem. He reassured them medically, but told Dorothy quite bluntly, "You do realize that you will be raising this child by yourself?"

"The next few years were very tough." Dorothy did get pregnant, but Kenny was having seizures, sometimes two or three a day. He was aware when they were coming and was able to let Dorothy know in advance. "We had tongue depressors taped to every wall in the house, always available for the inevitable."

"Our son Kevin was born on September 24, 1978. My time was pretty much consumed between our infant son and my handicapped husband." In her few spare moments, Dorothy could be found fighting with the Veterans Administration or the Army trying to get compensated for the pain and suffering they were going through because of Vietnam. "Taking care of the man I loved, day in and day out, was the easy part, the bureaucratic nonsense was the tough part."

Their search to find someone to help with Kenny's medical condition ended one day in Manhattan when they went to see a top liver specialist. His words were cutting, but real: "Doctors in the States have no idea how to treat Kenny, because he has an Asian strain of hepatitis. The only advice I can give him is to eat all the bacon he wants, because there is nothing we can do." By February 1980, Kenny was going downhill fast. It was a Friday in July when he came over to Dorothy and said, "I don't want to do this, but I have to go to the hospital." She stayed with him from seven every morning until eleven at night. Weeks later, during one of his more lucid moments (he had been slipping in and out of a coma), he whispered, "Dar, let me go." He was cradled in Dorothy's arms the Sunday night he passed away. Kenny was only 30 years old.

The next days were difficult. "I think if I didn't have Kevin to take care of I probably would have put a gun to my head." Dorothy, a 26-year-old widow, had a tremendous support system of friends and relatives. "I joined a bereavement group, which was a terrific place to talk to other adults about my emotions. I learned to get on with my life, living one day at a time." Added to her loss were the deaths of Kenny's two best friends: Kenneth died of a heart attack at the age of 39, and Neil was 43 when he died of AIDS.

"All I know is that I would live my life all over again in a heartbeat. I can't picture it any other way. Kenny thought of himself as the richest man in the world. He died happy and content, knowing so much love. Even with his illness, we probably had more in our eight years than most people have in a lifetime."

Today, Dorothy spends her days dealing with life and death situations working as a 911 operator. Kevin is in his third year at the University of Buffalo studying to be an el-

ementary school teacher. Kevin is now almost the age Kenny was when Dorothy and Kenny met. "Every day, there are moments from our lives that trickle back into my memory. Kenny will always be a part of me. His love stays alive in our son, Kevin."

Dorothy requested to have Kenny's name added to the Memorial Wall in Washington with others whose lives were ended prematurely because of the war in Vietnam. Her request was denied. The only names now added to the Wall are those who died of combat injuries suffered in Vietnam—not those who died of medical illnesses. Instead, Kenny's name was added to a small memorial wall in a local park surrounded by trees.

Dorothy has her son Kevin to remind her of her husband's love. They were on their first date when Kenny told her that he was a Vietnam veteran and had only five years to live.

I Pray My Son Will Never Know War

"For me, there's no getting away from war." Wide pools of sadness fill Thai's eyes. "War will always be a part of who I am." Thai was born in 1967 in the Quang Tri province—a place of death. Quang Tri was the site of the Demilitarized Zone, a creation of the 1954 Geneva Peace Accord that divided Vietnam into two parts. From 1954 to 1975, the Ben Hai River served as the demarcation line between the South and the North. The area just south of the DMZ was the scene of some of the bloodiest battles of the Vietnam War; tens of thousands of soldiers died there. During the war, Khe Sanh, Dong Ha, the Rockpile and Hamburger Hill—all battlegrounds near the DMZ—became household names in the United States. Today, for most, they are only faint memories. But not so for Thai. These names continue to represent a present-day reminder of her terrifying childhood.

"The war was a part of our everyday life when we lived in Quang Tri." Bombs blasting and machine guns firing were all normal, everyday sounds to Thai when she was a toddler. Finally, at the point when the war got too close to her village, her family fled southeast to Hue. Thai's childhood memories are clouded by layers of fear. "I was eight in 1975 when the liberation came. I'll never forget looking up at the Communists in their green uniforms as they stormed the streets of Hue. Or the smell of the city burning from the fires the ARVN set before they evacuated their bases. But mostly, I'll never forget the insane chaos during the mass departure to the South. The streets were thick and dark with panicked people." Fleeing the Communist advance, they left by the thousands, rich and poor alike. Most traveled by foot, but others grabbed any transportation they could find, from wheelbarrows to bicycles.

"We did not leave. I stayed in my home with my mother and helped to take care of my younger brothers and sister. We couldn't leave the house because it wasn't safe to go outside." The entire city was in a state of panic. Only hardship and silence remained when the exodus finally slowed down. "I remember two things about the few years after the war's end. One was studying my lessons for school and the other was waiting on long lines for food. There wasn't enough rice to go around so we ate corn and roots." The hunger she experienced in the past is reflected in her eyes today.

With much hard work and perseverance, Thai finished high school and went on to study French and history in college. She graduated in 1991. One day, she traveled back to Quang Tri to care for her grandparents' gravesite. While there, she met a mechanical engineer from the North. They fell in love, married, and decided to settle in Quang Tri, the province of her youth, where they now raise their son. Today, Thai spends her days as a tour director at the old battlefields of the DMZ, which forces her to relive unpleasant memories. "Some days it is hard to imagine the existence of those bloody ghosts of the past as I stand here amid the beautiful hills, valleys and fields. It is so peaceful now. I pray my son will never know war. But I think all the older soldiers must die before this can happen."

The war may be over, but death is still fairly easy to come by at the former DMZ. Despite the disastrous risks, impoverished peasants and farmers continue to probe the red clay in their relentless search for scrap metal—aluminum, steel and brass—and other items they hope to sell. Thousands have been killed this way when they encounter land mines, unexploded bombs, white phosphorus shells and other ordnance. The weapons often explode, adding more names to the war's casualty list.

Thai was born in 1967 in the Quang Tri province, a place of continual death. She lost her childhood innocence to the war. "If it wasn't for the war, I know my life would be happy—very, very happy," she says.

A year ago, a group of children were playing in the schoolyard where they played every day. A terrible storm had hit the area a few days before and the furious rain, wind and mud had carried a mine into the schoolyard. Soon, there were six new small gravesites to pray at in the province of Quang Tri—grim reminders that the war has not yet come to an end.

Thai tries to resume the cadence of an ordinary life by putting the war of her past aside. In the fading light of day at the desolate Khe Sanh combat base, still bare from the instruments of war, her face reveals another story. A story of emotional wounds that will never heal.

It Continued to Stalk Him

". . . although my brother came home with no visible scars from the war, that didn't mean he wasn't wounded."

On a cold, windy morning in December 1992, I went to the morgue at Jamaica Hospital to identify the body of my second-born son." Tommy's body had been found slumped over in a New York City subway car. He had died from an overdose of heroin. "The Vietnam War had finally killed him," sighs his mother, Harumi.

Death from war was not new to Harumi. She was born and raised in Japan. During World War II, one of the American bombs that fell on her country destroyed her sister's school, taking the young girl's life along with it. Now, some 50 years later, Harumi mourned again.

"Thomas was a restless teenager. He joined the Navy instead of finishing high school. At the time . . ." Harumi stops mid-sentence as the lingering memories of her son take hold, ". . . the Navy seemed to be the answer to all his problems. When he left for Vietnam, he was a clean kid." Jen, Tommy's younger sister helps her mother tell his story, "When he came home from the war, he was hooked on heroin."

Drug use in some units in Vietnam reached near-epidemic proportions. In 1974, a White House survey reported an estimated 81,300 American servicemen used heroin in Vietnam. When Tommy came home, he struggled to deal with the emotional wounds of the war. No matter how hard he tried to evade the enemy, it continued to stalk him. Heroin helped to deaden his pain.

"What the outside world didn't understand was that although my brother came home with no visible scars from the war, that didn't mean he wasn't wounded. The emotional wounds of the trauma he endured from Vietnam were as deep as any bullet wound." Jen's usually radiant face is now filled with deep shadows. "He tried for years to bury these wounds. He shoveled tons of heroin on the festering, open lesions. But, as much as he shoveled, and as many years as he shoveled, they never healed."

Jen and her mother Harumi still mourn their tremendous loss. Tommy went to Vietnam a
clean kid and came home a heroin addict. He died in 1992 from an overdose.

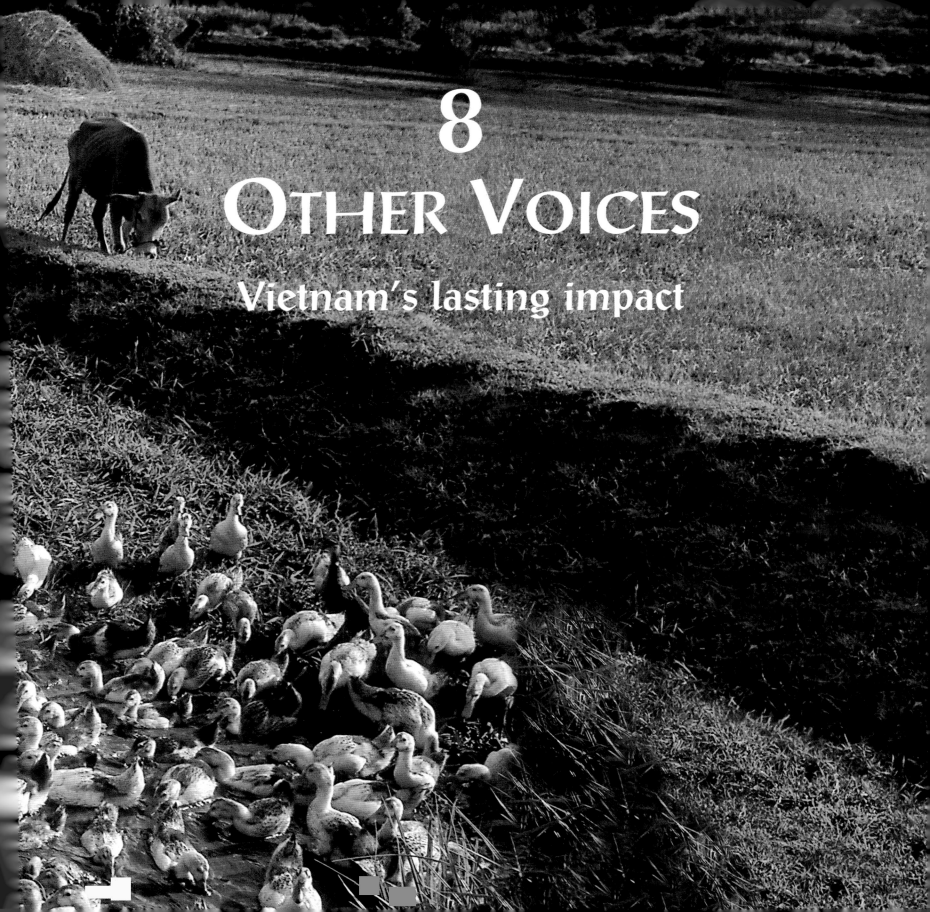

8
OTHER VOICES

Vietnam's lasting impact

Arnold spent years in Vietnam
working as a freelance journalist
and photographer pursuing stories
about the human impact of the war.
(photo courtesy of Arnold)

A Grasp for Life

By the time he was 27, Arnold was married, the father of two and a successful newspaper journalist. And he felt overwhelmed and suffocated. "My God, I was strangling. I had too much, too soon. I wanted to ditch the white picket fence and grasp for life." Born as the Second World War was breaking out, Arnold was too young to be called into service in the Korean War, and too old for Vietnam. This chronological good luck and all his responsibilities, however, did not stop this determined young journalist from dreaming of a glamorous job as a foreign correspondent in a war zone. His dreams became a reality one day in 1966 when Arnold's wife Phyllis spotted a press release squeezed in among the girdle ads on page 88 of the *New York Times*. The ad requested applicants for a program intended to train professional American journalists to live in Hong Kong and work in Asia. Out of 600 applicants, Arnold was one of six chosen. In 1968, he, Phyllis and their two children packed up and headed to the Far East.

When the training program ended two years later, Arnold had a difficult time getting a full-time job. He and his family had to decide whether to tough it out in Asia or head back to the States. "I was just getting started. It was ridiculous for me to go home. But I had to earn a living. Then a friend of mine who worked as a reporter for a major network made me an offer too good to refuse. He said if I paid for my own airline tickets, I could hitch along on his expense account and share his room and meals. Before I knew it, I was reporting from the middle of the battlefields of the Vietnam War." Six months later, while risking life and limb, Arnold was sending his freelance stories down the wire to the *Seattle Times*, *Newsday*, the *San Francisco Chronicle*, the *Philadelphia Bulletin* and the *Kansas City Star*.

For the next six years, Arnold traveled in Vietnam pursuing stories for three or four weeks at a time, and then returned to Hong Kong to be with his family and to file his stories. They sold well. "I didn't do political and big battle stories. When the herd went one way, I went the other." Arnold stares off to the wall in his den, which is filled with framed photos and stories that reflect a time and place called Vietnam.

> *"... and I remember thinking that I would have to multiply my fear by a thousand to begin to understand the level of fear of the soldiers who do this all the time."*

"I would go to the villages on the rim of the battle and learn what it meant to the lives of its people. I did this intuitively. There were no models back then."

For financial reasons, Arnold chose to wear two hats during the Vietnam War. One as a reporter of words, the other, as a reporter of images. "As a journalist, you can talk to the soldiers an hour or a day later and reconstruct the battle through their eyes. The visual face of war, however, doesn't wait until the battle is over. As a photographer, you have to be there when the action happens to capture it on film." Arnold regularly risked his life to get the picture and an extra 20 dollars.

"I wasn't scared most of the time. Actually, for the most part, I enjoyed my years in Vietnam. It was an exciting adventure." One of the more adventurous times Arnold fondly remembers was the week he spent with Captain Mac. "Mac was a professional military man, a killer. He and his A-Team of Green Berets were based on the Cambodian border and were supposed to stop any further infiltration into this area by the Viet Cong and the North Vietnamese." Arnold will never forget one night in particular when he went with them out on patrol. "It was a little after midnight, and there was no sound in the darkness. All of a sudden, from the quiet heavens, a B-52 dumped her load. The whole world lit up, as if it were coming to an end. All I could see and hear was the thunder, the flashes and the explosions. I remember how scared I was, and I remember thinking that I would have to multiply my fear by a thousand to begin to understand the level of fear of the soldiers who do this all the time."

"Later that same night, while we were asleep on the longhouse floor, a tremendous explosion literally picked me up and threw me down. The enemy had rocketed the longhouse. Shrapnel was flying everywhere. Hot slivers of metal zipped over my head and tore into the wall. By the time I realized what was happening, it was all over and two South Vietnamese soldiers were killed." Arnold's "grasp for life" had suddenly become a grasp for his own life. "All I could think about was my wife and kids."

By March 1973, the last U.S. troops had left Vietnam and Arnold's market for salable war stories disappeared. "American newspapers didn't care about what was happening in Asia as long as Americans weren't being killed there." Despite the sudden drought in his work, Arnold wasn't quite ready to go home. Instead, he stayed in Hong Kong working as the managing editor for *Asia* magazine. He and his family finally said their good-byes to Asia and headed back to New York in 1976. Arnold immediately began working for *Newsday*, where he continues to work today, bringing his experiences from Asia to his stories. "I write quite a lot of stories about Vietnam. It's an important part of my personal life and of the nation's political life. It is familiar."

The memory of Vietnam's life-giving, green rice paddies and mist-veiled highlands, its canopied rainforests and crashing and cresting sea have helped the more painful war memories fade into the background, but not disappear. Arnold's grasp for life resulted in a reverberation of negative consequences. He suffered terrible nightmares while in Vietnam, and these nightmares have followed him ever since, both day and night. "Once, on a gorgeous day in 1992, when I was in the middle of a game of tennis, I heard a ping. I was sure I was shot." The sound brought Arnold immediately back to Vietnam searching for a sniper in the treeline and blood from his rifle wound." A boyish smile forms on Arnold's face. "The ping I heard did get me six months on crutches, but not because of a bullet wound. My Achilles tendon had snapped while I was playing tennis." Gazing off into space, Arnold adds, "No one can come from Vietnam's war zone and leave untouched. Although I wasn't physically touched, I was spiritually moved and mentally triggered. Those experiences have all become a part of my consciousness."

No one left Vietnam's war zone untouched. Although he repeatedly risked his life for a story, Arnold claims he rarely felt scared in Vietnam. But still today, nightmares visit his sleep.

There But for the Grace of God

"*L*ife was so simple back in the 1950s. I spent my days singing harmony with the guys on New York City street corners." Nick's eyes sparkle as he tells the stories of his youth. "We'd practice for hours on end until we were good enough, then we did as most groups did back then—we worked for nothing. We played at church dances in hopes that someone might discover us."

Nick and his group, The Capris, were one of the lucky ones. His song—*There's a Moon Out Tonight*—became a smash hit. "It was a great time for all of us. We toured the country from the beginning of 1960 to the middle of 1961." After they had exhausted the run of this one-hit-wonder, Nick came home from the fame and excitement to a new reality. He needed to get a job. He worked at Idlewild Airport until 1965, when he was accepted into the New York City Police Department.

This was the same time that the Vietnam War was being played up in the American media. "It was a confusing time. I was puzzled by the war." Nick had joined the Army Reserves when he turned 18, so he did not have to worry about being drafted and sent to Vietnam. "Originally, I thought Vietnam was no big thing. We go to war, we win the war, the guys come home, and we cheer them on. Same as in all the John Wayne movies. Same as in all the other wars in our history. Boy, was I in for a rude awakening!"

"I think our country was in the dark about a lot of the events surrounding the war. In the dark about what really went on in Vietnam. Like the treatment our soldiers got when they returned to the States. The homeless vets. Post-traumatic stress disorder. All of it. As a cop, I probably saw more appalling situations up close than most people."

"One incident in October 1972 really sticks out in my mind." Fifteen policemen had been sent to police a rally in Central Park honoring Vietnam vets and returning soldiers. War protesters were expected. By the time Nick arrived, some barricades had been set up, but not much else was going on. "I remember we were standing around shooting the breeze when a few young people showed up wearing bandannas, tie-dyed shirts and peace symbols. They carried dummies dressed in American soldier fatigues with the words 'traitors' and 'baby killers' written across their chests. Soon those few protesters turned into a few hundred." Nick watched in amazement as the energy of the crowd changed from passivity to rage when four military buses containing soldiers pulled up. The buses were filled with men coming home from the war.

"As some of the soldiers started to get off the bus, the protesters became more agitated and started screaming obscenities. They called the soldiers 'baby killers' and 'war mongers.' And they shouted that they were an embarrassment to the United States. They even cursed at me for trying to protect the soldiers." Nick, after all these years, still tells this story with complete shock in his voice.

"Then they hurled balloons with blood-like red dye and rocks at the soldiers and buses. When the soldiers tried to get back in the buses, the protesters started banging and shaking the buses. There was no way to rationalize with this hyped-up crowd. The best we could do was try and keep them apart. Everything was so out of control, so surreal. All these years later, I still don't get it. These guys came home from dodging VC bullets to dodging rocks and packets of red dye. What happened to the cheers John Wayne used to get?"

Years afterward, when Doo-Wop music enjoyed a renewed popularity, Nick decided to start up the group again. In 1981, The Capris had another top hit, *Morse Code of Love*. "Before I retired from the police force in 1986, The Capris did a show for a chapter of the Vietnam Veterans of America." The evening began with a procession of veterans, most of them dressed in their service fatigues, coming out and carrying flags. A drum roll followed and one of the vets read a list of names. "The whole thing appeared very somber to me. I had no idea at first that the names being read were names of the war's dead. It was gut-wrenching to watch the pain, still so deep in the hearts and souls of those men."

"Our group was performing its usual lineup of songs, when I walked up to the mike and started talking." The room soon became pin-drop quiet. "From a place deep inside, I began by saying how thankful I was for the selflessness and bravery of the men in that room. As I spoke, the band began playing softly behind me. I then

As a policeman during the 1960s and 1970s, Nick observed the appalling treatment Vietnam veterans received when they returned home from the war. He and other police officers were sometimes cursed at for trying to protect the soldiers from protesters. *(photo courtesy of Nick)*

started singing *The Impossible Dream.* I dedicated the song not only to that room of veterans, but to all Vietnam veterans." As The Capris sang, a group of about 40 vets walked onto the dance floor, held each other's arms, and formed a circle. "I couldn't finish the song. Everyone was in tears. The tremendous emotion that filled the room was overwhelming. That one night made me realize that the war in Vietnam, which didn't affect me personally, had truly affected my spirit."

As a result of that experience, The Capris dedicated their latest CD, *Falling in Love Again,* to all Vietnam veterans. At every concert, after first giving thanks to the veterans for risking their lives for our freedom, they dedicate the song *Wind Beneath My Wings* to them. "For me, it's like saying, 'There, but for the grace of God, go I.'"

Nick and his Doo-Wop group, The Capris, thank Vietnam veterans and dedicate the song *Wind Beneath My Wings* to them at their concerts.

The Chicago Seven

*A*rrested three times in the previous eight months, 84-year-old David Dellinger, one of the Chicago Seven, says, "I had to fly back from Japan this past year to go to prison." The trial was cancelled, however, and David was released after only a few hours. Whether one thinks of David as infamous, or merely famous, one cannot deny that he has, and continues to have, an enormous living-color kind of life. Today, he calls himself an author, editor, teacher and nonviolent activist for justice and peace. Knowing him and his history, these titles prove to be only a small part of who he is.

The son of an affluent corporate attorney, David first became aware of society's wrongs at age thirteen when he fell in love with a poor Irish girl. "My mother discour-aged my relationship, and claimed that my sweetheart was a bad girl because, to use her words: 'I know the neighborhood she comes from.'" This incident taught David about economic and racial prejudices; it also helped to shape the rest of his life.

His formal education took place at Yale, where he received a bachelor's degree in 1936. He also studied at Oxford University, and took courses at Yale Divinity School and Union Theological Seminary for a year and a half. On his resume, however, he first lists the places where he received his informal education: Danbury Federal Correctional Institute and Lewisburg Federal Penitentiary, where he served three years for refusing to register for the WW II draft. When the draft law was passed in August 1940, David would

Accompanied by their attorney William Kunstler, Abbie Hoffman, David Dellinger and Jerry Rubin (left to right) arrive at U.S. Court House on March 22, 1969, to face charges stemming from the riots of the 1968 Democratic National Convention. *(photo courtesy of David)*

227

have been exempt from military service because he was a divinity student; all he had to do was register. But, "I saw the draft both as a coercive militaristic intrusion into the lives of the country's young males and as a calculated preparation for America's entry into a war that I didn't believe in. My exemption bothered me because it represented the same old business of my childhood all over again. It meant being treated, once again, as if I were somehow better than 'ordinary people' and that I deserved privileges that were denied to them."

To express his opposition to both the draft and the privileged exemption, David refused to register. Instead of choosing to continue his education, he chose to be sentenced to federal prison to live among hardened criminals. This was David's first time in prison, but not his last. As he puts it, he had "occasional refresher courses in other jails."

While incarcerated, David established friendships with some very tough criminals and learned that underneath, these men could be loving people. He believes in nonviolence and love as the most effective ways to resist injustice and to help its perpetrators and its victims. Even today, he regularly visits several long-term prisoners, serves on the Educational Advisory Board of a local prison and performs other volunteer work with prisoners and ex-prisoners.

A veteran of countless demonstrations and public protests, David is most famous for his anti-Vietnam War protests, especially the demonstration at the 1968 Democratic Convention in Chicago. The story varies, but on August 28, 1968, members of the anti-war movement gathered in Grant and Lincoln Parks in Chicago to protest for peace and the end of the war in Vietnam. Twelve thousand police, 7,500 Army troops and 6,000 National Guardsmen were also there. The press originally showed up to report on the Democratic Convention, but the news headlines came instead from what happened in the streets. In full view of the television cameras, widespread chaos reigned as the protest for peace turned to violence.

Chicago became a war zone. Although no lives were lost, hundreds of protesters were arrested, and both police and protesters were injured. Seven of the demonstrators were later tried together for conspiracy to incite a riot. The seven were Abbie Hoffman, Jerry Rubin, Rennie Davis, Tom Hayden, John Friones, Lee Weiner and David Dellinger. This group came to be known as the Chicago Seven. Bobby Seale, chairman of the Black Panther Party, was also involved, but his case was separated from the rest. Five were found guilty, though their sentences were later overturned on appeal. The media concentrated so much on the trial that it turned the Chicago Seven into prominent figures.

Things have quieted down a little for David and his wife, Elizabeth, who he met at a student movement in 1942 and married two weeks later. An activist herself, Elizabeth's main regret from her own long and interesting life is that she "has never been in prison." They both dart around the house with the energy and vitality of people half their ages. "Our lives have been so busy and fulfilling that the idea of retirement is out of the question." They still protest issues of importance to them, and they lecture at both American and foreign colleges, churches, spiritual centers, civic organizations and political events. David has published his memoirs, *From Yale To Jail*, and

David Dellinger, one of the "Chicago Seven," is still protesting at age 84.

Elizabeth is currently working on her autobiography. Sitting in her cozy rocker next to a pot-bellied stove in their rural Vermont home, Elizabeth says cheerfully, "It's the contact we have had with all the young people—their spirit is what keeps us going."

"What I've learned is you have to listen to people and keep learning new things all the time," says David, who quickly adds, "but still form your own judgment. Young people often have more to teach me than I do them. I certainly learn a lot from my own children and grandchildren." David and Elizabeth have six children (the last three were born at home with David acting as a mid-husband), fourteen grandchildren and three great-grandchildren.

David always knew the importance of leading a life that reflected his values. He speaks about this often, telling others that, "People should live their lives in accordance with the way they think society *should* be." David, more than most, has practiced what he preaches.

It Was a Great War for Journalists

"*I* remember listening to the 'whump-whump' of the rotor blades beating the air as Larry, Henri, Kent and Keizaburp took off in a helicopter," David says as his voice quavers. "I was supposed to be on that helicopter, but there wasn't enough room for me." He is referring to Larry Burrows, Henri Huet, Kent Potter and Keizaburp Shimamoto, four of the war's best known combat photographers. David, also a combat photographer, was covering the war for *Time* and *Life* magazines. "Their helicopter flew right into North Vietnamese anti-aircraft gunfire. A few moments after it took off, the chopper was hit, burst into flames and crashed. Their remains still lie somewhere in the thick of the jungle, about nine miles west of the Vietnam-Laos border."

During wartime, news photographers know that their jobs put their lives at risk—that they may be sacrificing their lives for a photograph. They are confronted with this truth each and every time they are pinned down in a rice paddy, below a merciless sun, hearing bombs striking in the distance. "Watching the randomness of the incoming artillery rounds was incredibly wearing. The 'pop-pop-pop' of gunfire is a sound I'll never forget." David shakes his head, his voice a little tight. "After you've been in Vietnam long enough, you go through a baptism of sorts that keeps you from freaking out every time a shell hits." Many photographers learn to deal with the rushing adrenaline of a combat situation by holding a camera to their eye. This simple act made them feel invisible and temporarily removed from the horror.

David, who graduated with a political science degree from Colorado College in 1968, did not have to go into the service. He could have avoided Vietnam altogether because a back injury made him exempt; instead, he chose to go as a photojournalist. He landed in Saigon in October 1970 to work on the assignment "Children of War" for *Time* magazine.

"It was a great war for journalists. If you didn't get killed in Vietnam, it was a charming place to be. It had all the elements of a Bogart movie." A forced smile touches David's lips. "The entire country was your subject, available 24 hours a day, seven days a week." David and other journalists working in the South could photograph men dying in battle by simply grabbing a cab outside their hotel room to get to the closer battles or by taking a helicopter to the front lines for the battles farther away. Then they could return to tea and toast served on white linen tablecloths adorned with delicate floral decorations. The North Vietnamese photographers were not as privileged. They were soldiers first and journalists second. In the grueling heat of the jungle, they wore uniforms, carried AK-47s and cameras. In the shadows of the forests and the rice paddies, they performed makeshift camera repairs and processed and printed photographs. A far cry from white linen tablecloths.

David left the battlegrounds of Vietnam in October 1972. "I never planned on having a career as a combat photographer, so when I got home I started looking for something else to do. I began freelancing and in late 1975 co-founded Contact Press Images, a photojournalist agency that distributes pictures worldwide." Since his experiences in Vietnam, David has worked in more than 60 other countries, where he photographed not only people at war, but also presidents, movie stars, kings and queens, and even the Pope. His work can be seen in the world's leading newspapers and magazines. The recipient of numerous awards, he now spends most of his time photographing feature stories and advertising. "I was married in 1984 and have a 25-year-old stepson and a twelve-year-old daughter. I don't accept assignments any more that take me away from home for a long time. I now choose to spend my time with my family in Virginia, not in a foreign war zone."

The Vietnam War, the most reported conflict in history, drew journalists and photographers from 22 countries. All told, 2,000 American journalists were stationed in Vietnam from 1954 to 1975. Forty-four were killed and 18 are still listed as missing. Their images and stories depicting the torment, pain, exhaustion and despair of this war continue to educate and intrigue the present generation and will endure for generations to come.

David is a photojournalist who voluntarily went to war. His weapon—a camera.

Turn Back
the Clock

*B*ill grew up in small-town America, and although he was born after World War II ended, he did not escape that war's wrath. "My father spent four years in the infantry and brought his all-consuming rage from the battlefields of Europe home to Indiana." Bill's face turns pale while he shares the experiences of his youth— experiences that deeply influenced the rest of his life. "We lived in a prison of chaos and unpredictability. I never knew which man I was coming home to—the loving dad or the violent father." Unlike most other rage-filled homes, theirs was free of booze and drugs, and even cigarettes and dancing. "Religion was the only thing allowed."

The one positive thing in young Bill's life was music. By the time he was fifteen, Bill and his brother Wayne were performing professionally at local country clubs. As things were finally starting to look up for the teenager, news of the war in Vietnam began to take center stage. "I knew I wouldn't go to fight, so I enrolled in college to get a deferment." Bill went to school during the day and performed up to six nights a week in clubs. Then, in one chance meeting, his whole life changed. Bill met six strangers who were headed west and they invited him to go to California with them. He packed up a few musical instruments, grabbed some money, and left his childhood behind without a look backward.

"My career took off quickly. I was playing piano for Linda Ronstandt and soon be- came her musical director." As Bill's career escalated, so too, did the amount of letters he received from the draft board. No longer in school, he was now rated 1A—eligible for the draft. "Just as we were about to go on the Steve Allen Show, Linda got a call from the FBI, and she dismissed me." That phone call changed everything; Bill was now on the run. "I was under a lot of pressure from my family to give it up, but the more I learned about the war from activists and returning vets, the more hardened I became against the military." Bill leans firmly back into his chair. "The idea of a five-year jail sen-

A musician and soldier, Bill, shown here in 1972, went AWOL to avoid being sent to Vietnam. *(photo courtesy of Bill)*

tence and a ten thousand dollar fine for objecting to military duty was never part of the equation."

Bill headed to New York. "At first I was panhandling for pizza money during the day and sleeping in phone booths at night. But after a few amazing connections, I landed a job as Janis Joplin's musical director. Shortly afterward, I came to the realization that I would never get ahead in my fairly public career if the FBI was always on my heels." Bill decided to head home to Indiana to try to

In the late 1960s, Bill was given the opportunity of a lifetime: he was asked to be Janis Joplin's musical director. This rather high-profile job was short-lived because the FBI was hot on his trail for draft evasion. Today, Bill continues his musical career in Canada.

resolve the draft issue. "It was resolved all right. On January 2, 1969, there I was, a hippie draft dodger wearing long hair and satin pants on a bus headed to Fort Knox." Five weeks after basic training, Bill sat in the day hall of the base watching Janis Joplin and her new band playing some of his arrangements on the Ed Sullivan Show.

"I lucked out and got a job in the service as a musician." Bill played piano for the officers, many whom had served in Vietnam. "Some of them privately shared horror stories of the battlefields of Vietnam with me. They swore they would never go back." He also played at the VA hospital. "I saw the war veterans dumped in the back wards, left alone and screaming in pain. These experiences strengthened my anti-war beliefs."

Bill and his girlfriend, Kristine, were married that June and were able to live off base, near Fort Campbell, Kentucky. But soon afterward, Bill was ordered to Vietnam. "I told them I wouldn't kill anyone and I tried desperately to get a compassionate reassignment—DENIED. Or an assignment to another country—DENIED. Or conscientious objector status—DENIED." Two weeks later, Bill was ordered to report to Fort Dix before being sent to Vietnam. Thousands of anti-war protesters were marching on the fort the day he and his wife arrived, and because of the possible threat of violence, Bill and Kristine were told they would not be allowed to spend their last night together as promised. "I totally freaked out. The only good thing in my life was Kristine. How could I say goodbye so suddenly, in only a few minutes? I cried so hard." Bill will never forget what happened next. "Kristine looked up at me and said, 'What are you going to do? Whatever you decide, I'm going with you.' I quickly changed into my civilian clothes. We were smuggled out of Fort Dix by one of the protesters. And with 90 dollars to our names, we hitched a ride to New York and another to Canada."

The couple made the best of the difficult situation, settled into their new home in Toronto, Canada, and in 1972 had a son, Jesse. "I eventually got work as the co-musical director of the *Jesus Christ Superstar* musical. Then one day, to my total disbelief, it was *deja vu*. The FBI had illegally crossed the Canadian border to try to kidnap me and bring me back to the States." Bill was warned, and he evaded them.

Bill and Kristine's lives eventually fell into place. Bill worked as a studio musician, made record deals, did commercial TV and radio, and played with various bands. In 1977, when President Carter introduced blanket amnesty for all draft offenders, he and his family decided to return to the States. "Whether you've been away to Vietnam or to Canada, it's hard to go back. Time factors into it. For me, it was eight years of my life and things in America had changed so much." Bill received varied responses to his homecoming. Some were overjoyed to see him, and some refused to look him in the face.

Bill and his family settled in California. "They were good times. I worked as the musical director for the Pointer Sisters for a while, then moved to Atlanta to manage a music studio." In 1980, they decided to return permanently to Canada. "The spirit in America had changed since the end of the war," Bill explains their decision. Once back in Canada, Bill started his own record label, a nationally-syndicated radio show, and created *The Jazz Report*, a magazine with a circulation of 7,000.

After all the years of alternating hard times and good times, Bill states confidently and without hesitation, "If I had the chance to turn back the clock, if I could choose again on that day in Fort Dix, I would absolutely do the same thing again."

Two Tall
White People

"It's funny where life takes you. My dad was a World War II veteran. I was an only child. Who would have thought that I would have voluntarily gone into a war zone after hearing his war stories?" Maddy pauses as she reflects on the hours she spent sitting by her father's side as he shared his war stories.

Maddy's experience in a war zone was quite different from her father's. She did not go to war as a soldier like her father, or as a nurse, Red Cross worker or journalist like other women. She went as a civilian. She accompanied her husband, Ken, who worked in Saigon as a systems analyst, and their two-month-old son, Shaun. "Ken and I met in Rhode Island a month after my dad passed away, and we were married a year later. At that time, there were a lot of ads in the newspapers encouraging people to work on government contracts in Vietnam. It was a great deal, because if you worked there for more than 18 months, your earnings were then tax free. At first we all moved to Hawaii, and Ken commuted back and forth to Vietnam. This separation soon became too much for us, so Shaun and I followed him to Vietnam in December 1967."

They landed in Saigon and were immediately whisked away to their new home—a company-owned villa. "The transition period was really tough, especially with an infant. Even though we were living in what seemed like a mansion, there were no screens on the windows. I had no

As civilians in Vietnam, Maddy, Ken and Shaun endured many of the hardships of war, but Maddy feels that their experiences made them people of character. Here they are with their maid and her family—an extended family of sorts—in Saigon in 1968. *(photo courtesy of Maddy)*

way to do laundry, and nothing we needed was ready-made. We had to hire a maid, a driver and a cook. I had to cut a photo out of a magazine to show to a carpenter so I could get a crib made for my son."

Less than two months after their arrival, on January 31, 1968, all hell broke loose in Saigon. The Tet Offensive created chaos and the city's residents were bristling with tension and fear. "There was no gas for cooking and no milk for Shaun. There was a 24-hour curfew—we couldn't even stick our heads out of our windows." Their villa was near the Presidential Palace—not an ideal place to live when the city is being bombarded with rockets—so they moved to another area farther away from the danger. "It's strange to look back from the safety of our home today, and try to explain why we didn't return to the States right then and there. But I guess it's human nature, you're there and your life is threatened, and somehow you adjust."

Once Tet ended, they settled into a somewhat regular routine. "Ken worked all day, and I was left at home with not much to do. I needed more stimulation, so I decided to take a job as a secretary. Shaun was two years old and his perception of our arrangement must have been pretty comical. He lived like a Vietnamese kid day and night. My blond-haired son spent all of his time with our maid and her family, and he spoke only Vietnamese. From Shaun's perspective, Ken and I were these two tall, round-eyed, white people who came home every night and tucked him into bed."

Saigon itself held all the intrigue, passion and insanity of a wartime capital. In the morning before sunrise, people were out on the street performing their slow dance-like *tai chi* exercises, and as soon as the sun rose those same streets teemed with bustling activity: girls wearing sheer *ao dais*, street hawkers selling everything imaginable, beggars tugging at passersby, uniformed soldiers carrying guns, old men pulling carts and young women dodging traffic on their bicycles. "Our life in Vietnam was good, yet lonely and isolated. There were the great restaurants, the French club with its gorgeous swimming pool and the fabulously glitzy nightclubs. But there was always the heat of the day. That heat wore at your body and soul. We always had curfews. We often went without electricity for long periods. And we had to filter our drinking water."

"I came from a working-class, blue-collar background and had practically never left home before I went to Vietnam. Vietnam showed me the wealth and privilege we really had back in America. It taught me to cherish my blue passport with the eagle on it, an eagle that meant freedom. We could leave anytime we wanted. The Vietnamese, on the other hand, were trapped by the decisions made between the Super Powers."

When Ken's contract ran out in January 1970, they left Vietnam. "We couldn't find jobs in Massachusetts, our home state, so we went to California. Ken landed a job as the director of a computer company. In 1975—the same year South Vietnam fell to the

Communists—our daughter Meghan was born." The stress they had endured over the years began to wear on their marriage and, by 1985, they were divorced.

Maddy remarried in 1987. Her new husband, Bob, died of a brain tumor in 1994, leaving her bereft. After his death, Maddy saved enough money to return to Massachusetts and buy a two-family house. Then she started thinking about what she should do with the rest of her life. "When I was young, I had been a cheerleader, a model and a secretary. Back then I didn't think, or really care much, about the rest of the world. But my experiences in Vietnam changed all that. I fell in love with the Vietnamese culture and the people. Their kindnesses helped to shape and form the rest of my life. I think I have more character and more empathy with the human race because of those few years I spent there. So, I decided to do some volunteer work with the Vietnamese in America." Maddy is now the director of education for a non-profit human services agency and works primarily with Southeast Asians.

Today, Maddy and Ken are together again, years after they divorced. Here they are with Shaun. He and his sister live nearby.

Ken stayed in California after their marriage fell apart, but years after their divorce, he called Maddy out of the blue. He wanted to know if there was any chance they could still be friends. "He called every Tuesday night for the next year. This gave us the chance to hash out a lot of things that we could not have years earlier. Then he came here to visit. I would have never thought this could have happened, but we are back together again, and things are really great. Shaun and Meghan are grown up, live close by and we are all a family again."

He Turned and Didn't Look Back

*T*he Vietnam War can be described as two separate wars—the one fought on the battlefields of Vietnam and the second fought on the streets and campuses of America. Millions of Americans waged the largest and most effective anti-war movement in United States history. They demonstrated in rallies, burned their draft cards and refused to join the armed forces, preferring jail or exile to Canada or Sweden. According to figures compiled by the Departments of Defense and Justice, the number of "draft dodgers" totaled 570,000 men. Jack was one of these young men.

"Funny where life's trail leads you." Jack's began in Philadelphia in 1945 with a bloodline going back to the Mayflower. "I was raised an all-American. I was an Eagle Scout, class president, prom king and a three-letter athlete in high school. I even earned a commission in ROTC at the University of Wisconsin." A wry smile crosses Jack's face, "So how did my patriotic life's trail lead to the Canadian border?"

By 1968, Jack had finished four years in ROTC and was commissioned a second lieutenant. He went on to graduate studies in American history. "By this time, I had a tremendous need to understand what the war was really all about. I began my quest by gathering evidence. I read the newspapers and magazines, went to all the demonstrations and watched the six o'clock news. All the contradictions, all the lies and deceit slowly became apparent and transformed me."

"I felt like one little guy in a big tidal wave. I kept asking myself, 'What does a patriotic human being do when his country asks him to commit war crimes?'" Jack sits back and stares off into the distance, "It's always easier to answer these questions *after* the war, not when you are in the middle of it."

"When I got my orders to report to Fort Gordon, Georgia, I packed a few clothes, some books, my dog Freddie and headed north instead. When I crossed the Canadian border on that sunny June day in 1970, it was raining in my heart. I remember

Instead of being sent to Vietnam, Jack left his loving family behind and took sanctuary in Toronto with his dog, Freddie. *(photo courtesy of Jack)*

saying to myself, 'What do I do now—no home, no friends, no family, no job? Why am I doing this? Because I don't want to kill someone?' I said goodbye to my homeland, turned and didn't look back."

Jack and Freddie settled in Toronto for the next seven-and-a-half years. He worked as an editor of AMEX-Canada (Americans in Exile in Canada) and finished his Ph.D. Jack became a prominent exile leader. He traveled throughout Europe and gave dozens of interviews, often appearing on the morning and evening news shows. He also participated in the Academy Award-nominated documentary *The War at Home*.

"When *Newsweek* magazine published their July 4, 1976 special bicentennial issue entitled *OUR AMERICA, A Self-Portrait at 200*, I was chosen to represent one of the nearly 50 people portraying the voice of America. There was The Hillbilly, The Boston Housewife, The Indian and me—The Deserter."

"I was an only child and was very close to both my parents. My dad had died when I was in Wisconsin. When I lived in Canada, I didn't have much money, so I didn't phone home often, but my mom and I wrote to each other three or four times a week. Then one day the phone rang. My mother had died. I was torn apart. I didn't know what to do. If I went to my mother's funeral, I would be put in jail. I didn't go."

In 1977, a blanket amnesty for all draft offenders was introduced by President Jimmy Carter. In December of that same year, two months after Freddie died, Jack crossed onto American soil. "I came home to no one and to nothing." For a minute or two, Jack is silent. "The only thing I knew for sure was that I needed to live within walking distance of the Library of Congress. I bought a little house in D.C. and have worked as a writer ever since."

"I was taught to love my country, but my country was fighting a war that by its very nature was criminal. This led me into a collision course with my government. My government considered me a traitor, a deserter, an outlaw." His voice thickens, "I don't believe I betrayed my country. I believe the leaders of my country betrayed my country's values. The decision I made almost 30 years ago was right for me. I feel sad about being in exile and not being with my mother when she died. But, I feel proud of my choice." Jack has received many death threats since his return to America.

Jack took advantage of President Carter's amnesty offer in 1977 and returned to the States, but with no one to embrace him. His father had died before he left for Canada, and his mother died during his absence. Today, Jack lives in Washington, where he is a writer.

CHINA BEACH

*S*and filters softly between my toes. I am on China Beach, the central coastline of Vietnam. The sea is flat. The sand is empty of footprints. A few sea baskets dot the miles of the white blanket of sand that form the beach. I feel the gentleness of the wind as I walk toward the sea.

I bend down and touch the sand. It smells sweetly of innocence and purity. The sand has forgotten the time when it smelled of violence and suffering and was soaked with blood and death. It has been able to forget, because the waves of time removed all evidence of the past.

I slowly drop to my knees and dig a hole deep enough to reach the old sand and I search my pocket for a letter I wrote in America. The letter describes the remorse and great pain I feel over my actions during the war—the letter asks for forgiveness. I place my letter into the hole and cover it with fresh, new sand. I sit silently. I cry.

I resume my walk. I smell the sea and feel the sand filtering softly between my toes. I look back over my unburdened shoulders and know that the circle is now complete. That I, and maybe someday all veterans from both countries, will be able to let go of the past and live in peace.

Finally.

RESOURCE GUIDE

This resource guide lists names and addresses of certified individuals and agencies that provide support services to those needing assistance in healing the wounds of war. Services include education, medical treatment, funding and counseling, including treatment for post-traumatic stress disorder and recovery programs for Americans, Amerasians and Vietnamese who live in the United States.

This resource guide is a list of sources, but is not necessarily an endorsement of these individuals or groups.

Five men reunited for the first time since the battlefields of Vietnam share warm embraces.

Veteran Support Services

ALCOHOL AND DRUG DEPENDENCY:

Al-Anon
Referral service for support
group meetings
(800) 344-2666

**Alcohol and Drug
Dependence Treatment**
Veterans Administration Office
US Department of Veterans Affairs
810 Vermont Avenue, NW
Washington, DC 20420
(202) 872-1151

Alcohol and Drug Helpline
(800) 821-4357

**Alcohol and Drug
Referral Hotline**
Information and referrals
(800) 252-6465

**American Council on
Alcoholism**
(800) 527-5344

**American Psychological
Association**
Consumer Help Line
(800) 964-2000
www.apa.org

**Drug Rehabilitation Services
Office for Children
and Families**
US Department of Health
and Human Services
200 Independent Ave, SW
Washington, DC 20201
(202) 205-8347

**National Institute on Drug Abuse
Hotline/HHS**
Information and referrals
(800) 662-HELP

**VA Drug and Alcohol Dependent
Treatment Programs**
810 Vermont Avenue, NW
Washington, DC 20420
(202) 233-4000

ARCHIVES:

Air Force History Support Office
200 McChord Street
Box 94
Bowlling Airforce Base, DC
20332-1111
(202) 404-2264

Marine Corps Historical Center
1254 Charles Morris Street
Washington Navy Yard, DC
20374-5040
(202) 433-3534

**National Archives of the United
States, Military Records**
8601 Adelphi Road
College Park, MD 20740
(301) 713-7250

**US Army Center of
Military History**
Bldg. 35
Fort McNair, DC 20319-5058

**Vietnam Archive, Texas Tech
University Library**
PO Box 41045
Lubbock, TX 79409-1045
(806) 742-3742

CHILDREN AND FAMILIES OF VIETNAM VETERANS:

The Access Group
Information on technology
services and devices, etc.,
for disabled children
(770) 514-7454

**Association of Birth Defect
Children (ABDC)**
930 Woodcock Road, Suite 225
Orlando, FL 32803
(407) 245-7035
hotline: (800) 313-2232
www.birthdefects.org

Among the emotional tributes and remembrances left behind at the Moving Walls is this lone card expressing years of unimaginable grief and sadness.

Federal Benefits for Veterans and Dependents
Superintendent of Documents
US Government Printing Office
Washington, DC 20402
(202) 512-1800

Gold Star Mothers
2128 Leroy Place, NW
Washington, DC 20008-1893
(202) 265-0991

Gold Star Wives
5510 Columbia Pike, Suite 205
Arlington, VA 22204
(703) 998-0064
(888) GSW-9788

Medical Care for Dependents or Survivors
US Department of Veterans
Affairs Medical Center
1055 Clermont Street
Denver, CO 80220
(303) 782-3800

Sons and Daughters In Touch
PO Box 1596
Arlington, VA 22210
(800) 984-9994
www.sdit.org

Veterans' Families of America
Albuquerque, NM
(888) 289-0953

CONGRESSIONAL COMMITTEES:

Bipartisan Veterans' Health-care Coalition
2134 Rayburn House Office
Washington, DC 20515
(202) 225-6416

House Committee on Veterans Affairs
335 Cannon Hob
Washington, DC 20515
(202) 225-3527
www.veterans.house.gov

Senate Committee on Veterans Affairs
Russell Building, Room 412
Washington, DC 20510
(202) 224-9126
www.senate.gov/~veterans

HOMELESS:

Center For Veterans Issues, Ltd.
3330 West Wells Street
Milwaukee, WI 53208
(414) 342-4284

HUD/VET Resource Center
PO Box 7189
Gaithersberg, MD 20898-7189
(800) 998-9999

National Coalition for Homeless Veterans
333 1/2 Pennsylvania
Avenue, SE
Washington, DC 20003-1148
(800) VET-HELP
www.nchv.org

WARE
2669 North Martin Luther
King Drive
Milwaukee, MI 53212

HUMANITARIAN:

American Red Cross
(800) HELP-NOW

Army Emergency Relief
(703) 545-6700

Gulf War Resource Center
(202) 628-2700 ext. 162
National Marrow Donor Program
(800) 654-1247

Operation Smile
(757) 625-0375

LEGAL:

Appealing Veterans Benefits Claims
Veterans Assistance Office
US Dept. of Veterans Affairs
810 Vermont Ave, NW
Washington, DC 20420
(202) 872-1151

National Organizations for Vets Advocates
Private attorneys representing
vets with disability claims
PO Box 2099
Topeka, KS 66601
(800) 810-VETS

US Court of Appeals for Veterans Claims
625 Indiana Avenue, Suite 900
Washington, DC 20004
(202) 501-5970
http://www.vetapp.uscourts.gov

LOCATOR AND REUNION SERVICES:

Army Worldwide Locator
US Army Enlisted Records
and Evaluation Center
8899 East 56 Street
Indianapolis, Indiana 46249-5301
(703) 325-3732

Wreckage of this B-52 in Hanoi is a permanent reminder of the war.

Navy Times Locator Services
6883 Commercial Drive
Springfield, VA 22159
(703) 750-8636

Services Reunions
(512) 438-4177
http://amf.org/text/8-56.htm

MINORITY VETERANS:

**Alaska Natives Prevention
and Treatment Services**
US Department of Health
and Human Services
5600 Fishers Lane
Rockville, MD 20857
(301) 443-1087

**American G.I. Forum-National
Veterans Outreach**
206 San Pedro, Suite 200
San Antonio, TX 78205
(210) 223-4088

Black Veterans for Social Justice
25 Chapel Street
Brooklyn, NY 11201
(718) 935-1116
http:/home.netcm.com/~blackvet/

**National Association of Black
Veterans**
3312 West Wells Street
Milwaukee, WI 53208
(414) 342-8387

Navajo Nations Veterans
PO Box 9000
Window Rock, AZ 86515
(520) 871-7914
www.navajo.org

POW/MIA:

**Defense POW/Missing
Personnel Office**
2400 Defense Pentagon
Washington, DC 20301-2400
(703) 602-2102
www.dtic.mil/dpmo

**National League of Families
of American Prisoners and
Missing in Southeast Asia**
1001 Connecticut Avenue, NW
Suite 919
Washington, DC 20036
(202) 223-6846
24 hour update hotline:
(202) 659-0133
www.pow-miafamilies.org

**VVA National POW/MIA
Committee**
1224 M Street, NW
Washington, DC 20005
(202) 628-2700 (ext. 111)
http://www.vva.org

POST-TRAUMATIC
STRESS DISORDER:

**American Psychological
Association**
Consumer Help Line:
(800) 964-2000
www.apa.org

**VA Affiliated National Center
For PTSD**
Locations in MA, VT, CT, HI
and CA
(617) 232-9500
www.dartmouth.edu/dms/ptsd

**VA Facilities for veterans
and dependents**
Call (800) 827-1000 for the
facility nearest to you

**VA Readjustment
Counseling Service**
Department of Veterans Affairs
810 Vermont Avenue, NW
Washington, DC 20420
(202) 273-8967

US DEPARTMENT OF
VETERANS AFFAIRS:

Department of Veterans Affairs
Office of Public Affairs
810 Vermont Avenue, NW
Washington, DC 20420
http://www.va.gov/
Benefits for veterans and dependents: (800) 827-1000

*(VA facilities are also listed in
the federal government section of
telephone directories, see:
Department of Veterans Affairs)*

**Agent Orange or Nuclear
Radiation Exposure:**
(202) 872-1151
Board of Veterans Appeals:
(202) 565-54436

**Central Office (main switch-
board):** (202) 273-5400
Center for Women Veterans:
(202) 273-6193
CHAMPVA: (800) 733-8387
Debt Management Center:
(800) 827-0648
Dental Treatment:
(202) 827-1151

Surrounded by hauntingly beautiful mountains, the airfield at Khe Sanh is still littered with bombs. Nothing has grown in the red soil since the war's end and the destruction and loss of thousands of lives is still felt in the air.

My Son served as the Cham intellectual and religious center from the 4th until the 13th century. After repeated pillaging in previous centuries by the Khmer, Chinese and Vietnamese, and bombing in the 20th century by Americans in response to the Viet Cong who used this site as a base during the war, only about 20 of the 68 original structures survive today.

Drug and Alcohol Dependent Treatment Programs: (202) 233-4000
Education and Training: (202) 872-1151
Educational Benefits: (888) 442-4551
Emergency Medical Preparedness: (304) 263-0811
Gulf War Helpline: (800) 749-8387
Headstones and Markers: (800) 697-6947
Health Benefits: (877) 222-8387
Life Insurance: (800) 669-8477
Loans: (202) 233-2044
Mammography Hotline: (888) 492-7844
Nursing Home Care: (202) 872-1151
Office of the Inspector General: (202) 565-8620
Office of the National Cemetery System: (800) 697-6947

Office of the Secretary: (202) 273-4800
Personnel Locator: (202) 273-4950
Readjustment Counseling Services: (202) 273-8967
Sexual Trauma Hotline: (800) 827-1000
TDD: (800) 829-4833
VA ON-LINE: (800) US1-VETS (871-8387)

VA Regional Offices, State by state:
All can be reached by calling (800) 827-1000

Alabama:
345 Perry Hill Road
Montgomery 36109

Alaska:
2925 DeBarr Road
Anchorage 99508-2989

Arizona:
3225 N. Central Avenue
Phoenix 85012

Arkansas:
Bldg. 65, Ft. Roots
PO Box 1280
North Little Rock 72115

California:
Federal Building
11000 Wilshire Blvd.
Los Angeles 90024

California:
8810 Rio San Diego Drive
San Diego 92108

California:
1301 Clay Street
Room 1300 North
Oakland 94612

Colorado:
155 Van Gordon Street
Denver 80225

Connecticut:
450 Main Street
Hartford 06103

Delaware:
1601 Kirkwood Hwy.
Wilmington 19805

District of Columbia:
1120 Vermont Avenue NW
Washington, DC 20421

Florida:
9500 Bay Pines Blvd.
St. Petersburg 33708

Georgia:
730 Peachtree Street, NE
Atlanta 30365

Hawaii:
PO Box 50188
300 Ala Moana Blvd., Rm. 1004
Honolulu 96850-001

Idaho:
805 West Franklin Street
Boise 83702

Illinois:
PO Box 8136
536 South Clark Street
Chicago 60680

Indiana:
575 North Pennsylvania Street
Indianapolis 46204

Iowa:
210 Walnut Street
Des Moines 50309

Kansas:
5500 East Kellogg
Wichita 67218

Kentucky:
545 South Third Street
Louisville 40202

Louisiana:
701 Loyola Avenue
New Orleans 70113

Maine:
1 VA Center
Togus 04330

Maryland:
31 Hopkins Plaza Federal
    Building
Baltimore 21201

Massachusetts:
JFK Federal Building
Government Center
Boston 02203

Michigan:
Patrick V. McNamara Federal
    Building
477 Michigan Avenue
Detroit 48226

Minnesota:
Bishop Henry Whipple
    Federal Building
1 Federal Drive, Fort Snelling
St. Paul 55111

Mississippi:
1600 East Woodrow
    Willson Avenue
Jackson 39269

Missouri:
400 South 18th Street
St. Louis 63103

Montana:
William Street off Hwy. 12 West
Fort Harrison 59636

Nebraska:
5631 South 48 Street
Lincoln 68516

Nevada:
1201 Terminal Way
Reno 89520

New Hampshire:
Norris Cotton Federal Building
275 Chestnut Street
Manchester 03101

New Jersey:
20 Washington Place
Newark 07102

New Mexico:
Dennis Chavez Federal
    Building
500 Gold Avenue, SW
Albuquerque 87102

New York:
Federal Building
111 West Huron Street
Buffalo 14202

New York:
245 West Houston Street
New York City 10014

North Carolina:
Federal Building
251 North Main Street
Winston-Salem 27155

North Dakota:
2101 Elm Street
Fargo 58102

Ohio:
Anthony J. Celebrezze
    Federal Building
1240 East 9th Street
Cleveland 44199

Oklahoma:
Federal Building
125 South Main Street
Muskoguee 74401

Oregon:
Federal Building
1220 SW 3rd Avenue
Portland 97204

Pennsylvania:
RO and Insurance Center
PO Box 8079
5000 Wissachickon Avenue
Philadelphia 19101

Pennsylvania:
1000 Liberty Avenue
Pittsburgh 15222

Philippines:
1131 Roxas Blvd.
Manila 1000

Puerto Rico:
150 Carlos Chardon Avenue
Hato Rey
San Juian 00918

Rhode Island:
380 Westminster Mall
Providence 02908

South Carolina:
1801 Assembly Street
Columbia 29201

South Dakota:
PO Box 5046
2501 West 22 Street
Sioux Falls 57117

Tennessee:
110 9th Avenue South
Nashville 37203

Seven million tons of bombs were dropped on Vietnam, leaving behind a countryside pockmarked with some 20 million bomb craters of all sizes. In many cases, these depressions have filled with stagnant water over the years and now harbor malarial mosquitoes.

A counselor offers comfort to a troubled vet at one of the Moving Walls.

Virgin Islands:
9800 Buccaneer Mall, Suite 8
St. Thomas 00802

Washington:
Federal Building
915 2nd Avenue
Seattle 98174

West Virginia:
640 Fourth Avenue
Huntington 25701

Wisconsin:
5000 West National Avenue,
  Bldg. 6
Milwaukee 53295

Wyoming:
2360 East Pershing Blvd.
Cheyenne 82001

VIETNAM VETERANS MEMORIAL:

**Vietnam Veterans Memorial
  Fund**
1012 14th Street, NW,
  Suite 201
Washington, DC 20005
(202) 393-0090

VIETNAM VETERANS OF AMERICA:

**Vietnam Veterans of
  America. Inc.**
1224 M Street, NW
Washington, DC 20005
(800) VVA-1316
http://www.vva.org

WOMEN VETERANS:

Center for Women Veterans
Department of Veterans Affairs
Washington, DC 20420
(202) 273-6193

**Women in Military Service for
America Memorial Foundation**
(703) 533-1155
www.womensmemorial.org
Memorial is located at the
  ceremonial entrance to
  Arlington National Cemetery

**Vietnam Women's Memorial
  Project**
2001 S Street, NW,
  Suite 610
Washington, DC 20009
(202) 328-7253
http://members.aol.com/vwm-
  pdc/Home.htm
Also offers a sister search
  program

OTHERS ON THE INTERNET:

**Advocacy and Intelligence Index
  for POW/MIA**
http://www.aiipowmia.com/

**AVVA (Associates of Vietnam
  Veterans of America)**
www.avva.org

Children of Vietnam Vets
www.geocities.com/pentagon/9125

**National Association of State
  Directors of Veterans Affairs
  (NASDVA)**
www.nasdva.com

**National Conference of Vietnam
  Veteran Ministers**
vetlady40@aol.com

**State Departments of
  Veterans Affairs**
http://www.nasdva.org

**Uniformed Services Family
  Health Plan (USFHP)**
http://www.usfhp.com

**US Court of Appeals for
  Veterans Claims**
http://www.vetapp.uscourts.gov

VVA National Office
www.vva.org

Texas:
6900 Almeda Road
Houston 777030

Texas:
One Veterans Plaza
701 Clay
Waco 76799

Utah:
PO Box 11500
Federal Building
125 South State Street
Salt Lake City 84147

Vermont:
215 North Main Street
White River Junction 05009

Virginia:
210 Franklin Road, SW
Roanoke 24011

Virgin Islands:
Box 12, RR 02
Village Mall
St. Croix 00850

Vietnamese and Amerasian Support Services

ARIZONA:

Tucson International Alliance of Refugee Communities
4228 East Grand Road,
Suite 4-B
Tucson, AZ 85712
P: (520) 881-4404
F: (520) 881-4191

CALIFORNIA:

Asian American Resource Center
1115 South E Street
San Bernadino, CA 92408
P: (909) 383-0164
F: (909) 383-7687

Asian Pacific Residential Treatment Program
1665 West Adams Blvd.
Los Angeles, CA 90007
P: (213) 731-3534
F: (213) 731-5618

East Bay Vietnamese Association
1218 Miller Avenue
Oakland, CA 94601
P: (510) 533-4224
F: (510) 533-4219
ebva@aol.com

Fresno Center for New Americans
4879 East King's Canyon Road
Fresno, CA 93727
P:(559) 225-8395
F: (559) 255-1656
fc039@fresno.com

Hmong American Women's Association, Inc.
4871 East King's Canyon Road
Fresno, CA 93727
P: (559) 251-9566
F: (559) 251-9511

Indochinese Resettlement and Cultural Center, Inc.
399 West San Carlos
San Jose, CA 95110
P: (408) 971-7857
F: (408) 971-7882
ircc@irccsj.com

International Mutual Assistance Association
4102 El Cajon Boulevard
San Diego, CA 92105
P: (619) 584-4018
F: (619) 584-3855
imaa@cts.com

Lao Family Community Development, Inc.
1551 23rd Avenue,
2nd floor
Oakland, CA 94606
P: (510) 533-8850
F: (510) 533-1516

Lao Family Community of Fresno, Inc.
4903 East Kings Canyon Road,
Suite 281
Fresno, CA 93727
P: (559) 453-9775
F: (559) 453-9705

A serene site today, the Hien Luong Bridge crosses the flowing waters of the Ben Hai River. Before it was bombed by the Americans, the original bridge at this site was painted red on its northern half and yellow on its southern, representing the demarcation line separating North and South Vietnam.

On the morning of April 30, 1975, the first Communist tanks crashed through the wrought-iron gates of the Presidential Palace in Saigon, and the South Vietnamese transferred power to the North, marking the war's end. Twenty-five years later, in front of these same gates, speeches, performances and a parade commemorate the anniversary with a celebration.

Lao Family Community
of Stockton, Inc.
807 N. San Joaquin Street,
  Suite 211
Stockton, CA 95202
P: (209) 466-0721
F: (209) 466-6567

Merced Lao Family
Community, Inc.
855 West 15th Street
Merced, CA 95340
P: (209) 384-7384
F: (209) 384-1911

Southeast Asian Assistant Center
5625 24th Street
Sacramento, CA 95822
P: (916) 421-1036
F: (916) 421-6731

Southeast Asian
Community Center
875 O'Farrell Street
San Francisco, CA 94109
P: (415) 885-2743
F: (415) 885-3253

Southeast Asian
Community Center
1415 Knoll Circle, Suite #108
San Jose, CA 95112
P: (408) 436-8438
F: (408) 436-8745

The Cambodian Family
1111 East Wakeham Avenue,
  Suite E
Santa Ana, CA 92705
P: (714) 571-1966
F: (714) 571-1974

The Union of Pan Asian
Communities
1031 25th Street
San Diego, CA 92102
P: (619) 232-6454
F: (619) 235-9002
mip@innercity.org

The Vietnamese Forum
2260 Quimby Road
San Jose, CA 95112
P: (408) 532-7755
vivoinfo@aol.com

United Cambodian
Community, Inc.
2338 East Anaheim Street,
  Suite 200
Long Beach, CA 90804
P: (562) 433-2490
F: (562) 433-0564

Unified Vietnamese
Community Council
709 North Hill Street,
  Suite 3
Los Angeles, CA 90012
P: (213) 680-1059
F: (213) 680-0087

Vietnam Chinese Mutual Aid
and Friendship Association
777 Stockton Street, #103
San Francisco, CA 94108
P: (415) 398-3726
F: (415) 781-6428

Vietnamese American
Chamber of Commerce
in Orange County
9121 Bolsa Avenue,
  Suite 203
Westminster, CA 92683
P: (714) 892-6928
F: (714) 892-6938
vaccac@yahoo.com

Vietnamese Community of
Orange County, Inc.
1618 West First Street
Santa Ana, CA 92703
P: (714) 558-6009
F: (714) 558-6120
vncoc@aol.com

Vietnamese Family
Community, Inc.
2551 Mission Bell Drive
San Pablo, CA 94806
P: (510) 620-0458

Vietnamese Federation of
San Diego
7833 Linda Vista Road
San Diego, CA 92136
P: (858) 268-1204
F: (858) 277-6146

Vietnamese Mutual Association
7621 Westminster Avenue
Westminster, CA 92683
P: (714) 894-3120

Vietnamese Voluntary
Foundation
2260 Quimby Road
San Jose, CA 95112
P: (408) 532-7755
F: (408) 532-1699

Vietnamese Voluntary
Foundation, Inc.
111 North California Street
Stockton, CA 95202
P: (209) 466-0644
F: (209) 466-0687

Vietnamese Youth
Development Center
160 Eddy Street
San Francisco, CA 94102
P: (415) 771-2600
F: (415) 771-3917

Vietnam Human Rights Watch
1311 South Rebecca Street
Pomona, CA 90720
P: (909) 623-2709

COLORADO:

The Vietnamese
Friendships Association
of Colorado Springs
4720 Jenson Lane
Colorado Springs, CO 80922
P: (719) 574-9818
tranc.lhuan@yahoo.com

Vietnamese Elderly
Association of Colorado
615 South Federal Boulevard,
  #103-105
Denver, CO 80219
P: (303) 922-3033
F: (303) 922-3033

DISTRICT OF COLUMBIA:

Asian American LEAD
3045 15th Street, NW
Washington, DC 20009
P: (202) 884-0322
F: (202) 884-0012

**Newcomers Community
 Service Center**
1628 16th Street, NW
Washington, DC 20009
P: (202) 462-4330
F: (202) 462-2774

FLORIDA:

**Asian Family and Community
 Empowerment Center**
2201 First Avenue North
PO Box 7881
St. Petersburg, FL 33713
P: (727) 323-0350
F: (727) 321-7176
aface@ibm.net

**Association for the
 Advancement of
 Vietnamese Americans**
3531 25th Avenue, North
St. Petersburg, FL 33713
P: (727) 321-1032
F: (727) 321-1032

HAWAII:

**Mutual Assistance
 Association Center**
1212 University Avenue
Honolulu, HI 96826
P: (808) 944-2610
phathana@kahala.net

ILLINOIS:

**East Central Illinois
 Refugee Mutual
 Assistance Center**
302 South Birch Street
Urbana, IL 61801
P: (217) 344-8455
F: (217) 344-8455

**Vietnamese Association
 of Illinois**
5252 North Broadway, 2nd floor
Chicago, IL 60640
P: (773) 728-3700
F: (773) 728-0497

KANSAS:

**Southeast Asian Mutual
 Assistance Association**
4101 East US Highway 50, Suite A
Garden City, KS 67846
P: (316) 275-2261
F: (316) 275-2672

**Vietnamese Mutual Association
 of Kansas**
2620 East Central
Wichita, KS 67214
P: (316) 686-5555
F: (316) 686-3440

Wichita Indochinese Center
2502 E. Douglas
Wichita, KS 67214
P: (316) 689-8729
F: (316) 689-8274

LOUISIANA:

Vietnamese Catholic Office
5069 Willowbrook Drive
New Orleans, LA 70129
P: (504) 254-5660
F: (504) 254-9250

MARYLAND:

**Maryland Vietnamese
 Mutual Association**
11501 Georgia Avenue, Suite 312
Wheaton, MD 20902
P: (301) 946-7911
F: (301) 942-1257

MASSACHUSETTS:

**Cambodian Mutual
 Assistance Association
 of Greater Lowell**
165 Jackson Street
Lowell, MA 01852
P: (978) 454-4286
F: (978) 454-1806
cmaa@cmaalowell.org

**Indochinese Refugees
 Foundation**
16 Rack Road
Chelmsford, MA 01824
P: (508) 934-4664
F: (508) 934-3084

**Springfield Vietnamese
 American Civic
 Association, Inc.**
433 Belmont Avenue
Springfield, MA 01108
P: (413) 733-9373
F: (413) 737-3419

**Viet-AID/Vietnamese American
 Initiative for Development**
1452 Dorchester Avenue,
 3rd Floor
Dorchester, MA 02122
P: (617) 822-3717
F: (617) 822-3718
Lnvietaid@aol.com

**Vietnamese American Civic
 Association**
1452 Dorchester Avenue,
 3rd Floor
Dorchester, MA 02122
P: (617) 288-7344
F: (617) 288-4860

MINNESOTA:

**Association for the Advancement
 of Hmong Women, Inc.**
1518 East Lake Street,
 Suite 209
Minneapolis, MN 55407
P: (612) 724-3066
F: (612) 724-3098

**Center for Asian
 Pacific Islanders**
3702 E. Lake Street,
 Suite 101
Minneapolis, MN 55406
P: (612) 721-0122
F: (612) 721-7054

**Intercultural Mutual
 Assistance Association**
16 Seventh Avenue, SW
Rochester, MN 55902
P: (507) 289-5960/292-6648
F: (507) 289-6199

**United Cambodian
 Association
 of Minnesota**
529 Jackson Street,
 Suite 221
St. Paul, MN 55101
P: (651) 222-3299
F: (651) 222-3599

**Vietnamese Minnesotans
 Association**
1030 University Avenue,
 Suite 160
St. Paul, MN 55104
P: (651) 290-4791
F: (651) 290-4785
vma@rptanet.org

Against all odds, two men—Toai, a former high commander of the Viet Cong, and Michael, a former U.S. army door gunner, display a close affection and a therapeutic embrace as they reminisce of times long ago.

Vietnamese Social Services of MN
1821 University Avenue, S-250
St. Paul, MN 55104
P: (651) 641-8907
F: (651) 641-8908

NEVADA:

Vietnamese Community Association of Southern Nevada
3300 Othello Drive
Las Vegas, NV 89121
P: (702) 734-3804
F: (702) 734-6948

NEW YORK:

Church Avenue Merchants Block Association, Inc.
1720 Church Avenue, 2/F
Brooklyn, 11226
(718) 287-2600

International Rescue Committee-NYC Refugee Employment Project
386 Park Avenue South
New York 10016
(212) 679-1105

The French-built Hoa Lo Prison became known to the world in the 1960s when American POWs were held there. Nicknamed the "Hanoi Hilton," and still in use until 1994, the property now contains a small museum and a 22-story hotel and office complex.

Key State Initiative Refugee Employment and Development Program of Bronx Community College
West 181 Street and University Avenue
Bronx 10453
(718) 731-5010

Refugee Assistance of the Flatbush Development Corporation
1033 Flatbush Avenue
Brooklyn 11226
(718) 469-8990

St. Rita's Asian Center
2342 Andrews Avenue
Bronx 10468
(718) 295-8175

Vietnamese American Cultural Organization
113 Baxter Street
New York, NY 10013
P: (212) 343-0762
F: (212) 343-0822

YMCA Elesair Project
215 West 23rd Street
New York 10011
(212) 255-4200

NORTH CAROLINA:

Montagnard Dega Association, Inc.
3116 Summit Avenue
Greensboro, NC 27405
P: (336) 375-8190
F: (336) 375-5614
mdadega@bellsouth.net

OKLAHOMA:

Asian American Service Association
11322 FE 21 Street
Tulsa, OK 74129
P: (918) 234-7431
F: (918) 234-3148

Vietnamese American Association
1444 NW 28th Street
Oklahoma City, OK 73106
P: (405) 524-2947/737-3902
F: (405) 524-2932/733-1721

Vietnamese American Association Refugee Center
919 NW 23rd Street,
Suite 101
Oklahoma City, OK 73106
P: (405) 524-3088
F: (405) 524-2932

OREGON:

Asian Family Center
4424 NE Gleason Street
Portland, OR 97213
P: (503) 235-9396
F: (503) 235-0341

IRCO
1336 East Burnside Street
Portland, OR 97214
P: (503) 234-1541
F: (503) 234-1259
irco@teleport.com

PENNSYLVANIA:

Indochinese American Council
4936 Old York Road
Philadelphia, PA 19141
P: (215) 457-0272
F: (215) 457-0557

International Service Center
21 South River Street
Harrisburg. PA 17101
P: (717) 236-9401
F: (717) 236-3821
isc1976@aol.com

Southeast Asian Mutual Assistance Associations Coalition
4601 Market Street
Philadelphia, PA 19139
P: (215) 476-9640
F: (215) 471-8029

Vietnamese United National Assoc. of Greater Philadelphia
1033 South 8th Street
Philadelphia, PA 19147
P: (215) 923-3430
F: (215) 923-4074

TEXAS:

**Research & Development
Institute**
10120 North West Freeway,
Suite 227
Houston, TX 77092
P: (713) 686-3717
F: (713) 686-4145
qumartin@aol.com

**Vietnamese Mutual Assistance
Association, Inc.**
7015 Greenville Avenue,
Suite 200
Dallas, TX 75231
P: (214) 691-1704
F: (214) 696-0275
vmaatx@aol.com

VIRGINIA:

**Vietnamese Resettlement
Association**
6131 Williston Drive,
Room 6
Falls Church, VA 22044
P: (703) 532-3716
F: (703) 532-3525

**Vietnamese Senior Citizens
Association**
6131 Williston Drive,
#107
Falls Church, VA 22044
P: (703) 532-0267
F: (703) 553-3916

WASHINGTON:

**Refugee Federation Service
Center**
7101 Martin Luther King, Jr.,
South, Suite 214
Seattle, WA 98118
P: (206) 725-9181
F: (206) 725-9175
training@rfsc.org

**Vietnamese Friendship
Association**
4913 47th Avenue, South
Seattle, WA 98118
P: (206) 725-9181
F: (206) 722-5358

Two youngsters peek out of their home near the old DMZ. The chalk drawings on the walls of their longhouse are ever-present reminders of a war that raged before they were born.

WISCONSIN:

**Eau Claire Hmong Mutual
Assistance Association**
423 Wisconsin Street
Eau Claire, WI 54703
P: (715) 832-8420
F: (715) 832-0612

**Hmong Educational
Advancements. Inc.**
2414 West Vliet Street
Milwaukee, WI 53205
P: (414) 931-8834
F: (414) 931-0545

**Hmong Mutual Assistance
Association of
Sheboygan, Inc.**
721 North 6th Street
Sheboygan, WI 53081
P: (920) 458-0808
F: (920) 458-0081
hmaas@powercom.net

**La Crosse Area Hmong Mutual
Assistance Association, Inc.**
2613 George Street
La Crosse, WI 54603
P: (608) 781-5744
F: (608) 781-5011
dltucker@centurytel.net

**Lakeshore Indochinese
MAA, Inc. of Manitowoc**
2411 Wollmer Street, #209
Manitowoc, WI 54220
P: (920) 684-1228
F: (920) 684-0461

Lao Family Community, Inc.
2331 West Vieau Place
Milwaukee, WI 53204
P: (414) 383-4180
F: (414) 385-3386

**Wausau Area Hmong
Mutual Association**
1109 North 6th Street
Wausau, WI 54403
P: (715) 842-8390
F: (715) 842-9202
wahma@pepros.net

Map of Vietnam

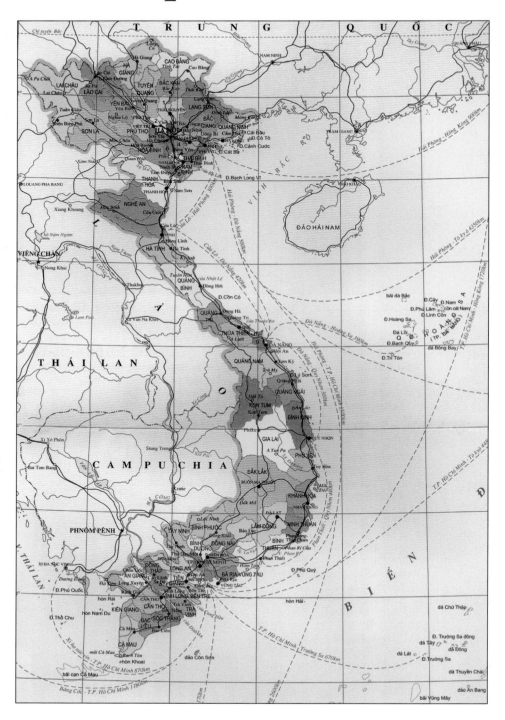

Chronology

111 B.C. The beginning of recorded Vietnamese history and of a thousand years of Chinese rule.

1500s Early in this century European colonial nations travel to Southeast Asia.

1883 France declares the "name of Vietnam" extinct and establishes Cochin China (in the south) as a colony, Annam and Tonkin (center and north) as protectorates.

1890 Ho Chi Minh is born in a small village south west of Hanoi.

1911 Ho leaves Vietnam, not to return for 30 years.

1914 World War I breaks out in Europe and ends in 1918.

1920 December, Ho Chi Minh joins newly formed French Communist party.

1930 Ho Chi Minh and his comrades form the Indochinese Communist party in Hong Kong.

1939 September, World War II begins as Germans invade Poland.

1940 June, France falls to Germany.
- September, Japanese troops occupy Indochina, but allow the French colonial administration to continue.

1941 Ho Chi Minh returns to Vietnamese soil to form the Viet Minh to fight the French and Japanese.
- December 7, Japanese attack Pearl Harbor.

1945 March, Japan unilaterally ends French rule in Indochina and establishes "independent" Vietnam under Emperor Bao Dai.
- April 12, President Roosevelt dies. Harry S. Truman becomes the next president of the United States.
- May 8, Germany surrenders.
- July, Potsdam Conference assigns Nationalist China and Britain responsibility for Vietnam, north and south of the sixteenth parallel respectively.
- August 18, Japan transfers power in Indochina to the Viet Minh.
- August 30, Bao Dai abdicates in favor of the provisional government and hands over the seals of office.
- September, Viet Minh, led by Ho Chi Minh, take power and declare a Democratic Republic of Vietnam.
- September 13, British forces under Major General Gracy land in Saigon and restore French control south of the sixteenth parallel.

- September 26, Lieutenant Colonel Dewey of the OOS is the first American killed in Vietnam.
- October, Ho Chi Minh appeals to President Harry S. Truman to support Vietnamese independence.

1946 November, amid growing tensions, French bombard Haiphong Harbor, killing 6,000 civilians.
- December, Viet Minh attack French forces in Hanoi. The Resistance war has begun.

1948 The French recall Bao Dai who is named head of state. Indirect U.S. funding of the war begins under President Truman.

1950 The Democratic Republic of Vietnam under Ho Chi Minh is recognized by the Soviet Bloc; Bao Dai's government is recognized by the United States and Great Britain. Both governments claim to represent all of Vietnam.
- July 26, U.S. gives France fifteen million dollars in military aid for the war in Indochina.
- U.S. Military Assistance Advisory Group (MAAG) is sent to Vietnam.
- The Korean War begins and ends in 1953.

1952 November 4, Dwight D. Eisenhower elected president of the United States.

1954 March 13 through May 7, the French suffer a major military defeat in the battle at Dien Bien Phu.
- June 16, Bao Dai selects Ngo Dinh Diem as prime minister of South Vietnam.
- July, at the signing of the Geneva Accords, the first Indochina War ends and Vietnam is temporarily divided at the seventeenth parallel. All Vietnam elections promised for 1956.
- October 9, French forces leave Hanoi.
- October 11, the Viet Minh take over the leadership of North Vietnam.
- October 24, President Eisenhower pledges support to Diem's regime.

1955 January, U.S. begins to give aid directly to Saigon government and agrees to train South Vietnamese army (ARVN).
- American-backed Diem rejects the Geneva Accords and refuses to participate in reunification elections.

- October 26, Diem becomes South Vietnam's president. Repression of remnant Viet Minh and their sympathizers.

1957 Insurgent Communist activity begins an offensive against the South.

1959 July 8, when Viet Cong attack Bien Hoa, the first American combat deaths in Vietnam occur.

1960 November 8, Richard Nixon is defeated by John F. Kennedy for the presidency of the United States.
- November 11, South Vietnamese army units unsuccessfully attempt to overthrow Diem.
- December 20, Hanoi leaders form the National Liberation Front for South Vietnam. The Diem government calls them the Viet Cong, short for Communist Vietnamese.
- U.S. military personnel in Vietnam stands at 900.

1961 President Kennedy sends Green Berets and military advisors to Vietnam.
- U.S. military personnel increased to more than 3,000.

1962 February, American military assistance command formed in Vietnam (MACV) under General Paul Harkins.
- U.S. military personnel number more than 11,000.

1963 Anti-Diem demonstrations by Buddhist communities spread across South Vietnam. The crisis intensifies when Buddhist monk Thich Quang Duc commits self-immolation on June 11.
- November, a military coup overthrows and kills South Vietnamese President Ngo Dinh Diem and his brother Nhu.
- November 22, John F. Kennedy is assassinated in Dallas, Texas. He is succeeded by Lyndon Johnson.
- U.S. military personnel number more than 16,000.

1964 June 20, General William Westmoreland replaces Harkins as head of MACV, all U.S. military operations in Vietnam.
- French President Charles de Gaulle calls for an end to foreign intervention in Vietnam and offers to mediate.
- August 2, North Vietnamese torpedo boats attack the Maddox and Turner Joy, an American destroyer in the Gulf of Tonkin. A second attack allegedly occurs on August 4, triggering United States entry into the war.

- August 7, Congress passes the Tonkin Gulf resolution giving President Johnson extraordinary power to act in Southeast Asia.
- November 3, Lyndon Johnson defeats Barry Goldwater for the presidency.
- U.S. military personnel number more than 23,000.

1965 February, U.S. forces at Pleiku are attacked by NLF. President Johnson authorizes Operation Rolling Thunder, a sustained air campaign against North Vietnam.
- March 8, 3,500 U.S. Marine combat troops land in Danang.
- April 17, students for a Democratic Society sponsor the first anti-war rally. Fifteen thousand students march on Washington.
- April 24, President Johnson officially declares Vietnam a "combat zone."
- May, teach-ins against the war are held at universities nationwide.
- June, Vietnamese Air Force commander, General Nguyen Cao Ky becomes the new premier of South Vietnam. A British newspaper quotes Premier Ky as saying, "Adolf Hitler is one of my heroes."
- October 15-16, anti-war protests are held in some 40 American cities, as well as in London, Rome, Brussels, Copenhagen and Stockholm. David Millar becomes the first U.S. war protester to burn his draft card.
- December 25, in an attempt to induce negotiations with the Communists, Johnson suspends the bombing of North Vietnam.
- U.S. military personnel increases to 184,300.

1966 January 31, Johnson resumes bombing.
- June 29, oil depots in Hanoi and Haiphong are bombed by American aircraft.
- American troops in Vietnam reaches 362,000 by the year's end.

1967 April, major peace demonstrations in cities throughout the U.S.
- September, Nguyen Van Thieu and Nguyen Cao Ky become president and vice president of South Vietnam.
- October 21-23, up to 150,000 demonstrate against the war in Washington.
- U.S. troops increase to 485,000.

1968 January 31, begins the Tet Offensive as North Vietnamese and Viet Cong attack South Vietnamese cities, towns and military bases.
- February 25, American and South Vietnamese troops recapture Hue after 26 days of fighting.
- March 16, My Lai massacre occurs.
- March, General Westmoreland is appointed army chief of staff and is replaced in Vietnam by General Creighton Abrams.
- Johnson orders a partial bombing halt over North Vietnam and announces he will not run for re-election.
- April 4, Dr. Martin Luther King Jr. is assassinated in Memphis.
- May, the Paris peace talks begin between American and Vietnamese officials.
- June 5, Senator Robert Kennedy is assassinated after his victory in the California Democratic presidential primary.
- August, Richard Nixon wins the Republican nomination for president in Miami, and Hubert H. Humphrey wins the Democratic presidential nomination in Chicago as the police battle demonstrators in the street outside the convention.
- Johnson stops all bombing of North Vietnam.
- November 5, Richard Nixon is elected president and commits the U.S. to a steady retraction from the Vietnam War.
- U. S. troop strength in Vietnam is 535,100 at year's end.

1969 June 8, President Richard Nixon meets with President Thieu and announces the first troop withdrawals of 25,000 from South Vietnam.
- September 3, Ho Chi Minh dies in Hanoi at the age of 79.

- October-November, massive anti-war demonstrations in Washington.
- November, the 1968 massacre of My Lai villagers is exposed.
- U.S. troop strength declines to 475,200.

1970 The draft lottery begins in the United States.
- April, U.S. invades Cambodia.
- Large anti-war protests spread across America.
- May 4, National Guardsmen kill four students at Kent State University in Ohio.
- U.S. troop strength drops to 334,600; ARVN troops total one million.

1971 February, American and South Vietnamese forces invade Laos in an attempt to sever the Ho Chi Minh trail.
- October 3, Thieu is re-elected as president of South Vietnam.
- U.S. military forces down to 156,800.

1972 June, Watergate break-in is discovered.
- November 7, Nixon is re-elected by a landslide against Senator George McGovern.
- December 18, after several aborted peace proposals, Nixon orders the bombing of the areas around Hanoi and Haiphong. Over a twelve-day period, 36,000 tons of bombs are dropped. When the bombing stops, the Communists agree to continue diplomatic talks.
- U.S. military personnel at 24,200.

1973 January 27, representatives of South Vietnam, North Vietnam, the NLF and the United States sign the Paris Peace Accords, ending the American combat role in Vietnam. The draft in the United States has also ended.
- March 29, the last American combat troops leave Vietnam.
- April 1, the last 591 acknowledged American POWs are released in Hanoi.

1974 January, President Thieu declares that the war has begun again.
- August 9, President Nixon resigns following the Watergate scandal. He is replaced by Gerald Ford.

1975 January, Khmer Rouge besieges Phnom Penh.
- March 10, ARVN retreat from the Central Highlands.
- March 26, the fall of Hue.
- March 30, the fall of Danang.
- April 3, President Ford announced that Operation Babylift would begin using American military transport aircraft. Other countries around the world join in the effort, and the evacuation of Vietnamese and Amerasian orphans begins.
- April 17, In Cambodia, Phnom Penh falls to the Khmer Rouge.
- April 25, South Vietnamese President Thieu resigns and leaves for Taiwan.
- April 28, Vice President Tran Van Huong transfers authority as chief of state to General Duong Van Minh.
- April 29, U.S. Navy begins to evacuate the last American personnel and South Vietnamese refugees.
- April 30, the North Vietnamese forces capture Saigon. Duong Van Minh surrenders, ending the war and reunifying the country under Communist control.

1976 November 2, Jimmy Carter is elected president of the United States.

1977 January 21, the day after his inauguration, President Jimmy Carter pardons most of the war draft evaders.
- May, U.S. and Vietnamese normalization talks open in Paris.
- June, Congress bans all aid, direct or indirect, to any Indochinese state.

1978 March, Vietnam issues severe restrictions on ethnic Chinese.

- November, Vietnam signs friendship pact with USSR. Exodus of ethnic Chinese begins.
- December, President Carter announces normalization of relations with China. December 25, Vietnam invades Cambodia and ends the reign of terror of Pol Pot's Khmer Rouge government.
- Thousands of "boat people" begin to flee Vietnam.

1979 February, China invades Vietnam.

1980 November 4, Ronald Reagan is elected president of the United States.

1982 November 11, the Vietnam Veterans Memorial Wall, inscribed with the names of more than 58,000 U.S. war dead, is unveiled in Washington.
- Vietnamese withdrawals from Cambodia begin.

1984 May, Vietnam veterans charge chemical companies with manufacturing Agent Orange. A federal judge announces 180 million dollar settlement against seven companies.

1985 Following the failure of the farm collectivization program, famine spreads in Vietnam.

1988 September, the United States and Vietnamese joint field investigations on MIAs begin.
- November, George Bush is elected president.

1989 Collapse of communism in Eastern Europe.

1991 Soviet Union ends aid to Vietnam.
- January 16, President Bush launches air war against Iraq. Six weeks later America and its allies emerge victorious.
- February, the U.S. and Vietnamese agree to open a temporary office in Hanoi to deal with the American MIAs.
- December, the U.S. ban on organized travel to Vietnam is lifted. Relations begin to normalize.

1992 April, U.S. eases trade restrictions on American dealings with Vietnam.
- Former anti-Vietnam war activist Bill Clinton is elected President of the United States.
- December 14, President George Bush permits American companies to open offices in Vietnam.

1993 President Clinton ends American opposition to foreign aid to Vietnam.

1994 January 27, the U.S. Senate urges President Clinton to lift the economic embargo on Vietnam, to help further MIA investigations.
- February 3, President Clinton announces the lifting of the U.S. trade embargo against Vietnam.

1995 July 11, the United States opens full diplomatic ties with Vietnam.
- July 28, Vietnam becomes a member of the Association of Southeast Asian Nations.

1996 Vietnam attends its first Olympic Games in America.

1997 May, Pete Peterson, a former POW, becomes the first Ambassador to Vietnam since the end of the war. And Vietnam's Le Van Bang arrives in Washington as Vietnam's Ambassador to the United States.

2000 April 30, Vietnam celebrates the 25th anniversary of the end of the war.
- November 16, President Bill Clinton becomes the first American president to visit Vietnam since President Nixon's visit in 1969. President Clinton's historic visit includes discussions of current and future relations between the two countries.

List of Color Plates

Listed below are descriptions of the uncaptioned color plates used throughout the book.

Acknowledgements

A journey that began with a spontaneous backpacking trip to the fascinating and extraordinarily beautiful country of Vietnam in 1992 was the inspiration for this book, which finally saw publication in 2002. The metamorphosis, although snail-like at times, evolved from a small slide show to gallery exhibits and eventually to what you now hold in your hands.

Along the way, many have helped to bring *Voices From Vietnam* from a small dream into an enormous reality, but without the voices and faces of the seventy generous and incredibly brave men and women in these pages, there would be no book. I thank them all for their proud courage in telling their stories and sacrificing their privacy to help others.

I am forever grateful for the generosity of the following people who have offered invaluable help in making *Voices From Vietnam* an actuality. I would like to thank them for providing brilliant editing, book designing, artistic eyes, computer savvy, support, advise, guidance and in some cases friendship and love. Their belief in the work has encouraged me through many times of uncertainty. They are: Eddie Adams, Hal Belmont, Chris Bowen, Allison Brandt, Philip Caputo, Evelyn Dannan, Cindy Falzone, Gasper Falzone, Roseanne Freilich, Amy Gannon, Sharon Golden, Steve Greenberg, Willis E. Hartshorn, Barbara Hoffman, Roz Howard, Anne Jackson, Jennifer Locke Jones, Anita Kirschner, Richard Klein, Robin Moore, Carole Naggar, Juliette Nguyen, Suzanne Nichols, Antonella Pergola, Roland Priebe, Frank Proschan, Frank Roff, Jan C. Scruggs, Esq., Patricia Shih, Harvey Stein, John Taylor, Rick Wright and Marilyn Young. And especially to Maria Distefano, Laurie Greenberg, Byron Noone, Lana Noone, Carl Pergola, Theresa Pergola and Robbi Wyenn. I could go on mentioning endless others who through the past ten years deserve my thanks, but the list would go on forever. The others know who they are, as do I, and to each of them I offer a tremendous silent thank you.

A special thank you goes to my book designer, Joe Gannon of Mulberry Tree Press, for his generosity in sharing his knowledge, his creative ingenuity, his ability to interpret my vision and mostly his extreme patience.

I would like to express my everlasting appreciation to two people whom I met while creating *Voices From Vietnam*. They are Bill Stilwagen, a Vietnam veteran and Susan A. Roth, a photographer and writer. Their support, encouragement and belief in me and the importance of this book helped me more than I can say. Bill has been there for me—from the very beginning until the very end. His knowledge of Vietnam, his help in finding resources and subjects for the book, and his expertise in editing until four or five some mornings, proved invaluable. And Susan, for her use of words, proficiency in editing, innate vision and clarity when viewing images and especially for her kindness, patience, and encouragement.

My remaining acknowledgments are first to my parents, Charlotte and Edward Pochtrager, who are together now, looking down from the heavens. I could never have accomplished this huge feat without the genes of creativity provided by them both. Thank you forever.

And second and above all, this book would never have happened without the endless love, patience and guidance of my husband, Michael, a Vietnam veteran. I am deeply grateful for his sustaining love and good will during my years of consuming involvement in the research, writing and photographing of this book. My appreciation and love for his compassion, support and belief in me go beyond what I can ever express in words.

Index